KU-522-075

The Great Wall of China

The Great Wall of China

by Jonathan Fryer

NEW ENGLISH LIBRARY

TIMES MIRROR

HERTFORDSHIRE
COUNTY LIBRARY
951·1
6954185

©Jonathan Fryer 1975
Published in Great Britain by New English Library,
Holborn, London EC1 N2JR in 1975

Filmset by Thomson Litho Ltd., East Kilbride, Scotland.
Printed by photolithography and bound in
Great Britain at The Pitman Press, Bath

All rights reserved. No part of this publication may be reproduced or transmitted,
in any form or by any means, without permission of the publisher.

45002349 4

Contents

List of Illustrations

PLATES

Between pages 48 and 49.

Ch'in Shih Huang-ti oversees the Burning of the Books and the Burying of the Scholars. *Bibliothèque Nationale, Paris.*

Han Dynasty engraving of the assassination attempt against Cheng of Ch'in.

Contemporary Chinese woodcut of towers in Wall.

The First and Last Gates of the Great Wall. *W. E. Geil.**

The 'First Gate in the World' at Shanhaikuan. A contemporary Chinese photograph.

Temple dedicated to the God of War at Luo Ma Pass. *W. E. Geil.**

Fortified settlement at Luo Ma Pass. *W. E. Geil.**

Chinese drawing showing tamping of earth. *J. Needham.*

Meng T'ien, who supervised the building of the Wall.

Ruins of the Wall in North-central China. *W. E. Geil.**

A house built into the Wall. *W. E. Geil.**

Li Ssu, Ch'in Shih Huang-ti's chief adviser.

Two views of the Tibetan Loop. *W. E. Geil.**

The Fortress of Chia Yü Kuan. *W. E. Geil.**

Dr Geil posing with the 'last brick' of the Great Wall in 1908. *W. E. Geil.**

The Rataling Gate in the Wall. *Radio Times Hulton Picture Library.*

The Wall as drawn by T. Allom and engraved by J. Sands. *Radio Times Hulton Picture Library.*

* Photographs by W. E. Geil are taken from *The Great Wall of China* (1909) and reproduced by permission of the publishers, John Murray Ltd.

Between pages 112 and 113.

Nineteenth-century German cartoon. *Collection Claude Estier.*†

Kuomintang sentries posted along the Wall during the Sino-Japanese war of 1937–45. *Wide World.*

Chinese map showing eastern end of the Wall. *Harvard University Library.*

Chinese poster showing Chairman Mao viewing the Middle Kingdom. *Collection Claude Estier.*†

Chinese troops marching along the Great Wall. *Radio Times Hulton Picture Library.*

View of the Wall from the foothills behind Peking. *Private collection.*

President Nixon viewing the Wall in 1972. *Associated Press.*

Ruined Watch-tower north of the Tun Wang oasis. *A. Stein.*

Remains of the Wall east of Tower (above). *A. Stein.*

LINE ILLUSTRATIONS

†Illustrations from the collection of Claude Estier are taken from *Histoire de la Chine en 1000 Images* (Cercle Européen du Livre, Paris; 1966).

For
Yip Bao-dong
who did so much to break
down the barrier of
misunderstanding between
East and West.

The author and publishers wish to thank those whose work is quoted here. Wherever possible, permission has been obtained, but in those cases where proper credit has not been given, the publishers will be happy to make an amendment in future editions.

Introduction

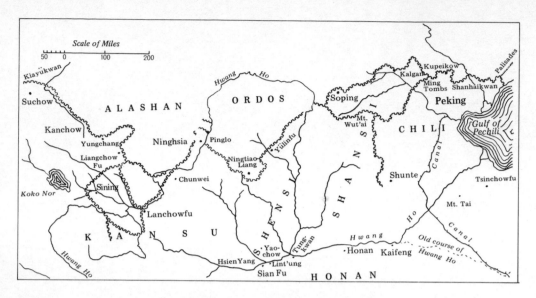

Fig. 1. Sketch-map of the Great Wall of China.

Introduction

For over four thousand years China has enjoyed a rich and developing culture, the longest continuous civilisation in the history of the world.

In both the sciences and the arts, the Chinese have made a great contribution to the knowledge of mankind. Often their inventions and techniques were hundreds of years in advance of the West.

Collections inside and outside the Middle Kingdom bear witness to the achievements of a culture that remained relatively free from outside influences until the nineteenth century. This culture is sufficiently distinct to make an impression on most non-Chinese, even if sometimes it is aesthetically baffling to Western eyes.

In recent years Red Guards on the rampage in Peking, and the late Bruce Lee starring in Kung-fu films from Hong Kong, have become the main images conjured up by the word China in many people's minds. Yet much of the old mystique remains. Politicians, academics, tourists and delegations of every kind have scrambled to get into China since the thaw in external relations following the Cultural Revolution of 1966–8. No other country commands such curiosity and attention.

The sheer size of China demands respect. Ever since Kaiser Wilhelm of Germany warned of the Yellow Peril, invoking vague and exaggerated memories of Mongol hordes sweeping into Europe, the West has looked upon the hundreds of millions of Chinese with fear as well as fascination.

The Great Wall is the paramount symbol of China's standing and achievement. Its importance goes far beyond the fact that it is a colossal human feat – the longest man-made construction in the world, stretching round one-twentieth of the circumference of the earth. The Chinese recognise this and dutifully take almost every foreign visitor to see it.

There is an ancient Chinese story that the first emperor of the unified Middle Kingdom rode up to the moon on a magic carpet to get a better view of his domain. Seen from this vantage point, his territories looked rather vulnerable, so he decided to build a barrier round the empire to keep his people in and barbarians out.

At first he thought the barrier should be shaped like a horseshoe, with the open end facing the coast, but then he realised that the high mountain ranges protected the west, and the Yangtse River blocked any threat from the south. The sea guarded the east, so all he had to worry about was the north.

Coming back down to earth again, the emperor summoned his bravest general and ordered him to build a great wall, a 'Wall of 10,000 li' (about 3000 miles), which would ensure the future of China for ages to come.

So the Great Wall was built, and when news of its existence reached Europe nearly 2000 years later, it captured the imagination of many from Voltaire to Dr Johnson.

The legends surrounding the Wall are numerous and colourful, but the true history of the barrier is one of bloody conflict and human suffering. Hundreds of thousands of men lost their lives because of the Wall, but the emperors and generals concerned with the mammoth structure were convinced that hundreds of thousands more would have died at the hands of the barbarians had the Wall not existed.

The notion of the Wall as a barrier put up by a nation determined to turn its back on the world is a neat idea of Chinese isolationism, but far from true. The aim of this book is to clarify some of the misconceptions, to produce a clear picture of the Great Wall seen in the wider context of Chinese society and ideology.

It is a changing picture, for the Wall is not a homogenous construction but a conglomeration of barriers built at different times for different reasons, and little of what we can see today is the same fortification as that built by the First Emperor.

Although the book traces the story of why the Wall was built, and how it was built, it is nevertheless largely a book about people. The characters dealt with range from the First Emperor, Ch'in Shih Huang-ti, and his Machiavellian adviser, Li Ssu, to the present leaders of the People's Republic of China, and the scenario depicts their various attitudes to the Great Wall and the world outside.

In tracing the historical development, I have been selective about the periods I have chosen. The book does not claim to be a complete history of China. Five fundamentally important periods have been described; individually they show the living conditions and mentality of the people and the role of the Great Wall at each time, while collectively they show the overall trend from ancient society to the present day, and the degree to which modern China has maintained its traditions.

The number of characters appearing in the book has also been restricted. Chinese names are confusing at the best of times to the non-specialist Western reader, and in large quantities become impossible to remember or distinguish.

The romanisation of all Chinese proper names and terms conforms to the Wade-Giles system apart from place names, for which I have used the most common spelling (e.g. Peking for Pei-ching). The Wade-Giles system is at least as misleading a guide to Chinese pronunciation as any other romanisation form, but has the undeniable advantage of being widespread. With much regret, I have not used the modern P'in-yin system recently introduced in China, which is representationally more correct but produces unrecognisable names for the Western reader familiar with the Wade-Giles version (e.g. Mao Zi-dong for Mao Tse-T'ung).

Translations used in the book are my own, unless otherwise stated. I have deliberately been free in my translations to put them into modern English which flows with the rest of the text, thus hopefully avoiding the erroneous cuteness of translations which try to transpose literally Chinese phrases and idioms into English, often clouding the real meaning.

Since China reopened its gates to Western journalists and photographers, people in the West have had plenty of opportunity to see what the Great Wall is like – or rather, of seeing those fifteenth and sixteenth century sections in the hills behind Peking, which have formed the background in so many photos of visiting foreigners from Richard Nixon to the Albanian ping-pong team. Some of the illustrations in the book show how surprisingly different other less well-known parts of the Wall are.

At the time of writing it seems highly unlikely that any Westerner (or Chinese, for that matter) will have the chance of making a journey along the Wall, as did the American traveller William Edgar Geil, whose idiosyncratic account[1] at the turn of the century is still a classic. What is certain, though, is that the Wall will continue to fascinate, as it did Dr Johnson two hundred years ago.

[Dr Johnson] expressed a particular enthusiasm with respect to visiting the wall of China. I catched it for a moment, and said I really believed I should go and see the wall of China had I not children, of whom it is my duty to take care.

'Sir,' said he, 'by doing so, you would do what would be of importance in raising your children to eminence . . . They would at all times be regarded as the children of a man who had gone to view the wall of China . . .'[2]

Jonathan H. Fryer
1975

1 Geil, William Edgar, *The Great Wall of China* (Sturgis and Walton; New York, 1909).
2 Boswell's *Life of Johnson*, 10 April 1778.

1

States in Strife

CHAPTER ONE

States in Strife

I N the beginning there was chaos. Then in the year 279,479 BC P'an Ku appeared, creator of Heaven and Earth. Every day of the 18,000 years of his life he grew ten feet in height, and the sky was raised accordingly. His tears became the Yellow River and the Yangtse; his breath was the wind. When P'an Ku died, the different parts of his corpse formed the five sacred mountains of China. Out of his eyes were born the Sun and the Moon. His flesh became the seas and the rivers and his hair gave birth to the plants and the trees.

The first rulers of the universe were the Twelve Emperors of Heaven, each reigning for 18,000 years, succeeded by the Eleven Emperors of the Earth, who occupied the throne for a similar period. Nine Emperors of Man followed, who wielded power for 45,600 years. Sixteen kings – of whom we have only sparse details – ruled over succeeding centuries until the arrival of the Three Sovereigns: Fu Hsi, who had the head of a man and the body of a snake, invented fishing and established the rites of marriage; Niu Wa, the Queen who rebuilt the fallen sky and brought peace to the Earth submerged beneath the Flood; Shen Nung, the Divine Cultivator, with his human body and ox-head, who taught Man how to work the land. Between them the Three Sovereigns taught the Chinese their arts and crafts and provided the basis for their rituals.

Until fairly recently the full-bodied legends of Chinese tradition were accepted as historical truth by the average Chinese. Mythology and history were totally blurred, and it is still a matter of dispute as to where one ends and the other begins. There has never been a great quest for objectivity and scientific fact in the oriental tradition such as in the West. Reality and irreality are but variants of the same thing; one should never be sure of anything.

Archaeology in China became a serious science in China only in the early 1930s, when large numbers of 'oracle bones' (tortoise or ox-bones used for divination by fire) were uncovered in large quantities near An Yang Hsien in Honan province. Their existence had been known to the leading Chinese novelist Liu Eh at the turn of the century, but it was some time before proper digging took place, by which time many of the oracle bones had been taken by profiteers who ground them into a fine powder to be sold in the drug-shops of Peking as a miraculous cure for a whole spectrum of diseases. The bones and other discoveries in the same area established beyond doubt the existence of the so-called Shang Dynasty (c. 1500–1100 BC) which 'enlightened' historians in the nineteenth century had ridiculed as being a figment of the legend-writers' fertile imaginations.

With its damp and seasonal climate, China had none of the archaeological advantages of the great Middle Eastern civilisations where ancient relics have been preserved in excellent condition under the sands or in dry, sealed tombs. None the less a reasonably clear picture of the Chinese past has emerged during this century. Until the Chinese Revolution of 1949, the oldest Chinese anthropoid was thought to be Peking Man, whose 500,000-year-old remains were dug up at a village called Chou Kou Tien thirty miles south-west of Peking in the 1920s (and which disappeared in 1941, rumour has it into the knapsack of an American GI). Since then far older bones have been discovered, such as the Yuan-mo Man from the south-western province of Yunnan, thought to be as much as two million years old. Archaeological evidence is very patchy, however. Although paleolithic remains have been found in Inner Mongolia and parts of Shensi, the bulk of early material discovered is neolithic. Primitive tools and ornaments have been dug up in places throughout China, as well as some magnificent painted pottery whose swirling designs in red, black and white show a resemblance to those discovered in southern Russia, suggesting some sort of cultural link between China and central Asia around 2000 BC.

From the earliest times walls have played an important role in China. The first settlements of neolithic times were surrounded by ramparts of pounded earth, and until the Communist Revolution walls were an essential part of any village. Indeed the Chinese word for a city (ch'eng) also means wall. Of course most prehistoric civilisations surrounded their settlements with walls, to keep wild animals and marauders out, and in many cases to lessen the feeling of vulnerability felt by people leaving cave-dwellings for a more exposed domicile. Yet no other civilisation seems to have adopted walls as enthusiastically as the Chinese. Not only would every town or village be surrounded with walls, but also the houses and temples, usually windowless in the walls facing the street, so that in many old Chinese towns one has the feeling of wandering around a huge maze.

Given this obsession with walling everything off, it is perhaps not surprising that the Chinese should conceive the outrageous idea of building a huge wall around their country as well. They even projected their wall-consciousness beyond the realm of the mortal world into the kingdom of the gods, whose cities and palaces were also surrounded by walls. The God of Walls and Moats is himself an important figure in the divine hierarchy whose territory is not only the dividing line between the secure inside and the dark world outside but also that between Life and Death. It is, they believed, the God of Walls and Moats who informs a dying man of his fate, telling him that his hour is come in accordance with the entry in the Book of Hades. The God's two assistants, half beast, half human beings with the fearsome names of Ox-head and Horse Features, were said to escort the parting soul to the frontier hall between our world and the next. Such gods were of fundamental importance to the lives of the people of the Shang Dynasty, and most of the oracle bones used in prophecy bear requests for advice from Heaven ('If we went into battle, would we be victorious?' 'Is the time right for starting our harvest?') requiring yes/no answers that were deduced by means of cracks caused when the bone was thrust into the flames of the soothsayer's fire.

The Shang Dynasty allegedly reigned through thirteen generations until about 1100 BC when the tyrannical last ruler, Chou Hsin, was dethroned. He has been colourfully portrayed by ancient historians as an ogre and debauchee of unimaginable proportions. But it must be remembered that teaching by models, or examples, has been at the core of the Chinese educational system since earliest times. The good and evil of human behaviour are stereotyped in extremes, either to be emulated (as in the case of Yü, the miraculous founder of the Hsia Dynasty which was the undocumented predecessor to the Shang; or, latterly, as in the case of Communist Party Chairman Mao Tse-Tung) or to be reviled (such as the last Shang ruler, Chou Hsin, or the 'revisionist' President of the People's Republic of China, Liu Shao-ch'i). Chou Hsin, last Shang ruler, was a man of phenomenal strength, with eagle eyes and acute powers of hearing, combining eloquence and brilliance with pure viciousness. To please his consort, Chou Hsin made a lake of wind surrounded by groves of trees from which joints of meat were hung. Scholars were subjected to fearful humiliation and tortures, and Chou Hsin had his own uncle's stomach slit open to see if it was true that a sage had seven openings in his heart. Ironically, because of recent archaeological discoveries, we in the twentieth century know far more about Shang Dynasty customs than intervening dynasties did, and can therefore appreciate that the spring festivals which marked the religious beginning of the year were filled with sexual overtones and fertility practices for ritual as well as carnal reasons. But by the eighth and seventh centuries BC Chinese society had developed a highly puritanical official moral stance that has remained ever since. Rigid moral codes were a protection for a new society wishing to ensure for itself a permanence of existence and were, in many ways, abstract counterparts to the walls of earth and stone that surrounded the settlements.

The conquerors of the declining Shang Dynasty, a federation of tribes called Chou, were semi-barbarians when they took over control of the North China plains. As was to happen time and time again in the course of Chinese history, the conquerors adopted the established Chinese civilisation with a vigour often outmatching that of their predecessors. The Chou tribes emanated from the Wei Valley, where they had experienced close contact with the nomad tribes of the west, and therefore knew what they had to fear from that direction. For nearly nine hundred years the Chou Dynasty (c. 1100–221 BC) ruled over China, yet this statement is deceptive for their rule was frequently nominal, particularly as time advanced and individual fiefdoms and petty states fought among themselves for hegemony. For hundreds of years China was to know no peace. A situation existed where local leaders were locked together in a continuous jostling for power, while in the background always lurked the possibility of invasion from the western nomads or other alien groups. Out of this conflict and fear were born the frontier walls of the different rulers' domains, which would eventually coalesce into the Great Wall.

The Chou ruler existed in a fundamental relationship with the forces of Nature. The Chinese believed that man's destiny depended on the balance of the natural world. When things were in equilibrium, life went well. When the natural balance was upset, things went badly. It is easy to see how this belief came about, viewed in the context of the constant flux of seasons that characterises the climate of northern China. The Chou king (known as the Son of Heaven) was the link between the divine and the human, and therefore the agent by whom the balance could be achieved. It was part of his duty to perform the necessary sacrifices and rituals at the appropriate times, and as such he was educated to be of a pure and semi-divine nature himself, which often put him completely out of touch with the reality of the outside world.

The Chou conquerors made use of the principle of divine relationship between king and heaven for justifying their action against the Shang, saying that the decadent behaviour of Chou Hsin made him no longer worthy of the Mandate of Heaven. The Chou rulers continued the ancient Shang rites to avoid running the risk of offending the gods. Right up until the end of the Chou period, for example, a 'bride' was given to the Yellow River. A beautiful girl, dressed in fine clothes and jewels, was cast out into the swirling waters on a marriage bed, to be sucked under to appease the fickle river.

During the early stages of the Chou Dynasty the administration ordered the construction of a line of watch-towers along the northern and north-western frontiers as a system of defence and communication. These towers were close enough together for messages to be flashed from one to the next, though it was several hundred years before anyone thought of joining them together by a wall. Paradoxically the watch-towers were instrumental in the decline of centralised Chou power, thanks to a foolish royal practical joke which will strike a chord with any reader brought up on Victorian cautionary tales. The Chou Dynasty had been in power for three centuries by the time King Hsüan (827–782 BC) ascended the throne. During his reign, a child medium appeared who strode round in a trance saying repeatedly, 'Mulberry bows and wicker quivers, these will bring about the downfall of Chou!' Consternation spread throughout the superstitious royal court, and urgent enquiries led to the discovery that in the whole of China there was only one couple who were renowned for their archery equipment made from mulberry wood and wicker. The King immediately ordered this couple to be killed, but they were warned in time and escaped to the wild area of the west. Along the way they came across an abandoned baby girl (a not uncommon phenomenon in a civilisation that prayed that every baby be a boy). The couple were compassionate and adopted the girl, who is known to history as Pao Ssu.

By the time Pao Ssu had grown into a young woman her adopted parents had died and King Hsüan had been succeeded by his son. At the time of Pao Ssu's flowering into maidenhood, the people of the remote region where she lived had offended the new Chou King, and decided to make amends by sending him a beautiful consort. Pao Ssu, as an orphan with enchanting looks, was an obvious choice, and she was duly shipped off to the royal harem in 779 BC. The first time the king called for his new consort to come to his inner rooms he became infatuated with her. So great was his passion for this strange girl from the west that he promoted her to the position of queen over the heads of the consorts, including his first wife. This action caused outrage among the senior courtiers, who said that such interference with the natural law of things was bound to lead to disaster. And indeed on 29 August 776 BC (the first scientifically verified date in Chinese history) a solar eclipse occurred to prove the point. Worse was to come.

While the advisers consulted on ways of appeasing heaven for this gross impropriety, the young king was far more concerned with a domestic problem that was ruining his pleasure. The beautiful Queen Pao Ssu never smiled. Pao Ssu, for all her captivating beauty, was a woman of rather perverse pleasures; she took particular delight in listening to the King ripping pieces of costly silk to shreds, but even that bored her after a time, and she sat in the palace looking glum and bored. The King tried every conceivable way of amusing her, summoning the best clowns or musicians, or arranging magnificent excursions by boat along the river. Pao Ssu remained unmoved, her lips pursed, a frown on her face. The King was being driven to distraction by his lover's unhappiness. In despair, he admitted that he could think of nothing else to entertain her, and offered a thousand measures of gold to anyone who could make Pao Ssu laugh.

The King's chief minister came to the rescue, showing a keener sense of psychology and his own benefit than of his state responsibilities. He reminded the monarch of the emergency alarm system that had been devised, whereby lighting beacons on top of the frontier watch-towers would warn the capital of a threatened barbarian invasion. In a relatively short space of time the message could be flashed across hundreds of miles of territory, and the various vassal lords who owed allegiance to the Chou King could rush to the capital's defence. The minister believed that a false alarm would be a practical joke of such enormous proportions that Pao Ssu would be forced to laugh. The fires were lit, and the lords arrived in haste with their assembled forces. Looking down from the battlements the royal party watched the astonished faces of the faithful leaders as a court official announced that there was no danger after all. Pao Ssu burst into gales of laughter, and the chief minister was given his gold. The King's relief was short-lived, however.

The King had a son by his first wife, a boy who should have been the rightful heir to the Chou throne. Cast out from his heritage when Pao Ssu became Queen, the young prince determined to redress the situation. He entered into an alliance with a barbarian tribe who had every reason to grasp an opportunity of acquiring for themselves some of Chou's territory. The prince and the nomads assembled an army and marched on the Chou capital. The warning beacons were lit, but none of the vassal lords arrived – once bitten, twice shy. Hopelessly outnumbered, the King and his forces were easily defeated in battle. The King was killed, Pao Ssu disappeared to an unknown fate and the capital was sacked by the invaders. The victorious prince ascended the throne, but soon found his allies were not content with helping him to power and then retiring back to their lands. He turned to the vassal lords for help in getting the nomads out of Chinese territory, and they realised it was in their own interest to aid him. But even if the vassal lords were prepared to acknowledge the new king as titular, ritual head of the land, they were determined that the Chou rulers would never again enjoy major power. Aware of his weakness without the full support of the vassals, the King moved his court away from the smouldering ruins of the old capital to a site further east along the Yellow River where he would be safer from outside threats.

The King's withdrawal eastward was covered by the forces from a state of only half-Chinese origin called Ch'in, located well to the west. The ruler of Ch'in (which was later to form the first Chinese empire, and from which our word 'China' is derived) was rewarded with a large area of land that belonged previously to the Chou ruler. Probably the Chou King felt that a strong Ch'in state could form a useful buffer zone between the barbarians and China proper. Thus the rulers of Ch'in came into possession of the fertile Wei Valley, cradle of the Chou Dynasty, and a well-protected base from which they could eventually extended their power.

At the end of the eighth century BC China entered a period of interstate strife that was to last for 500 years, with a confusing series of wars and intrigues during which traditional values of chivalry and allegiance to the throne subsided in a welter of self-interest and butchery. Sometimes states would work together, particularly in the face of outside aggression, and several of the earliest defence walls along the northern frontiers were joint efforts, for only then could an adequate labour force be raised. In 658 BC, for example, Ch'i, Sung and Ch'ao built a wall against the northern barbarians in what is now Hopei province. The states of Han, Wei and Cha'o were all active wall-builders. Han built a wall along its southern border to keep out the armies of Ch'i, and Ch'u built a wall on its northern border to hold back the forces of Ch'in. Ch'i built a 300-mile barrier along its southern frontier as defence against Ch'u, as well as to keep out the flood waters of the Yellow River. The existence of these walls made the eventual construction of the Great Wall feasible as they were to form a large part of it. In general, though, these early walls were of only minimal defensive effectiveness as the enemy found it relatively easy to outflank them.

Shortly after the flight from the western Chou capital, there were fifteen major states on the scene (of which four were basically non-Chinese, including Ch'in) plus a host of tiny fiefdoms. This number had been whittled down to eleven principal contenders by the end of the fourth century BC, as shown in the map opposite, together with their frontier walls.

In theory, the Son of Heaven was still the supreme lord of the land. He alone was entitled to use the title king (*wang*), and the feudal lords still came to pay ritualistic homage to him, bringing tribute articles, often of religious significance (such as rushes for straining wine). As the weakness of the Chou house became obvious, various feudal lords held sway not only over their own states but elsewhere, recognised by the other rulers as having achieved hegemony. As time wore on, the less respectful they became to the Chou king, and the more they presumed for themselves, so that by 325 BC all the surviving rulers were calling themselves kings.

A feudal lord was judged largely by his education, unlike many of the feudal barons of medieval Europe centuries later. Foremost among the required talents was a full grasp of the principles and ritual of social conduct. A gentleman's behaviour towards the ruler or

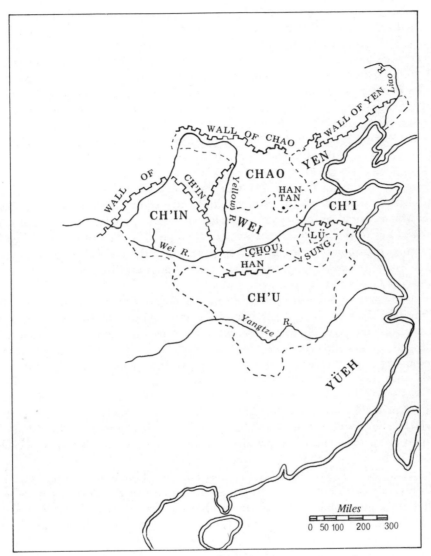

FIG. 2. The warring states and their walls, fourth and third centuries BC.

senior members of his own clan was regulated down to the tiniest detail. The social inferior was expected to behave with a maximum of elaborate respect, and the superior individual was to act with great chivalry, even in times of victory. It was not done to rub the vanquished foe's face in the mud, for that was to go to extremes, and extremes were contrary to the maintenance of harmony between the world of men and the cosmic order. Even so, by the end of the seventh century BC, chivalry was beginning to give way to more practical considerations. About the only state left where the ancient code of conduct was still respected was Sung, ruled by the descendants of the defunct Shang Dynasty. When the Sung army went to war against Ch'u (638 BC) they came across the enemy in the process of crossing a river. The advisers attendant on the Duke of Sung urged him to give the order to attack while the Ch'u forces were in such a weak position. The Duke refused, saying such action was outside the bounds of chivalry, and only when the Ch'u army was properly lined up on the other side of the river did the Duke sound the attack—and was utterly defeated. 'Man of Sung' became synonymous for buffoon in popular speech because the men from Sung clung to the old traditions in practice as well as in theory. The *Tso Chuan*, a Chinese history book compiled around 300 BC, from which the Duke of Sung story is taken, is full of accounts of the politicking, back-stabbing and flagrant disregard for higher morality or the wishes of Heaven as shown by divination.

The long years of bloodshed and destruction had one very salutary effect however, making the period of interstate strife one of the most significant stages in the pattern of Chinese development. Out of the turmoil were born most of the major Chinese schools of philosophy, as men of intellect struggled with notions of what had gone wrong and how things could be put right. These men were rarely pure philosophers in the Western sense of the word, concerned with finer points of existence or meaning in tiny detail. They were involved in a search for solutions to very real everyday problems, and were often, therefore, as much political thinkers and economists as philosophers. Several sought a perfect code under which a sage ruler would infallibly govern a united and peaceful China. Others claimed that all such systems were worthless and that the only way to achieve peace was to tune oneself in harmony with the forces of the universe.

Confucius (551–479 BC), probably the most famous Chinese personality known outside Asia before Chairman Mao and currently the bête noire of the Peking government, was the earliest of the great philosophers of whom historical records remain. Named K'ung Tzu in Chinese, he was a wandering scholar who tried to sell his philosophical wares to rulers of several different states in the hope of finding one who would be prepared to put into practice his ideas of a perfect society. That perfect society was a highly idealised conception of what ancient Chinese society had been like, a Golden Age which bore very little resemblance to historical fact, but which was acknowledged by Confucius and his followers to be a model for emulation. The Confucianists were reactionaries in the true sense of the word; progress was to go back to the ways of the former kings. It is understandable that in times of strife and misery thinkers should try to learn from the lessons of past centuries, but the obsessional reverence for the past dogged Chinese society for the next two millennia, and was all too often used by officials as an excuse for resisting any form of modernisation or change in the status quo of power and corruption.

Confucius' beliefs were handed down in a collection of aphorisms or Analects that stressed the need for strict observation of the rules and conduct of relationships between Man and Heaven, and between different ranks of men, such as ruler to subject, father to son, elder brother to younger brother, and so on. If these regulations were followed, and the king followed the advice of his wise counsellors, then harmony would be restored to the world, according to the Confucianists. The doctrine was most effectively developed by Mencius (372–289 BC), who had as little effect upon his contemporaries as his master had exercised a hundred years before. The book he left behind him, though, became one of the major canons in the vast body of Chinese literature learnt by rote by every Chinese schoolboy until the present century. Mencius illustrates his points by means of anecdotes and parables that convey early Confucian thought more easily than the Master's own epigrams. Mencius developed the idea that Man is basically good but easily misguided. His philosophy was paternalistic and never questioned the divine right of the monarch; Nature deems it that there are those who rule and those who are ruled.

The Confucianists deplored the necessity for wars, and the way in which they were conducted when they took place. They deplored the necessity for walls, and the way that the workforces who built them were treated. Adherents of another philosophical school went much further, and deplored society altogether. These were the followers of Yang Chu, who Mencius says was the most popular sage of the period, though virtually no record exists of Yang Chu's exact teaching. No doubt later scholars were instrumental in destroying his legacy for Yang Chu propounded anarchistic hedonism which undermined the whole concept of human order so sacred to the intelligentsia. By Yang Chu's standards, self-interest was a virtue, and he would not be prepared to do anything to help the authorities to get the world out of its mess. Under the violent conditions of the period, where it was difficult enough to keep body and soul together without meddling in political affairs, it was a reasonable enough idea.

A group of thinkers who had a far more lasting effect upon the Chinese mind (if such a thing exists) were the Taoists. The Tao is by nature indefinable, beyond the limitations of mere words. As the opening lines of the Taoist classic, *Tao Teh Ching*, say, any Tao that can be uttered in words just isn't the Tao. The mystical truism makes the curious even more so, and several thousand volumes have appeared in print purporting to be elucidations of the doctrine, though many of these volumes are plain misleading or else manuals of magic and hokery-pokery, the refuge of many failed mystics. 'Tao' (pronounced 'dao') means 'the way', the way to the goal and the goal itself, as well as (and here the logical mind will balk, which is an essential part of the process of realisation) the no-way and the no-goal. Many of the terms and the concepts of Taoism were later adopted by Zen Buddhists. To the Taoists, all distinctions and values were meaningless. Everything is in a constant state of flux. What goes up must come down, therefore ambition and struggle are pointless, and one should passively accord oneself with the Tao.

Fig. 3. Design symbolising the interaction of the Yin and the Yang.

The Taoist symbol of interlocking black and white is more helpful than most words. It illustrates the essential duality of existence; not only are there two characteristics (the Yin, feminine, dark, passive; the Yang, masculine, bright, active) but each has a drop of the other, and there is constant movement between the two. Taoism is a very selfish philosophy, though it does not set out to be in the way that Yang Chu's hedonism did. It is also a philosophy for intellectuals because usually only by supreme mental effort (or relaxation) can one sufficiently rid oneself of the cares and values of the world to arrive at enlightenment. Taoist masters who looked after their own salvation were invariably more satisfied than those who tried to convert others. The author of the *Tao Teh Ching*, allegedly a semi-historical figure called Lao Tzu who lived sometime during the sixth century BC, was one of many who eventually gave up the struggle. Leaving the capital by means of Han Ku Pass he was welcomed by the Warden of the Pass, who was also a Taoist. The warden tried in vain to persuade the master not to abandon the people of China who had so much to learn from him, but all he could manage was to persuade Lao Tzu to write the *Tao Teh Ching* for posterity. The task finished, Lao Tzu felt he could stay no longer and, mounting his black buffalo, he rode slowly off into the west through the Jade Gate (Kiayükwan), turning his back for ever on China, an extreme and terrible fate in Chinese eyes. 'Nor is it known where he died', the Han Dynasty historian, Ssu-ma Ch'ien, comments drily. When the Jade Gate was incorporated into the Great Wall as its western terminal many years later, the significance of passing through its portals into the wilderness outside became even greater.

Another major 'gentle' philosophy in the times of strife was Mohism, often incorrectly described as being something like Christianity. The Mohists preached pacifism and love, not for any altruistic reasons but because they believed that the world would run more smoothly that way. If a man loved everybody as much as he loved his own family then there would be neither wars nor walls, they reasoned. Although Mohism was almost as popular as Yang Chu's hedonism in Mencius' times (*c.* 300 BC), it too was snuffed out.

Had any of the main philosophies described above become the state philosophy at the expense of all the others, it is quite likely that the Great Wall would never have been built. As it happened, however, a school of thought grew up which became the ideological backbone of the state of Ch'in which strengthened itself until it was able to conquer all others and establish the first real Empire of China, so exclusive and populous that a project so vast as

28

the Great Wall could not only be conceived but also put into effect. The philosophy adopted by Ch'in was Legalism.

The Legalists worked from the fundamental precept that man is basically evil and therefore had to be guided by means of a totalitarian system of rules and punishments. The Legalist philosophers (infinitely more realistic than any of their rivals) made no attempts to disguise the fact that they worked to make the rulers they served into the masters of China, which would in turn make the philosophers themselves powerful ministers. Laws were made the basis of society, applying to all from the highest officials to the common peasant. The ruler was the sole, supreme human authority. Unity of will and direction would lead to strength. Opposition was not to be tolerated, and one of the first things the Legalist ministers did when they came into power was to try to obliterate all rival schools of thought.

The Legalist proposals for the world were nothing short of revolutionary. The hereditary aristocracy was condemned as anachronistic and was to be replaced by a meritocracy, with military prowess being an important index of merit. Agriculture and the army were the dual foundations of Legalist society – one can begin to see why the Legalists never received the vitriolic condemnation from Chinese Communist historians as they have from liberal counterparts. Traditional culture and beliefs were not only unhelpful, they were positively dangerous. In the words of the Legalist philosopher, the Lord of Shang: 'If a state has the ten evils, viz: ritualistic conduct, music, poetry, history, virtuous behaviour, morality, filial piety, brotherly obligations, integrity and sophistry [all good Confucian aims], then the ruler will be unable to get his people to fight and the state will fall to pieces.'

Totalitarian socialism (of a kind) was called for, and for the most practical of reasons:

> Encourage the poor with incentives so they become richer, penalise the rich so they become poorer. If a state administration manages to make the poor rich and the rich poor, then the country will be very strong and will end up on top.
> By nature, people are spoiled by love, but made obedient by severity.[1]

Lord Shang (*d.* 338 BC), the greatest exponent of Legalism, was born in the state of Wei as a member of the cadet branch of the ruling family. He was taken on as an assistant to one of Wei's chief ministers, and proved himself to be of considerable ability. When this minister looked as though he was about to die the ruler of Wei asked him whom he could recommend to take over the post. Without hesitation the minister replied that his young assistant was the most capable person, but the ruler was far from pleased. Seeing that his advice was not going to be followed, the minister then recommended that the yong man be killed, for he knew that his keen assistant would seek to fulfil his ambitions in another state if he could find no outlet for his talents in Wei, inevitably making him antagonistic to his home state. Having executed his duty as a minister, the old official then hurried to his young assistant to warn him to flee without delay. The youth wisely took heed and moved into the neighbouring state of Ch'in, which had gained a reputation as the state most receptive to foreign talent.

1   *The Book of Lord Shang.*

Lord Shang soon ingratiated himself with the Ch'in authorities, and rose rapidly up the official ladder.

Ch'in was of great strategic importance because it acted as a buffer between the Chinese states and the barbarians. It had characteristics of both cultures, and as such was looked down on by the other Chinese feudal domains. Even as late as 361 BC, the date of Lord Shang's arrival, Ch'in was not invited to the conferences attended by the rulers of the other states, and a noble of the state of Wei later expressed to his ruler what many others thought.

> Ch'in has the same customs as the Jung and Ti barbarians. It has the heart of a tiger or wolf. It is avaricious, perverse, greedy for profit and totally without sincerity. It knows nothing about etiquette, proper relationships and virtuous conduct, and if there is the slightest opportunity for material gain, it will disregard its relatives as if they were animals.[2]

The feudal rulers of the other states were alarmed by Ch'in's failure to follow the accepted codes of behaviour and ritual, but their basic worry was the fact that Ch'in policies were in many ways opposed to feudalism as such, and thus threatened the status quo. In fact, Ch'in had reaped many advantages from being half Chinese and half barbarian. One striking feature was that the Ch'in armies employed cavalry like the nomads (the Chinese were restricted to chariots), which gave them much greater mobility than their rivals. Inevitably though, the Ch'in rulers claimed descent from the powers of high Chinese antiquity, no less than the mythical Yellow Emperor, who was credited with clearing the North China plain of wild tribes called Miao so that the Chinese could settle in peace. The founder of the royal line of Ch'in was down in the historical records as the son of the Yellow Emperor's granddaughter, who had conceived 'immaculately' after swallowing a magic egg dropped from the sky by a fantastic bird.

Lord Shang's first aim when he reached a position of power inside Ch'in was to overhaul the last vestiges of feudal privileges enjoyed by the noble classes. Redistribution of land was chosen as an obvious method of cutting across traditional boundaries and breaking down petty loyalties. When the local ties were destroyed, there would be nothing to stop the populace turning its devotion wholeheartedly towards the central power. The ancient system of land control in China was the 'well-field' pattern, so called because the land was divided into units of nine fields arranged like a noughts-and-crosses board, which in Chinese is the character for a well. Eight families would each farm one square, the ninth portion going as a tithe to the local ruler. It is far from certain how generally this idealised pattern existed in China, particularly during the long centuries of fighting when all rigid systems tended to collapse. As Mencius called for a return to the well-field system in his book at the end of the fourth century BC, it would be fair to assume that it had pretty well disappeared.

Lord Shang's idea was to divide the population of Ch'in into mutually responsible

2   Ssu-ma Ch'ien, *Records of the Grand Historian.*

groups of five or ten families. They were obliged to help each other in agricultural work or in cases of difficulty, and, moreover, were required by law to reveal any crimes or grave faults committed by any member of the group. Unlike the situation in modern China, where to bring someone's shortcomings to the notice of the group and the authorities is to fulfil a moral duty to the community and to the man himself, in the state of Ch'in people had the encouragement of stiff penalties if they failed to denounce any misdemeanour. Anyone who knowingly neglected to report the crime of a member of his group was liable to the same punishment as the offender himself. It is therefore not surprising that Ch'in quickly gained a reputation as the state where precious jewels could be left in the street with confidence as no one would dare to pick them up, a situation looked on with grudging envy by the other states.

One of the strongest factors in the success of Lord Shang's measures was their universality. Aristocratic privilege above the law was a thing of the past. There was little point having rigid rules for the masses if corruption, abuse of power and extravagance were tolerated in the upper echelons. Inevitably some members of the nobility, spoilt by years of comfort and security, felt that in practice they would be exempt from severe punishments, but they were quickly disillusioned. Even the Crown Prince of Ch'in found himself in trouble. Knowing that overall power would be in his hands upon his father's death, he assumed that he could ignore Lord Shang's new regulations with impunity. Lord Shang balked at punishing the future ruler personally, but applied the law of mutual responsibility, so that the Prince's chief tutor was executed and the assistant tutor branded with a hot iron. The Prince never forgave Lord Shang for this action, which was to prove the cause of the Legalist minister's later downfall. However, the people of Ch'in had been shown once and for all that the law was practised as well as written.

Under Lord Shang's ministry, Ch'in became a magnet for foreign talent. Pragmatic men of intelligence moved into the state in the hope of finding employment, and farmers, craftsmen and immigrant workers of all kinds sought a haven of security in Ch'in as an escape from the world of conflict outside. Many natives of Ch'in protested strongly at this influx of foreign workers, but the government was fully aware that the foreigners could play an important role in the advance of the state to the position of kernel of the first Chinese Empire, and it turned as deaf an ear to the protesters as it did to the dispossessed aristocrats. The severity of the laws and brutality of the punishments soon led to a state where few people dared raise their voices in objection, and outwardly all was calm.

Upon Lord Shang's advice, the old ruler of Ch'in moved his capital eastwards to be nearer the heart of Chinese civilisation, choosing the site of Hsien Yang, which had been the former Chou capital. Trade prospered in the city, and its residents were able to enjoy rare luxuries such as silks, jade and spices brought by the wave of immigrants. But in 338 BC the tranquility was broken when the old ruler died. Power naturally passed to the Prince whom Lord Shang had indirectly punished, and who had not by any means forgotten the incident In revenge he claimed that Lord Shang was plotting to overthrow him, accusing the minister of high treason punishable by death. As the ruler was the supreme authority, Lord Shang knew there was no way of appeal, and decided to make good his escape. Hurrying away from Hsien Yang, Lord Shang tried to put up in a wayside inn for the night. However, under Ch'in law a traveller was required to have a passport authorised by a magistrate if he wanted to leave his home town. For the innkeeper to put up the minister without such a permit would be a crime. Thus Lord Shang found himself a victim of his own law, and hurried on into the night to get away from the state that he had helped to make so strong.

Lord Shang made for his native state of Wei, but found no welcome there. Wei had been having trouble with the barbarians as well as with its neighbour Ch'in, and the last thing the Wei ruler needed was a political refugee wanted by his enemies on charges of treason. Lord Shang's choice of Wei is even more surprising considering the fact that he himself was responsible for making Ch'in such a powerful threat to Wei's very existence. In 353 BC, Wei workforces had built a long wall running north-south in Shensi, along the banks of the Lo River to the north-east bend of the Yellow River, which was as much to try to keep the Ch'in armies at bay as to deter barbarians. Ch'in forces eventually broke through this barrier and occupied the territory around it, so that the Wei ruler had to command another to be built.

Hounded out by the Wei authorities, Lord Shang decided his only alternative was to go back to Ch'in and make a last stand on his own estate. Unable to gain much support for his resistance, he was soon overpowered. Following the articles of the penal code which he himself had drawn up, his body was torn to pieces by galloping horses, and all his family wiped out so that there would be nobody left to seek revenge or carry on his name. Despite the harshness of Lord Shang's rules and his ignominious end, the historical records say that the people wept for him. They acknowledged the benefits that his measures had brought to Ch'in; they had only to look over the borders to the neighbouring states to see the misery, bloodshed and poverty brought about by inefficient rule, selfishness and internal strife. They were not impressed by the fine words of philosophers who wandered round China condemning Legalism and preaching the doctrines of humanity. What use were humanity and filial piety if there was constant war and starvation? Legalism worked. Legalism brought food and a roof over their heads. Yes, they had only to look at the other states to see how true were the words of the hedonist sage Yang Chu:

> A hundred years is the utmost a man can expect to live. Helpless infancy and a drivelling dotage take up half of that, while sickness, suffering, losses, troubles, fear and worry form the rest. What is a man's life about? Wherein is its pleasure? Once dead he is a stinking, putrid mess – but how much worse to live for eternity![3]

The rulers of the feudal states were well aware that Ch'in now posed a severe threat to their existence. Throughout the fourth century BC they made attempts at anti-Ch'in alliances, but these alliances invariably fell apart as soon as matters of importance to the individual states of the alliance came into play. Ch'in had also organised an effective network of spies and saboteurs who helped to sow dissent among the allies. The various kings and

3   *The Book of Yang Chu.*

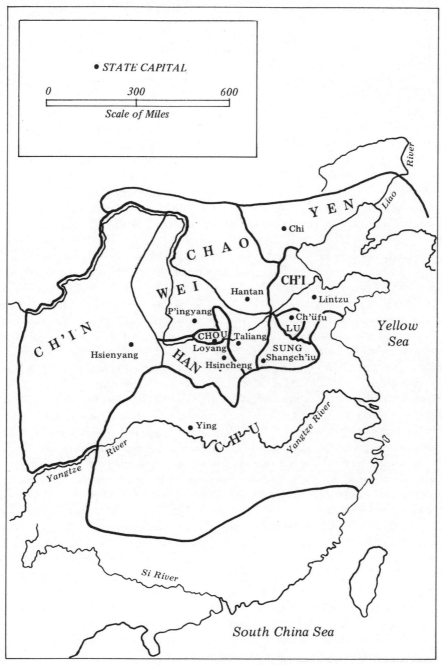

STATE CAPITAL

0   300   600
Scale of Miles

YEN

Chi

CHAO

WEI

CH'I

Hantan

Lintzu

P'ingyang

Ch'üfu

LU

CHOU Taliang

CH'IN

Loyang

SUNG

Hsienyang

HAN

Shangch'iu

Hsincheng

Yellow Sea

Liao

River

Ying

CH'U

Yangtze River

River

Yangtze

Si River

South China Sea

FIG. 4. ·The warring states (c. 300 BC).

33

dukes knew that Ch'in's strength came from its internal organisation which was stringent in its application of laws but flexible in its willingness to experiment with new ideas and accept talent from abroad. Oddly enough, the other feudal rulers never tried to imitate this blueprint for success but instead thought in terms of defeating Ch'in militarily, whereas in fact it was Ch'in that started to destroy and absorb the others.

Some of Ch'in's advantages were geographical. Its territory was protected by mountains and girdled by the Yellow River. Far from being a drawback, its position bordering the wild nomad lands meant that the Ch'in armies were highly experienced at dealing with barbarians in warfare. Their records show that there was a string of major encounters down to 327 BC when the Ch'in forces captured twenty-five walled towns belonging to the Jung barbarians, who must have been abandoning their nomadic habits for a more settled existence. Still later, during the reign of King Chao-hsiang of Ch'in (306–251 BC), the Ch'in people constructed another long wall, this time as a protection against another tribe called the Hu. The Ch'in army was in fact three armies working in unison: one, composed of able-bodied men, looked after battles and defence; another, made up of able-bodied women, looked after transportation of provisions and construction of defences; a third, made up of old people and invalids, looked after the livestock and collected food. Discipline within the army was severe, but soldiers were properly looked after and given incentives. This was a marked contrast to the situation in other states where bands of badly equipped soldiers wandered round the countryside pillaging. Military success was rewarded by the highest honours, and the common soldiers of Ch'in got the tangible benefit of financial bonuses for every enemy head they could produce, a custom adopted from the western barbarians.

Chivalry had no part to play when the Ch'in military machine took to the battlefield. Terror was seen as the most powerful deterrent to the enemy, and Ch'in victories were marked by battlefields covered with the bodies of massacred prisoners. Chinese historians have always been prone to rounding up battle casualty figures to impressively huge numbers, so that the phrase 'and a hundred thousand heads were chopped off' is almost *de rigueur* part of a battle description. But even allowing for this exaggeration, the casualty lists recorded in the state annals bear witness to remarkable scenes of carnage. When the army of the state of Chao was starved into surrender in 259 BC, for example, the Ch'in generals are said to have ordered the slaughter of 400,000 men, virtually the entire male population of Chao. Such tactics naturally induced some of the smallest states to submit to the Ch'in armies without putting up much of a fight. Those who hoped for a negotiated settlement were shown the futility of their wishes by the example of the hapless king of Ch'u, who had been invited to the Ch'in capital for talks. On his arrival he was arrested and kept prisoner until his death.

The greatest symbolic victory of all came in 256 BC, when the last king of the Royal House of Chou, the Son of Heaven himself, was removed from power. In one of the easiest military exercises of the whole Ch'in conquest of China, the armies marched into the Chou capital and brought an end to the ritualistic, nominal rule of the Chou Dynasty. With the Chou figurehead fallen, the Ch'in king was well on the way to claiming the Mandate of Heaven. The story was put about that the Ch'in had captured the Nine Tripods of Yu, the mystical tripods allegedly forged by the legendary Emperor Yu, tamer of the Flood. These tripods were the most important symbols of imperial power, but as some years later the Ch'in authorities carried out an extensive search of the river bed of the Huai tributaries to try to find them, it seems likely that the Chou ruler had ordered them to be thrown into the river rather than have them fall into Ch'in hands.

The Ch'in armies moved across the map of China, absorbing the other states as a silkworm devours a mulberry leaf, to borrow a phrase from the Han Dynasty historian, Ssu Ma-ch'ien. In 246 BC occurred an event of enormous significance, the ascent of a thirteen-year-old boy to the throne of Ch'in. He was later to be known as Ch'in Shih Huang-ti, the First Sovereign Emperor of China or 'Only First', and to be remembered as the man who conceived the idea of the Great Wall of China. The Great Wall and its building were to play a crucial role in his reign, and the Wall remains as a testament to a man who played a foremost role in the shaping of East Asia.

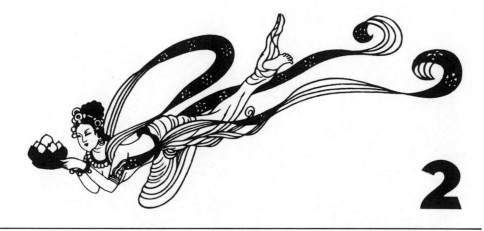

2

The Great Wall of
Ch'in Shih Huang-ti
(246-210 BC)

CHAPTER TWO

The Great Wall of Ch'in Shih Huang-ti (246–210 BC)

Iɴ September 1974, articles appeared in the *Red Flag* (the Chinese Communist Party's principal journal) comparing Chairman Mao to Ch'in Shih Huang-ti, the first Emperor of China. The parallels were taken further. Chou En-lai, the Prime Minister, was likened to Li Ssu, the Emperor's closest adviser, and the *Red Flag* said helpful political lessons for the present could be drawn from the history of the Ch'in Dynasty and its leaders. Considering the reverence with which Chairman Mao is regarded, and the reputed character of Shih Huang-ti, this might seem rather an odd parallel, but the People's Republic presents Shih Huang-ti in a far more favourable light than did the traditional pre-revolution histories. Mao Tse-tung acknowledges in his own writings how much he learnt from the life and legacy of the First Emperor, who not only gave China its most striking monument in the form of the Great Wall but also laid the foundations for nearly two thousand years of Chinese Imperial history.

If the classical historians are to be believed, the First Emperor (until 221 BC known as Cheng) had extremely dubious origins. His mother was a courtesan, a beautiful young woman who was an exquisite dancer, and who had been taken as a concubine by a wealthy travelling merchant called Lü Pu-wei. The merchant Lü went to the state of Chao to investigate business possibilities somewhere around 262 BC, though the chronology of the story is rather vague and full of discrepancies, as is often the case in early Chinese history. While on Chao, Lü Pu-wei had the opportunity of visiting the royal court at the capital, Han-tan, and there made the aquaintance of a young man called Tzu-ch'u, one of the numerous grandsons of the King of Ch'in. Tzu-ch'u had been sent to Chao by his grandfather as a hostage, a common practice in ancient China to ensure that one state would not engage in any treacherous dealings against another. The King of Ch'in could not have cared very much for his grandson's safety, however, as Ch'in and Chao were engaged in bitter struggle, and Tzu-ch'u was consequently having rather an unpleasant stay in Chao at the time Lü Pu-wei met him. The merchant realised that the situation could be turned to his own advantage, and according to the Han Dynasty historian, Ssu-ma Ch'ien, he took the youth to one side. Lü pointed out that although Tzu-ch'u's father had been named Heir Apparent, there was little hope of Tzu-ch'u himself ever ascending the throne of Ch'in, as many of his twenty-odd brothers were older than he was. The very fact that Tzu-ch'u had been sent to Chao proved that he was considered dispensable.

Lü Pu-wei put a proposition to Tzu-ch'u whereby the merchant would go to Ch'in to plead the young man's case. Lü would finance any necessary bribes out of his own pocket, on the understanding that if he succeeded in helping Tzu-ch'u to the throne he would be rewarded with a high official position. During the course of their discussions, Tzu-ch'u noticed a beautiful dancing concubine, who belonged to Lü Pu-wei. He fell in love with this girl, and asked Lü Pu-wei to give her to him. Lü Pu-wei agreed, no doubt realising that the action would form a closer link between himself and the Prince. There was no mention of the fact that the girl was expecting a baby, and it is quite possible that at the time of the handover the pregnancy was at such an early stage that nobody was aware of it. In due course, during the winter of 260–259 BC, a baby was born, a boy of whom Tzu-ch'u seems to have regarded as his own child. This baby was to become Ch'in Shih Huang-ti, First Emperor of China.

Meanwhile, Lü Pu-wei had gone to Ch'in to carry out his plan to win support for Tzu-ch'u. He bribed his way into favour at the royal court of Ch'in, and apparently even had private discussions with the principal wife of the Heir Apparent, Tzu-ch'u's father. The wife was, despite her exalted position, a very unhappy woman, because unlike her husband's concubines, she had no children. Lü Pu-wei told her that her own future position was far from safe, for when her husband became king, the mother of his chosen heir would inevitably usurp her own high standing. Lü therefore suggested that she adopt one of the younger children of the concubines, and that this youth be groomed for eventual power. The youth to be chosen for this honour would of course be Tzu-ch'u, so that the baby Cheng (allegedly merchant Lü Pu-wei's own son) would be put in eventual line for the throne.

Events happened even more quickly than Lü Pu-wei could have hoped. When the Crown Prince of Ch'in ratified his wife's adoption of Tzu-ch'u, Tzu-ch'u was summoned back to Ch'in, though according to another version he was able to get home only in 257 BC when he managed to escape from Chao during some interstate feuding. In 251 BC the old King of Ch'in died, and Tzu-chu's father ascended the throne for a reign of only a few months before also going to his grave. Tzu-ch'u therefore found himself king in 250 BC, and true to his agreement, appointed Lü Pu-wei Grand Counsellor of Ch'in. Cheng, the bastard Prince, was officially declared Heir Apparent.

Sinologists could argue until eternity as to whether the charge of Prince Cheng's illegitimacy is true or not. There can never be a definite answer, and in all honesty the truth is not as important as the fact that the story was accepted as true. It is quite possible, as some writers have suggested, that the whole thing was the invention of Han Dynasty historians wishing to slander the brief Ch'in Dynasty, founded by Cheng, which the Han replaced. But there is reason to believe that the story was already in circulation during Cheng's lifetime, and very possibly reached his ears. If so, it was just one of many adverse influences upon the future emperor's psychological well-being which were to have such a profound effect upon the way he dealt with state affairs, including the building of the Great Wall.

Prince Cheng had little time to be adequately prepared for the heavy duties of monarchy as his 'father', Tzu-ch'u, died after little more than three years on the throne of Ch'in. In 246 BC, at the tender age of thirteen, Cheng became king of the fastest growing military power of East Asia and, not surprisingly, left most of the decision-making to the Grand Counsellor Lü Pu-wei, who had assembled a formidable team of advisers, including a highly talented young man called Li Ssu who had arrived in Ch'in the year before and was eventually to win the nickname amongst Western historians of China's Machiavelli.

The Taiwanese play, *The Great Wall* (1963), by Winifred Wei, gives in its stage directions a fairly representative picture of the boy King three years after he had come to power.

In a moment the moon-shaped door is pushed open and he enters. He is a boy of sixteen but looks much older. His eyes at times look bold and self-assured but at other times frightened and uncertain. His manner is often offensively supercilious and then syco-phantically humble. His hazardous childhood has woven fear, suspicion and hatred into his character, but given him the ability to hide his real feelings.

What had given the young King his complex nature and prematurely aged him? No doubt the sudden responsibility of being king had taken its toll as much as his 'hazardous childhood', but there was a further factor for concern, namely the behaviour of his mother. On the death of her husband, the Queen Mother resumed her affair with her ex-master, Lü Pu-wei. But Lü Pu-wei quickly tired of her, as his exalted position gave him easy access to younger, more attractive women, and he was also concerned that the boy King would hear of the relationship. However, the Queen Mother was insistent in her demands, the historian Ssu-ma Ch'ien recorded, and Lü Pu-wei sought a solution to the problem in the form of a professional gigolo called Lao Ai. Stories of Lao Ai's virility and enormous penis had passed along the grapevine of the capital, and Lü decided to take him into service. He organised wild orgies, at which Lao Ai would prance around naked, even (so went the rumours) spinning a cartwheel on his penis. Lü made sure that the Queen Mother learnt of this, rightly assuming that she would want Lao Ai for herself.

Lü thereupon introduced Lao Ai to the court, and induced someone falsely to accuse Lao Ai of a crime which carried the penalty of castration, letting the Queen Mother know that under those circumstances Lao Ai would be able to serve as a eunuch in the women's quarters. The Queen Mother then bribed the official in charge of the 'silkworm room' where the castration took place (so called because of the near-darkness similar to the rooms where silkworms were kept) so that on Lao Ai the operation was not fully completed. His beard and eyebrows were plucked so he appeared to be a eunuch, then he went into service in the women's quarters, soon becoming the Queen Mother's lover. She even bore him two sons,

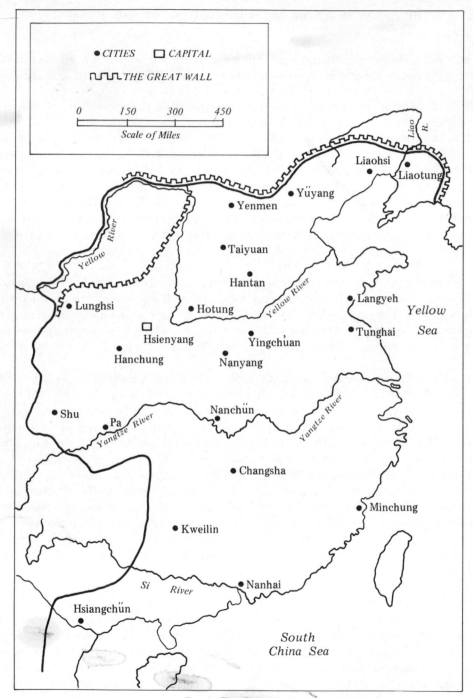

FIG. 5. The Ch'in Empire.

42

and had to be hidden away during the pregnancies so the people of Ch'in would not hear about the affair.

At first the adolescent King Cheng was unaware of the full extent of his mother's strange behaviour, and he put full trust in Lü Pu-wei. The state of Ch'in was continuing to run smoothly, and Cheng put his seal on many documents relating to new construction works, including roads and canals. In 244 BC the existing walls of Ch'in were strengthened, and new fortifications built at three passes where nomads were most inclined to raid. Lü Pu-wei was becoming increasingly worried about the Queen Mother's secret life however, and indeed, in 238 BC, the bubble burst.

Public events of that year centred around the coming of age of King Cheng, who donned the symbolic cap and sword of manhood and took on more direct rule. Inevitably someone inside the court then felt obliged to tell the ruler of his mother's relationship with Lao Ai. King Cheng acted swiftly, but Lao Ai heard that the secret was out, and started an abortive rebellion. Once caught, he suffered the fate of being torn apart between two chariots. Lü Pu-wei was implicated in the affair, and was sent into exile in 237 BC, where he committed suicide by drinking poison two years later.

The sequence of events shattered King Cheng's confidence in both his family and his advisers, and he learnt to rely almost entirely upon his own judgement until Lü Pu-wei's former assistant, Li Ssu, won his confidence. King Cheng began to show increasing signs of paranoia as he aged, suspicious of everybody, fearful about his own mortality and developing a tendency to over-protect and hide everything, including himself, behind high walls and elaborate magic.

One of the King's first reactions to the whole Lao Ai and Lü Pu-wei affair was to sympathise with those Ch'in officials who called for the expulsion of foreigners from the kingdom. Li Ssu vigorously and successfully argued against this move in 237 BC, thereby saving his own position as well as that of other foreign advisers and technicians who had done so much to make Ch'in strong. It is worth digressing slightly at this stage to look at Li Ssu's character, because it was he who kept up the strength and momentum of the first Ch'in state and later the Empire of China while his ruler's ability and mind disintegrated, particularly during the years of most intensive work on the Great Wall (214–210 BC).

Li Ssu was in his early thirties when he came to Ch'in in 247 BC. He was born in Ch'u and had studied under the famous Confucian philosopher, Hsün Tzu. Ssu-ma Ch'ien wrote of him:

When a young man he became a minor official in his district. In the toilet of the offices where he worked he noticed that there were rats that ate up the filth. Whenever a man or a dog approached, the rats were frightened off. But when he went into the granary, he found other rats eating up the grain. Those rats lived in the great side-galleries and showed no sign of fear of man or dog. Li Ssu sighed to himself 'A man's ability is like the situation of these rats; it's merely a matter of where he puts himself'.[1]

1   Ssu-ma Ch'ien, *Records of the Grand Historian.*

Fortified by this observation, rather like Robert Bruce and his spider, Li Ssu decided to educate himself as well as was possible, and put himself at the feet of Hsün Tzu, the most distinguished Confucian philosopher of the day who differed greatly from Mencius and the old school in that he taught that Man was basically evil and acquired goodness only by training. Li Ssu seems to have accepted this notion of natural evil without adopting the rest of the philosophy, and therefore moved without much difficulty to Legalism, with its ideas of enforced good conduct through laws and punishments.

Having finished his studies, Li Ssu decided that the ruler of Ch'u was not of sufficient merit to be served, and that none of the central states was markedly better. Therefore he decided to travel west to Ch'in, and bade farewell to his master Hsün Tzu.

I have heard that one should not be slow off the mark when the time is ripe for action. That moment has arrived, now that thousands of chariots are at war and the affairs of men are in the hands of travelling politicians. The King of Ch'in [Cheng's father, Tzu-ch'u] now wants to swallow up the whole world and assume the title of Emperor. This is the moment for commoners to come to their senses, for it is the golden age for travelling politicians.[2]

Tzu-ch'u died the year after Li Ssu arrived in Ch'in, but the fact was of little importance for Li Ssu. He wanted to see the King of Ch'in, no matter who that might be, become Emperor of China, preferably with Li Ssu himself at his right hand, and was therefore perfectly prepared to do everything to aid the young Cheng, particularly after Lü Pu-wei's demise helped his own advancement.

Sometimes between 237 BC and 221 BC, Li Ssu was appointed Minister of Justice, for he had established himself as a leading voice in the Ch'in court by the time the final great military sweep led Ch'in to control of the Empire. In 230 BC, Ch'in annexed the state of Han following the machinations of Li Ssu. Of course it was King Cheng's wish to carry through his forefathers' plan to take over the other states, but Li Ssu probably brought matters to a head. Han rulers, aware of their state's inferiority compared with neighbouring Ch'in, had deliberately given an impression of quiet subservience, but when Han officials learnt that Li Ssu was pressing for an invasion of their state they sent a protest memorial to King Cheng of Ch'in. The memorial was written by a member of the Han royal family, an eloquent writer named Han Fei Tzu, a famous philosopher in his own right, and a former fellow student of Li Ssu. The King of Ch'in was familiar with Han Fei Tzu's writings, and was extremely favourably impressed, which very probably awakened Li Ssu's jealousy. The exact contents of this fine piece of prose are of little concern here, except for Han Fei Tzu's reference to the long walls that the Han army had built in defence, which he claimed meant that even if the Ch'in army were to attack Han, it would be unable to annihilate the Han people even if they fought for a year.

Li Ssu retaliated with a suggestion to King Cheng that the Han king be invited for

2 Ibid.

talks and then be held prisoner for ransom of a large area of Han. He also asked that General Meng Wu (father of General Meng T'ien who was to supervise the building of the Great Wall) lead a diversionary force which would confuse the other states as to Ch'in's actual intent. King Cheng of Ch'in accordingly sent Li Ssu off to Han to speak with the Han King, but the latter refused to see him. Li Ssu returned to Ch'in in disgust and succeeded in securing the death of Han Fei Tzu, who was being held prisoner there. Han Fei Tzu's confidence in the ability of the Han walls to keep out the Ch'in armies proved singularly over-optimistic, as Han was swallowed up without much difficulty. The state of Chao, which had never fully recovered from its bloody defeat several years before, followed Han's fate two years later in 228 BC. In occupying Han and Chao, Ch'in gained control not only of Han's rather ineffective Long Ramparts (walls) but also a wall built by King Wu Ling of Chao (325–298 BC) as a defence against the northern barbarians. The Ch'in ruler knew it was to his advantage to keep up this wall in a good state of repair, and it is very likely that he had already started thinking of combining the stone defences of the states he was conquering, though no one will ever know exactly when the vision of the Great Wall entered his head.

The other states, meanwhile, were extremely worried by the course of events and several rulers had come to the conclusion that it was obvious that diplomacy had no effect on unscrupulous Legalists, and that therefore the only hope for the continuing existence of their own fiefdoms lay in assassinating Ch'in's able young ruler. Foremost among these plotters was the Crown Prince of the northern state of Yen, which lay adjacent to the unfortunate state of Chao. The Crown Prince of Yen was already familiar with his adversary as he himself had been a hostage in Chao at the same time as Cheng's father, Tzu-ch'u, and so knew both Tzu-ch'u and the infant who had now grown into the King of Ch'in. The Crown Prince of Yen had even been a hostage in Ch'in and had been so appalled by his treatment there that he had fled back home in fear and resentment.

The Yen Prince's grievance was exacerbated by the knowledge that the forces of Ch'in were closing in on his state, and he decided it was time some preventive action was taken. Eventually he managed to find a man of courage and learning called Ching K'o, who was a brilliant swordsman as well as a scholar – just the sort of stereotyped hero who today appears in innumerable blood-and-guts films made in Hong Kong.

The Yen Prince first contacted Ching K'o at the time that the state of Chao was on the verge of collapse. He outlined a plan by which a man of great bravery would go to Ch'in and try to get admitted into the King's presence. The envoy would then attempt to persuade the King to return all the territory occupied by the Ch'in armies to its former rulers. If this appeal failed (as it was bound to do) the man would stab King Cheng. The Crown Prince of Yen was convinced that once the King was dead, Ch'in would be weakened by the subsequent factional in-fighting, which was, in fact, a very accurate projection of what was to happen.

At first Ching K'o was not sure that he was up to the task, worthy though the aim might be. The Crown Prince made great efforts to try to persuade him with gifts ranging from sacrificial beasts to beautiful girls, all to no avail. Then in 228 BC Chao fell to the Ch'in invaders. The Yen Prince implored Ching K'o to go ahead with the plan. Ching K'o relented, but said that it would be very difficult to gain an audience with the King of Ch'in unless he were the bearer of some very precious gift, and suggested taking the head of a Ch'in general who had turned against King Cheng and fled to Yen for asylum.

The Yen Prince was far from happy with the idea of disposing of a general who had come to him seeking refuge, but Ching K'o solved the problem by going to see the general personally and putting the case before him. The general wept and bemoaned the fact of his exile. Then in a magnificent gesture of traditional chivalry, he cut his own throat.

Ching K'o brought the head of the noble general to the Crown Prince, who gave him a dagger coated with a potent poison that was guaranteed 'to kill any person whose clothing it caused to be stained with blood'. As an assistant Ching K'o was given an intrepid thirteen-year-old lad who had already killed a man, and the two were taken to the river marking Yen's southern boundary, escorted by the Crown Prince and others, all dressed in white (the Chinese colour of mourning). As he left, Ching K'o sang the song:

> How the wind whistles
> Cold over the River Yi;
> The lusty warrior sets forth
> Never to return.

When he arrived in Ch'in, Ching K'o gave presents to a court official, who helped him obtain an audience with the King by saying that he bore a treacherous general's head as witness to Yen's desire to become an obedient vassal of the Ch'in kingdom. The King was pleased but wary, and ordered a thorough search of the two emissaries, which showed that they had no weapons hidden in their clothing. As the two approached the royal daïs, the boy started to shake with fear, and with a clatter dropped a map-scroll he was carrying. The King looked suspicious, but Ching K'o calmly said that the boy was just a common northern lad not used to regal finery, and was trembling merely out of awe at the King's majesty.

Ching K'o slowly picked up the map and began to mount the daïs, but courtiers restrained him, saying that no one was permitted to approach the King so closely. Ching K'o protested that to show the King properly the resources of Yen, he must point out the finer details. The King overruled the courtiers and beckoned him up.

Then, as Ching K'o unrolled the map before the King, there was a flash of metal as he grasped the dagger concealed within the scroll. Ching K'o leapt at King Cheng, grabbing his target's sleeve with his left hand and thrusting the dagger forward with his right. King Cheng's reactions were instantaneous. He jumped backwards so that the blow failed, and his sleeve tore off in Ching K'o's hand. The King tried to draw his sword but it was large and cumbersome, and in his shocked state he could not get it out of its scabbard. The courtiers stood around horrified and helpless, as by Ch'in law they were forbidden to carry

46

arms inside the audience hall. The historians say they stood open-mouthed as Ching K'o chased the panic-stricken king around the room.

A quick-thinking physician present hurled his medicine bag at Ching K'o, who was temporarily caught off-balance. This gave the King the necessary second's respite to push his scabbard backwards and draw out his sword. He struck at Ching K'o, cutting deep into his left thigh. Ching K'o threw his dagger at the King in a last desperate attempt, but it missed and struck a pillar. The would-be assassin was soon overpowered and killed.

The King was later subjected to two more direct attempts on his life, forcing him to forbid anyone from getting anywhere near him. He moved around constantly, each night sleeping in a different one of his palaces or residences, which eventually numbered 270 around the capital alone. Later he constructed covered tunnels linking the palaces, so that no one would know where he was, and it was an offence punishable by death to reveal his whereabouts.

In 225 BC however, there were still important military campaigns to supervise. The Ch'in armies moved into Wei, thereby completing their control of the northern states, and acquiring a long stretch of wall running along the northern frontier. The patchwork of walls was beginning to appear as a whole, and no longer as the isolated defences of individual states.

The final victories of the Ch'in conquest of China were rapid. Ch'u was annexed in 223 BC; Yen in 222 BC and Ch'i in 221 BC. Thus for the first time a man had achieved what all past rulers had dreamed of – to be master of all China from the sea to the barbarian fringes. The Ch'in Dynasty, it was declared, was designed to last for ever. King Cheng of Ch'in decided he needed a grander title, and chose 'Shih Huang-ti' (First Sovereign Emperor). The Grand Counsellor and others pressed the new Emperor to set up his relatives as puppet rulers of the different states comprising the empire rather than to risk trying to run the vast territories from a central capital straight away. Minister of Justice Li Ssu strongly opposed this return to feudalism, and the Emperor accepted his advice.

Although the Emperor was only thirty-eight when he unified China, he had already started to become obsessed with the idea of his own death, and had a morbid premonition that his work would be undone unless the most complicated accords were made with heaven. His vain attempts to find the sacred Tripods of Yu has already been mentioned, but there were many other similar concerns that took up an ever-increasing amount of his time.

Although Legalism had remained the fundamental philosophy of Ch'in throughout the third century BC, the Emperor himself was greatly attracted by a totally different philosophy known as the Five Elements School, which had been founded in the pre-unification state of Ch'i. The Five Elements were Earth, Wood, Metal, Fire and Water, and a chief tenet of the philosophy was that each period of history was underlain by the dominating power of one element, and that the Five Elements followed one another in a definite and never-ending cycle. Metal would be replaced by Fire, Fire by Water, and so on.

The long and shaky Chou Dynasty dealt with in the previous chapter had Fire as its element. Consequently, as the interstate wars intensified, there was a scramble by the feudal rulers to acquire for themselves the patronage of the element Water, which would by rights supersede. Proponents of the Five Elements School took advantage of the situation by travelling from one state to the next giving advice and performing various dubious rites that would allegedly bring the element Water to the fore. The Grand Historian Ssu-ma Ch'ien recorded how Shih Huang-ti set about obtaining the mystical patronage of Water for his new empire.

Black [the colour connected with water] was given pride of place as the colour of clothing, pennants and flags. Six [the number symbolically associated with water] was made the standard number. Both tallies and official caps were six inches in measurement, while chariots were six feet. Six feet made one pace, and chariot teams had six horses. The Yellow River was renamed Power Water, for it was as the beginning of the power of water. Everything was decided hard and fast by law.

Shih Huang-ti, in any case, applied Legalist methods to his mystical beliefs. None the less, the Emperor had a most inauspicious start to his reign. He is said to have ascended the sacred mountain of T'ai on a pilgrimage, only to be greeted by a rainstorm. Then, when he tried to visit Hsiang Mountain where the divine daughter of the legendary sovereign Yü was reputed to live, he was buffeted by a strong wind. This so incensed him that he ordered 3000 convicts to cut down every tree on Hsiang Mountain and paint the whole thing red, the colour worn by criminals.

Like many paranoids, Ch'in Shih Huang-ti combined his fear of death and defeat with a tendency towards megalomania. This manifested itself in a policy of building monuments to his own glory everywhere possible. The Great Wall of course was to be, and remains, the most awe-inspiring construction in the world, which would be a symbol of his own enormity as well as a useful defence. Yet it was also a symbol of fear, fear not only of the barbarian tribes to the north that might sweep down into the Chinese empire at any moment, but fear also of the unknown, against which he tried endlessly to protect himself. We shall never know whether he realised that when all was done, it could never permanently hold back either.

Immediately before he sent his best general off to the northern border zone to oversee the building of the Great Wall, Shih Huang-ti embarked on his most absurd project of all – the search for the elixir of immortality. It is easy to imagine the sentiments of Li Ssu (appointed Grand Counsellor at an unspecified date between 219 and 213 BC) and the other hard-headed advisers of the Legalist court when their First Sovereign Emperor, founder of a political system supposedly destined to last for ever, disappeared on quests for magic mushrooms. The Emperor became a prey for soothsayers and charlatans, and was far more likely to grant an audience to a magician than to people on official business.

The main propagators of the belief in immortality were members of degenerate Taoist sects, who gained enormous influence during the Ch'in Dynasty. The original Taoist

From Page 1: Ch'in Shih Huang-ti (seated) oversees the Burning of the Books and the Burying of the Scholars during the literary inquisition of 213 BC.

Opposite: Han Dynasty engraving of the unsuccessful assassination attempt against King Cheng of Ch'in before he became Ch'in Shih Huang-ti. The assassin's dagger can be seen piercing a pillar (bas-relief from Shantung province).

Bottom Left & Right: The First and Last Gates of the Great Wall at Shanhaikuan and Chia Yu Kuan.

Below: Contemporary Chinese woodcut showing stylised fortified towers in the Great Wall.

Above: Temple dedicated to the God of War at Luo Ma Pass in the Great Wall.

Left: Fortified settlement at Luo Ma Pass, not far from Tsunhwachow.

Below Left: Chinese drawing showing the method used to build walls by tamping earth between frames, a technique common along sections of the Great Wall.

Below Right: Meng T'ien, the general who supervised the building of the Great Wall.

Opposite Page: 'The First Gate in the World' at Shanhaikuan, as it is today.

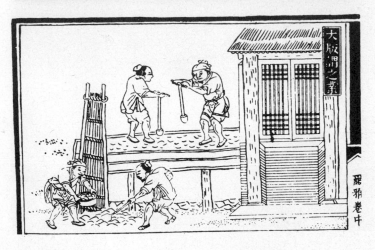

Opposite Page: The Great Wall has suffered severe erosion in the loess country of north-central China, though some magnificent ruins remain (top picture). The lower view shows a house built into the Wall.

Right: Li Ssu, Ch'in Shih Huang-ti's chief adviser.

Below & Bottom Left: Two views of the Tibetan Loop of the Great Wall, discovered by W.E. Geil in 1908.

Bottom Right: The magnificent fortress of Chia Yü Kuan, the first sign of 'civilisation' for Chinese travellers returning from the West. The fortress acted as the western terminus of the Wall for much of its history.

秦李斯

Right: Dr Geil posing in 1908 with the 'last brick' of the Great Wall, little realising the existence of Han Wu Ti's extension, whose ruins are to be found as much as 300 miles further west.

Below: The Rataling Gate in the Great Wall.

Bottom of Page: The Great Wall of China drawn by T. Allom and engraved by J. Sands.

philosophers had said that he who retires from the world of men and achieves an under-standing of the falsity of distinctions and other such questions could attain union with the Tao, and thus become a True Man, liberated from the cares and pains of the world – a victory of spirit over matter. The degenerate schools, however, said that one could become a True Man by breathing exercises, or by consuming various magic substances, of which the most eagerly sought was the elixir of life. The new Taoist theories were mixed with the beliefs of the Five Elements School to form a magic code to immortality which Ch'in Shih Huang-ti found irresistible.

The Emperor's first serious attempt to find the secret of eternal life was in 219 BC, when a magician called Hsü Shih came to him from the area that now forms Shantung province. Hsü Shih told the Emperor of three magical mountains that existed in the middle of the Eastern Sea. There dwelt Immortals, the gullible Emperor was informed, and the elixir of life grew there as a fungus. Hsü Shih said he had tried to land on these islands himself, but that when he approached they had disappeared into the sea, although he had later encountered a sea god who asked for 3000 boys and 3000 girls as a price for reaching the mountains. The court officials present at the interview scoffed at these ideas but dared not upset the Emperor, who was so deeply impressed that he financed an expedition for Hsü Shih to sail to the mystical islands of P'eng Lai with his 6000 young people. The adventurers were never seen nor heard of again, though legend has it that they reached Japan and settled there. Ch'in Shih Huang-ti does not seem to have been too much disillusioned by this experience though, as in 215 BC he sent off three more men in search of Immortals.

Although there is an infuriating lack of exact information about Shih Huang-ti, and no known contemporary portrait, his character emerges as a complex entity consistent only in its unpredictability. He was an impetuous and emotional man, as different from his minister Li Ssu as sand and water, but recognising the other man's abilities. Ssu-ma Ch'ien describes the Emperor as 'having a high pointed nose, slit eyes, pigeon breast, wolf voice, tiger heart, stingy, cringing and graceless'.

The description is typical of the spite and imagination of Ssu-ma's historical writings. Other writers have given a more favourable impression of Shih Huang-ti, such as the French author René Grousset who described him (in *The Rise and Splendour of the Chinese Empire* (1952)) as 'a personality without equal...not only a conqueror, but an administrator of genius ... an achievement equal to that of Caesar and Alexander the Great ... He was one of the mightiest geniuses to whose lot the reshaping of humanity has fallen.'

The truth is probably somewhere between these two extreme views, though the Emperor could suit either description depending on his mood. It would be fascinating to know his exact state of mind when he ordered the building of the Great Wall, but the best one can do is conjecture. The Wall was an idea that appealed to the Emperor's fantasies, and the pragmatists at court supported it as a useful defence project and as an excellent place to send troublemakers, who were marched off to join the workforce.

The classic reason quoted for the building of the Great Wall is that it was designed to keep the barbarians out, but the reality was not quite so simple. At the time, the barbarians were at one of their most disorganised stages, and posed little real threat to the Empire. The Wall would act as a formidable insurance policy against further aggression, yet security reasons did not seem to have justified the vast expenditure of capital and manpower. The Wall provided an effective break against a sweeping nomad cavalry charge, but was this worth the employment of over one million men and the deaths of thousands during the construction?

A somewhat more plausible reason for the mammoth human endeavour was that the government of Ch'in wanted to find gainful employment for the thousands of disbanded soldiers who had formerly been engaged in interstate warfare. Yet all the popular literature of the period and for centuries after pointed to the fact that soldiers returning from the wars, far from posing a threat to the new Empire, wanted to take advantage of the novel security to farm peacefully and rear their families. The traditional reasons for the building of the Great Wall do not bear close scrutiny. The sino-geographer, Owen Lattimore, is probably nearer the mark when he said that the Great Wall was the 'outward limit of desirable expansion' of the Chinese people. It was an arbitrary line drawn between the nomads and the Chinese, a line that wandered for well over 1000 miles across the wide transition belt between the two cultures.

Approximately 500 miles of this dividing Wall were constructed by Ch'in Shih Huang-ti between 221 and 210 BC. The rest of the structure, approximately 1300 miles in length, was made up of already existing state walls incorporated into the main body. Eventually the Great Wall was to stretch for nearly 4000 miles, more than one-twentieth of the earth's circumference, changing its course and purpose with the succeeding dynasties but retaining a majesty and mystery all its own.

Ssu-ma Ch'ien, however, treated the building of the first Great Wall like a summer picnic:

> After Ch'in had unified the world, [General] Meng T'ien was sent to command a host of three hundred thousand to drive out the barbarians along the north. He seized territory south of the river from them and built a Great Wall, constructing its defiles and passes in harmony with the nature of the terrain.

Ssu-ma Ch'ien dates the assignment of General Meng T'ien to oversee the building of the Wall as 214 BC, only months or even weeks after the Emperor's last great futile search for the elixir of life. Ssu-ma's account almost supports the popular legend that the Wall was built in a single day, but in fact the workforces were toiling solidly for the remaining four years of the Emperor's life, reinforced constantly by new conscripts. Behind the casual historical statements and the bland statistics lie the accumulated effort and suffering of men toiling in extreme seasonal heat and cold, lashed by rain and hail, and housed in inadequate makeshift camps, a colossal army of labourers, shaping granite blocks, digging trenches and forcing the Wall up hillsides so steep that succeeding generations said that the bricks must have been tied to the tails of mountain goats.

50

General Meng T'ien followed in the already hallowed line of distinguished men of foreign origins who served the Ch'in royal family with great loyalty. His father, Meng Wu, was Adjutant-General of Ch'in state, and had led the conquering army against Ch'u in 223 BC. Meng T'ien's brother, Meng Yi, was also a high official, one of the select group of men who had direct access to the Emperor. The most credible reconstruction of Meng T'ien's methods for building the Wall suggests that he began by setting up supply bases along the projected route, probably quite different from the line of the Wall as we know it today, as almost nothing of Ch'in Shih Huang-ti's wall remains. These supply bases numbered thirty-four in all, and were essential to nourish the workforce as the barren terrain through which the Wall passed was of little agricultural use. Men could not be spared in large numbers to develop the land near the Wall to supply the builders with locally grown food, besides which the work camps had to be as mobile as possible.

The frontier zone therefore had to be provisioned by transport columns coming from the fertile plains. A complex system of trails brought pack-animals in convoy bearing food and essential materials. Much of the food destined for the builders of the Wall never reached its destination, however, as banditry was rife in the distant north and consignments just disappeared along the way. One account says that of 182 loads of grain sent from the Shantung peninsula to the Wall, only one arrived. The resultant food shortages accelerated an already high death rate which led to violence between workers and overseers and fanned the fires of rumour that the workmen were being deliberately starved or fed on lime to reduce their appetites. Men dropped from exhaustion and malnutrition, and their bodies were thrown into the trenches where the foundations were being laid in a form of impromptu burial. Some people were bricked up inside the Wall as it progressed to act as Guardian Spirits, though it is unlikely that there were sacrifices or mass live burials as certain chroniclers would have us believe. It was thought that the spirits of the dead men buried inside the structure would appease the demons of the Far North, who were believed to be opposed to the building of the Wall, and that they would keep guard on sections of the barrier.

Once the supply bases had been set up, the engineers turned their attention to completing a line of watch-towers along the frontier. These towers were generally about 40 feet high and 40 feet square at the base, tapering to 30 feet square at the summit, and were designed to be the length of two arrow-shots apart so that all of the intervening territory or Wall was under cover. Some of the towers were those used by the Chou Dynasty for their beacon system, repaired and modernised. The towers could hold a small garrison, and protruded from the Wall like the turrets of a medieval European castle, enabling the archers to fire at people along the base of the Wall. The towers were stocked, when possible, with enough provisions to withstand a four-month seige.

At the height of the Wall's usefulness there were as many as 25,000 such towers incorporated in its length, as well as several thousand others that were free-standing further north as outposts to warn of marauding bands. They were sited on hilltops and at valley entrances to give maximum strategic value. Even today the hills outside Peking are dotted

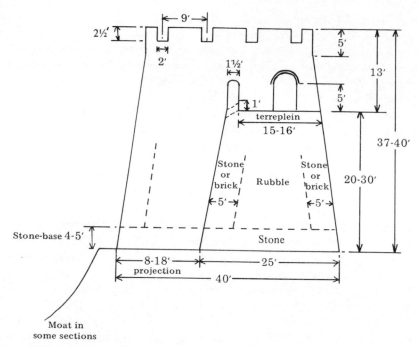

FIG. 6. Dimensions of the walls and towers in the eastern part of the Great Wall.

with towers that give the impression of a formidable defence system, though the situation further west is much less inspiring. Finally, the towers were joined together by a stone barrier, a 'demon curtain' to keep out evil spirits and potential invaders. This construction constituted the first Great Wall.

The earliest Chinese walls were made of tamped earth (terre pisé), and large stretches of Shih Huang-ti's Wall were probably constructed this way. Large wooden frames or boxes were used, dry earth being rammed into them at successively higher levels as the wall rose. According to Professor Joseph Needham, in his massive contribution to Western knowledge, *Science and Civilisation in China* (1954 et seq.), rubble stone without binding material was used as the foundation of early walls. A layer of thin bamboo stems was placed between each pisé block to speed up the drying-out process. Other authorities suggest that even in Ch'in times, more sophisticated methods were already being used, possibly similar to those employed by Ming engineers on the Great Wall nearly two thousand years later. Parallel trenches were dug into the rock about 25 feet apart, along which granite foundation blocks were laid. A brick facing was built up on top of these blocks upwards of 20 feet high, and the centre cavity filled with pounded earth. The granite blocks of the foundation were as much as 14 feet by 4 feet, while those of the stone facing (if stone was used) might be 5 feet by 2 feet by 1½ feet. Bricks that were used in facing were moulded from a particular kind of clay and baked.

The mortar used in parts of the Wall was said to be so hard that a nail could not be driven through it. The secret of mixing this 'magic mortar' has been lost, and like many rare and ancient substances it acquired mystical qualities over the centuries. It was used by pharmacists (along with ground oracle bones and herbs picked on the first snowy morning) as a cure for a whole range of diseases and complaints. Even in the early years of this century people could be seen chiselling away at broken parts of the Wall to get some of the precious ingredient. The recipe for mortar medicine, as given to the erstwhile American traveller, W. Edgar Geil, said that for internal use a pill the size and shape of a lotus seed should be swallowed as a sure cure for stomach ache. Externally, the mortar could bring instant relief for cuts or burns. A patient was instructed to take sufficient of the magic mortar, pulverise it, mash an unborn mouse into the powdered lime and apply. Should the unborn mouse prove hard to come by, oil could be used as a substitute.

The builders of the third century BC pounded the earth between the two wall faces until it was solid, then made a brick top which would serve as a roadway along which five horsemen were supposedly able to ride abreast. The gradient was so steep in parts though, that the top of the Wall was stepped, making rapid movement impossible. But the Wall was never really intended to be travelled along for more than short distances.

The most familiar parts of the Great Wall behind Peking rise and cascade across mountainous country that was difficult enough to penetrate even without a stone barrier blocking the way. Further west, however, the picture is very different. There the Wall traversed the fertile loess country, land whose earth is made of yellow silt, highly porous and so fine that when rubbed between the fingers it disappears into the skin. Thousands of square miles of north-west China are loess country, an excellent agricultural area due to the capacity of loess to hold moisture, thereby ensuring reasonable harvests even in dry years. This area, however, provided scant material for making a wall, but Meng T'ien's engineers used a variant of the terre pisé method by erecting wooden frames into which the loess, mixed with water, was poured. As it dried out, it was rammed into a solid structure. In other places they just cut away ditches on either side of a strip of loess, leaving a rampart of the earth itself. If stone or brick were available, they would face the loess to make it more durable, but this was often not the case. The net result was a wall much weaker than its eastern counterpart, and often much lower. It must have been a fairly poor deterrent, and was of much more use as a frontier delineation between China and the outside world. The elements eroded much of the western Wall, and sections facing the prevailing wind disappeared altogether. The nineteenth-century traveller. Abbé Huc, was able to cross the Wall in the west without dismounting from his horse, though Geil in 1908 found parts still standing which were 15 feet in height.

As the construction teams moved westwards, the conditions became even less inviting than in the north-east. In the Ordos region, General Meng T'ien had to clear out the Hsiung-nu barbarians before that section of the Wall could be built. The nomads offered little resistance, though, and when they had moved out, the Emperor ordered thousands of Chinese settlers to go in and cultivate the area. The colony failed after a few years and the Hsiung-nu soon took it over again.

From the Ordos the Wall progressed along the edge of the desert of Chinese Turkestan, though exactly what route it took we cannot know as so much has disappeared and bits and pieces exist looped within each other. Meng T'ien's wall finished at Kiayükwan after a section running through the A-la mountains from Liang Chou. Roughly 1800 miles in length (if projections of its route are correct) this Great Wall had three sections. The first ran from the sea to the Yellow River, the second through the loess country and the last to Kïayükwan. Much of this included walls already in existence, and the Great Wall as it stands today is a hotchpotch of later additions and alterations (see Appendix 2 for breakdown).

Western travellers, fond of statistics and trying to convey the unparalleled majesty of the Wall to people at home, came up with a host of figures and comparisons, mostly misleading and often based on comments made by helpful Chinese guides who shared their countrymen's contempt for accurate data. One of the most vivid pictures conjured up was that of the young Englishman, John Barrow, who accompanied Lord Macartney's ill-starred mission to China in 1793. He estimated, on unimaginable evidence, that the Great Wall contained more masonry than all the houses of England and Scotland – and that was without including the towers! The Western world was held in awe by the sheer bulk of the legacy of Shih Huang-ti's creation. Of course the Romans knew how to build walls, Hadrian's Wall in England is testament to that, but only the Chinese produced anything so colossal as the Great Wall.

3

Legends of
the Great Wall and
the Fall of Ch'in

CHAPTER THREE

Legends of the Great Wall and the Fall of Ch'in

INEVITABLY the imaginative legend-writers and story-tellers of China seized on the Great Wall as a fount of source material for their art. Many of the most popular tales speak of the miraculous tools that Shih Huang-ti possessed, which enabled him to build the Demon Barrier in such a short time. In the stories Shih Huang-ti takes on an even greater role than history records in the building of the Wall. Indeed, it would sometimes seem he had built the whole thing himself.

One of the Emperor's major assets was said to be his 'Drive the Mountains Whip', a flick of which would move a whole range of mountains, or make the flood waters of the Yellow River stand back to enable the workmen to get on with their job. A gigantic shovel enabled the Emperor to throw up a mile of earth in three scoops. But the greatest of his fabulous aids was his Magic Horse, a jet-black beast with a red mane and flaming tail, whose eyes shone like beacons in the night and whose hooves could carry its rider 300 miles in a single day. If needs be, the horse could fly, carrying Shih Huang-ti along the northern frontier, stamping nine or ten times every mile. Each time the Magic Horse's hooves touched the ground a watch-tower sprang up. Thus Shih Huang-ti was able to build the entire Great Wall within twenty-four hours, though it would have been difficult to make that story sound convincing to the man who worked on the Wall for so long that grass started to grow in the dust in his hair.

Another legend has the horse moving at a much slower pace. The animal was allowed to wander freely, with a weight tied to his tail, so that a track was marked in the dust as he dragged the weight along. The Emperor's engineers followed the horse, building the Wall along his winding path. One day a dust-storm blew up, and the builders lost sight of the magnificent steed and could not find his tracks in the swirling dust. The overseers decided to carry on in a straight line, until they had gone another twelve miles or so, and the storm cleared and they realised they had been going in completely the wrong direction. A scout was dispatched to locate the horse, whom he found quietly grazing just near where they had lost him. So the builders abandoned the latest stretch of Wall and rejoined the proper course. At least this story offers an explanation as to why there are twelve miles of Wall that veer off from the main structure at a seemingly pointless tangent.

Many people believed that the Magic Horse was in fact a dragon in disguise; after all, didn't the horses's hair brush up the wrong way, just like a dragon's? The Great Wall itself was also likened to a dragon, a wise and benevolent creature in Chinese mythology. A dragon, too, was responsible for some of the most violent curves in the Wall. The workmen were resting one hot summer's afternoon when a dragon came along for a nap. He curled up against a newly-completed section of the Wall, but so great was the bulk of his body that the Wall was pushed out of shape into undulating curves.

Not all the stories and legends connected with Shih Huang-ti's masterpiece are so light-hearted or amusing. One moving account of the personal suffering caused by the giant undertaking has come down through the ages in numerous different versions of the story of a devoted young wife called Meng Chiang-nu. A beautiful and talented girl, she married a brilliant adolescent scholar who had passed the highest academic degree in the education system at the tender age of sixteen. Soon after the couple married, the Emperor ordered the building of the Great Wall, and Meng Chiang-nu's husband was conscripted into the labour force because of his political views. The story continues in a third-century version, translated by Arthur Waley.

At the time of taking leave from his wife
he did not speak for long,
For he hoped as it were between morning
and evening to come back to his home.
Who could think that he would suddenly meet
disaster by pestle and hammer,
His soul be dissolved, his life finished –
that he should perish at the frontier wall?
After he had taken leave and reached the
Long Wall
The officials in charge of the work there
treated him with bitter harshness.
When he died his body was at once built into
the Wall,
His wandering soul strayed far amid the
thorns and the brambles . . .[1]

Meanwhile, Meng Chiang-nu stayed at home, waiting in vain for news of her long-departed husband. One winter night his spirit came to her while she was asleep, and told her that he was freezing to death. The spirit begged her to make some winter clothes and bring them to him at once. But before she could reply the spirit spoke again, saying that it was already too late, for her husband, unaccustomed to hard labour, had succumbed to the strain and had been buried in the Wall.

1 Waley, Arthur (trans), *Ballads and Stories from Tun-huang* (George Allen & Unwin; London, 1960).

When Meng Chiang-nu awoke the next morning, she decided to gather together some padded winter clothing and go to the Wall to try to find her young spouse, in the hope that he had survived, despite the dream's ending. Her journey was long and arduous, through wild territory full of dangers for a young woman travelling alone, but finally Meng Chiang-nu arrived at the right work camp. She ran between groups of workmen, asking them if anyone knew her husband. A man from the same province as she leant on his long-handled axe and sadly told her that the young scholar had indeed passed away some time ago.

That night, as she lay in fitful sleep, Meng Chiang-nu was visited again by the spirit.

> 'Weary and destitute on this long journey
>   you came on purpose to see me,
> Bravely meeting wind and frost,
>   wasting your energy.
> A thousand times farewell!
>   Go quickly home;
> A poor soldier under the earth
>   will never forget you.'
> When his wife heard this, she burst
>   into great sobbing:
> 'Little did I know that you my lord
>   had perished at the Long Wall!
> But how am I to know what part of
>   this Long Wall to look in?'
> Chiang-nu smote herself and wailed
>   to mighty Heaven,
> Making plaint that so good a husband
>   had perished all too soon.[2]

The story then goes on to describe how the heavenly deities heard her crying, and looked down with pity and compassion. Suddenly there was a great rumble and a gaping hole appeared in the Wall. The bones of not one but thousands of dead workmen were exposed to the icy winds – all victims of Shih Huang-ti's monstrous creation. How could she find the remains of her loved one, to take them back into central China where she could give him a proper burial, without which his soul would never rest?

The gods told her to make a cut in her finger and without hesitation she drew a knife across her delicate hand, then walked among the skeletons letting her blood drip over the bones until she reached a spot where the red blood sank into one of the skeletons, and she knew that these must be the remains of her beloved husband. Gathering up his bones, she prepared for the long journey home.

2   Ibid.

At the time, Shih Huang-ti was passing by on a tour of inspection, surrounded by officials and soldiers. We take up the story in a new translation.

> . . . noble and numberless with spears,
>   pikes and swords like a forest of hemp,
> With ladies of honour and maidens in pairs
> With canopies and fans bright like
>   the sun and the moon.
> In the middle stood an imperial baldaquin
> Under which sat the wicked Emperor.[3]

Shih Huang-ti, always partial to feminine beauty, spotted the lovely Meng Chiang-nu and let his eyes wander over her willow-like figure, her pale moon face and her beautiful hair, now tousled by the wind and her journey. He was captivated, and immediately pronounced his wish to make her a lady of his court. Whatever she thought of this proposition, she could hardly refuse, as the alternative would be a sentence of death for having caused part of the Great Wall to collapse. Anxious above all else to ensure the successful burial of her husband, the faithful widow brushed aside her revulsion for the imperial tyrant and agreed, on the condition that she be allowed to observe one hundred days' mourning before joining his other concubines. Shih Huang-ti reluctantly accepted these terms, imposing on her the condition that she make him a gown, promising that when this was completed she would be given leave to go and bury her husband. Unfortunately however, the Emperor was so enchanted with the embroidered gown that Meng Chiang-nu produced for him that he reneged on his promise and refused to let her go. Meng Chiang-nu was commanded to join his harem at once, but she again won time by asking that her husband be given an immediate state funeral on the shores of the Eastern Sea. The Emperor agreed to this proposition as well, and attended the ceremony with the court officials dressed in all their finery. The assembled crowd gasped in horror as they witnessed Meng Chiang-nu's final victory when she leapt into the sea to join her husband's released soul.

The Emperor turned yellow with rage, but then declared:

> 'To live for love alone is a rare
>   feat in this world of ours;
> So few girls like this can be found
>   these days.
> Let a monument in stone be built
>   overlooking the coast

---

3   Needham, J. and Hung-Ying, Liao (trans),. 'The Ballad of Mêng Chiang-nu, Weeping at the Great Wall', *Sinologica*.

> In memory of Meng Chiang-nu
>   who leapt into the sea.
> Now go and make ready my royal
>   chariot,
> For soon I am to return to my court.'[4]

The story received a late addition with the coming of Western technology to China, for according to local legends the gaping hole in the Wall caused by Meng Chiang-nu was never closed, and remained to provide the gap through which the Peking–Kalgan railway passes.

The detail of a section of the Wall falling down recurs in many stories. Undoubtedly the real reason for collapse had more to do with earthquakes and other natural phenomena than the passionate whims of minor gods. One such accident did indeed happen just before the Emperor visited the Wall during a tour of the northern provinces. The workmen at the time believed they had disturbed a sleeping dragon underground, and later generations nodded their heads and said that the spirits of the other world were showing their disapproval of Shih Huang-ti. It is quite conceivable that certain sections of the Wall, built at break-neck speed over extremely difficult terrain by bands of weary, underfed and inexperienced men, were structurally not as sound as they should have been. The Great Wall is a massive piece of masonry of breathtaking proportions, but architecturally it is relatively unsophisticated, especially in the western reaches, if compared with something like the pyramids of Egypt.

Shih Huang-ti is blamed by history for the barbarity of conditions under which the workforces lived, while General Meng T'ien, who had more direct control in the matter, is even now regarded as a national hero, largely because of a totally falacious tradition that he was responsible for inveinting the writing brush, the precious tool of Chinese scholars. However, even Shih Huang-ti, for all his superstitions and disregard for human life (other than his own), balked at one barbarous suggestion put forward by one of his oracles. The Emperor characteristically consulted soothsayers during the Wall's construction, particularly when it seemed to be falling behind his own demanding schedule. The diviner calmly replied to the Emperor's anxious questions that the project would be successfully completed only when 10,000 men had been buried inside it. Shih Huang-ti found an ingenious and acceptable alternative to this mass slaughter by finding a man whose name included the character for ten thousand (*wan*), and having him buried behind the brickwork instead. All progressed smoothly.

The building of the Great Wall was met with universal dismay among the common people. A ballad from the lyrical *Book of Songs* captures the mood of the peasantry when large building projects were under way, though the particular northern defences mentioned were constructed long before Shih Huang-ti's time.

4 Ibid.

The King has ordered General Nan-chung
To go and build a fort on the frontier.
To bring out the great concourse of
    chariots,
With dragon banners and standards so
    bright . . .
Long ago when we started,
The wine-millet and cooking-millet
    were in flower.
Now that we are on the march again
Snow falls upon the mire.
The King's service brings many
    hardships.
We have no time to rest or bide.
We do indeed long to return;
But we fear the writing on the tablets.[5]

Throughout the ages of the Chinese past the peasantry has borne the brunt of life's misfortunes and paid the price of their country's achievements. The Ch'in Dynasty was no exception, for while the members of the court of Shih Huang-ti were able to instigate their intrigues in relative luxury, the agricultural masses lived a hard and impoverished existence. They laboured against recurring climatic disasters and crippling demands from the state that brought frequent financial ruin and the break-up of the all-precious family unit. Behind the glorious façade of the imperial experiment of the Ch'in and succeeding Han Dynasties, the people groaned long and hard. One of the rare documents that goes beyond the history of Kings and battles records:

At the present time, out of each peasant family of five persons, at least two are taken away by official press-gangs for state works. A family is incapable of farming more than 100 mou [five hectares], with a total harvest of no more than twenty hectolitres. In spring the peasants work the land, in summer they hoe, in autumn they harvest, in winter they gather in. They go off to cut wood, they serve the authorities, they work in press-gangs. In spring there is no way they can escape the wind and the dust, in summer the heat and the sun, in autumn the foul weather and the rain, in winter the cold and frost. They do not have a single day of rest throughout the four seasons. And I haven't mentioned their private affairs. They are expected to give travellers a fitting send-off, and to go out and meet visitors. They go in mourning for the dead, keep up to date with the progress of those who are sick, feed orphans and raise the children of their own family group. Even if they are fatigued by all this, they still have to suffer

5   Waley, Arthur (trans), *The Book of Songs* (George Allen & Unwin; London, 1937).

62

calamities of floods or drought, as well as the cruel requirements of an exacting government, taxes out of season, orders in the morning and counter-orders in the evening. Therefore those who have possessions have to sell them at half their real value, and those without have to borrow money under agreements whereby they will have to repay twice the amount plus interest. That is why there are people who abandon their fields and who sell their children or grandchildren to pay their debts.[6]

Another contemporary writer called Li K'uei, writing in the *Ch'ien Han Chou*, estimated that a peasant family in Ch'in and Han times was bound to make a loss, given the economy of agricultural production coupled with state demands:

Nowadays a peasant usually supports five people. He cultivates about five hectares. The average harvest per hectare per year is thirty 'zhe', i.e. 150 zhe of millet for the whole farm. The 10 per cent tithe means he is left with 135 zhe. The food required per person per month is around $1\frac{1}{2}$ zhe, so that for five people over the year ninety zhe are eaten. That leaves forty-five. As each zhe is worth thirty cash, the net value is 1350 cash. If one deducts from this figure the amounts needed for sacrifices to the ancestors and the Spring and Autumn offerings – reckoning 300 cash – 1050 cash are left. Clothes for a man cost on average 300 cash a year, in other words 1500 cash for the family of five. There is thus an annual deficit of 450 cash, without counting for sickness costs, funerals, mourning expenses and other forms of taxes . . .

One of the events most dreaded by families during the Ch'in period was the arrival of conscription officers, calling up labourers for giant state projects. The Great Wall was just one of a series of huge public works, though of course it was by far the biggest, and soon became the most frightening for potential workmen because of the fast-spreading and well-founded rumours of the high death-rate. The Emperor and his ministers had decided that the new Empire should have a communications system worthy of a state the size of China, so that while hundreds of thousands of men slaved on the Great Wall, others were laying down a network of roads, which fanned out from the capital of Hsien Yang to the furthest corners of the Empire. Some of the roads were reputedly as much as 300 feet wide, paved with stone and bordered with cypresses. A central avenue was reserved for the Emperor when he travelled to tour his realm. One road ran along the coast from Shan Hai Kuan to south of the Yangtse, but most roads led direct to Hsien Yang. The rebel armies were to find this of great help when they overthrew the Ch'in Dynasty some years later.

The Emperor's workers also dug new canals and enlarged existing waterways. With the aid of this efficient transport system, Shih Huang-ti was able to pursue a colonisation policy as far south as Kuangtung province (around Canton), then a humid and inhospitable area full of malaria and other diseases, and therefore a useful place to send into exile criminals,

6 Chäo Tsuo, second century BC.

dissident scholars and other undesirables who could not be more gainfully employed on the Great Wall.

Soldiers would arrive in a village to conscript the workers, marching them off to the north where they encountered a climate and working conditions even worse than they were used to. Some died on their way to the Wall, and many thousands more while they were working there, earning the Wall the gruesome epithet 'The Longest Cemetery on Earth'. The ordinary men would carry their belongings slung on a pole balanced on their shoulders, whereas the wayward scholars and criminals were forced to wear chains and other impediments to movement during the journey, so that they were almost invariably weakened even before they began the ordeal of building. Such treatment of the labour force for such an important project would support the notion that the punitive aspect of the Great Wall was quite significant, as well as showing a singular disregard for economic restraint.

Shih Huang-ti was anxious that the Great Wall should not be a razor's edge between the Chinese and the barbarians, a locked door outside which the nomads would muster in discontent, ready to strike at any moment. He attempted a policy of accords with the tribes who lived nearest the Wall, in order to create a buffer zone of 'friendly barbarians' between China and the wild north and west. This policy proved fairly successful for a while, but then turned sour when the friendly barbarians began to abandon their nomadic life and imitate Chinese styles. This transformation meant they were far more interested in the luxuries that China had to offer. The friendly barbarians therefore became far more of a threat to peace than the true nomad tribes, who had very little time for the Chinese with their silk clothes that tore after only two or three hearty rides across the steppes.

One of Shih Huang-ti's main reasons for fearing the nomadic tribes was a prophecy that Hu would be the downfall of his empire. There was a tribe called Hu in what is now Manchuria, but at the time they were relatively insignificant militarily. The Jung and the Ti, the two powerful tribes who wrought so much havoc during the Chou Dynasty, had disintegrated and dispersed. The Hsiung-nu were becoming the major barbarian grouping. Like the Hu, the Hsiung-nu were livestock herders who spoke a range of Turkic languages. The Hsiung-nu were later to strengthen and become the Huns who swept across Eastern Europe, possibly turning their attention to the West because of the existence of the Great Wall, but during Ch'in Shih Huang-ti's reign, they lived in Inner Mongolia. A third and even less important group were the Yueh Chih, a confederation of tribes strung out across Chinese Turkestan to the borders of Tibet. Only the Hsiung-nu had significantly encroached on Chinese territory, and they were fairly swiftly pushed out of the Ordos by General Meng T'ien's army.

The line followed by the Great Wall had to be fairly arbitrary. In the north there was no great natural divide such as a river or a sheer range of mountains to mark the end of China proper, but instead a transition zone of infertile land gradually becoming the Gobi. There was no attempt to get as much land as possible inside the barrier, no desire for great imperialist expansion at this stage. The only important consideration was to include as many water sources and river systems as possible to guarantee water supply. The nomads were far more grieved by the resultant loss of access to water for their herds than they were by being shut off from the lush fields and rich culture of China. However, as the geographer Tom Tregear has pointed out, there is a close correlation between the line of the Great Wall and the 15 inch (rainfall) isohyet, an isohyet that divides the pasturalists of the north-west from the arable farmers of the south-east.

The Wall was essentially a cultural frontier, a barrier between the ways of life of those who rode horses, wore animal skins, smelt and had no learning, and those who wore silk, made books and cultivated their minds as well as their fields. All within the barrier practised the same basic habits and rituals and spoke dialects of Chinese. The peoples outside the Wall, on the other hand, spoke all manner of heathen tongues and had such revolting mores as drinking milk and eating cheese. The people in the transition zone on the Chinese side were forever being tempted into leading nomadic lives themselves because of the geographical conditions, and the administration in Hsien Yang felt this had to stop. The people of the frontier areas must look inwards to the plains and to the Emperor, and thousands of settlers were sent off to help make the land more productive and to bring the people more into line with the cultural uniformity. Despite the Communist Chinese championing of minority cultures in recent years, much the same sort of thing is going on in the remote parts of the republic today. 'All north of the Great Wall is the country of bowmen', proclaimed Emperor Wen of the Han Dynasty (second century BC); 'all south of the Wall is the country of hats and girdles'. The difference between the two cultural areas existed before the Wall was built, but its construction exaggerated this difference as well as the Chinese fear of the alien peoples beyond.

At each end of Shih Huang-ti's Wall, terminals were built. At the western extremity was Kiayükwan, the 'Barrier of the Pleasant Valley', often known as the Jade Gate because it was here that the first caravans bringing the imported jade so highly prized by the Chinese came into the country. It also has the name Barrier of the Gate of Demons (Kuei Men Kuan) – presumably one used the name most appropriate to the direction in which one was travelling. The local people also referred to it as 'China's Mouth', so that those who have passed through on their way to foreign lands are 'outside the mouth', and those who stay behind are 'inside the mouth'.

An inscription at the western terminus reads 'The Martial Barrier of the World'. It was the setting-off point for many Chinese travellers and exiles, and therefore the scene of many painful departures and poetic reminiscences.

> Looking westwards we see the long long road
> > leading to the new dominions,
> Only the brave cross the Martial Barrier.
> Who is not afraid of the vast desert?
> Should the scorching heat of Heaven
> > make him frightened?[7]

7 Inscription at Kïayükwan, the western terminal of Shih Huang-ti's Wall.

To die outside the confines of the Wall was considered a major catastrophe. The dark outer regions were more the realm of demons and spirits than the world of men, and therefore there was no guarantee that any man who met his fate there would ever rest in peace. This induced a state of panic among some exiles and prisoners of barbarians, who saw their chances of getting back home to die gradually whittling away. Some of the mood is conveyed by a lament by General Li Ling, writing about a hundred years after Shih Huang-ti. The General had been forced to surrender to the Hsiung-nu after his army had been wiped out.

> All day long I see no one but barbarians around me. I have to use skins and felt to protect myself from the wind and the rain and have only mutton and whey to satisfy my hunger and thirst. I have no friends with whom to pass the time of day. The whole country is rigid with black ice. I hear nothing but the moaning of the autumn wind, beneath which all greenery had disappeared. I cannot sleep at night, but toss and turn, listening to the sounds of Tartar pipes and the whinnying of Tartar horses.[8]

The fear of death outside the Wall grew with the arrival of Buddhism in China (the first monks arriving during the later part of Han Dynasty), for Chinese Buddhists believed that the soul which left a dead body on the wrong side of the Wall would never enter a newborn babe inside China, but would be condemned to an eternity of barbarian reincarnations. According to Peter Lum, writing in *The Purple Barrier* (1960), when a body was brought back into China proper in a coffin, a live cock would be tied to the cart to help guide the soul through the Great Wall.

At the eastern end of the Wall, at a town called Shan Hai Kuan, boats loaded with large rocks were sunk in the bay, and the Wall was thus carried on into the sea for a way. From the shore to the town runs a wall made of red earth and faced with brick. The traveller enters through the Hsia T'ien Ti Yi Men ('The First Gate Under Heaven'). A dedication tablet reads 'Heaven made the Sea and the Mountains', but the traveller's mind may wander to Shih Huang-ti and Meng T'ien, the men who made the Wall. Also in the east is the Willow Palisade, a barrier of willow trees that had existed since earlier times. This palisade was renovated by Shih Huang-ti, and cut off the Liaotung peninsula from the northern tribes.

While General Meng T'ien was occupied with the Great Wall, the Emperor had many other important duties to look after. He was worried about security within the Empire, and to deter insurrection he commanded that all weapons not needed by the imperial armies should be collected, brought to the capital and melted down. As a large proportion of the population of the feudal states was accustomed to being armed for self-defence, as well as during times of war, the measure caused much discontent. Men felt themselves weakened, and those who had previously led armies into battle deplored their loss of power and status.

The Emperor and his Minister Li Ssu followed many of the methods used by the Legalist philosopher, Lord Shang, in the pre-unification state of Ch'in, ensuring obedience

8 Li Ling, letter written *c.* 99 BC.

66

by harsh but consistent laws. Standardisation and harmonisation became the key administrative policy, not only in legal procedure but also in weights and measures, customs and language. Standardisation eased commercial life considerably. Transport had always been an enormous problem between the states, as was the complicated system of tariffs and customs. The wheels of carts and carriages cut deep ruts into the loess roads of the North China Plain, but harmonisation of axle lengths now meant that vehicles could travel through different regions without changing their undercarriages.

An extremely important measure was the standardisation of the way of writing Chinese characters, which up until Shih Huang-ti's time had been different in the various regions. A uniform method of writing was introduced which has endured for over 2000 years, despite modifications in the twentieth century. This meant that Chinese throughout the length and breadth of the nation could understand each other's writing even if the spoken dialects were mutually incomprehensible.

The eminent historian C. P. Fitzgerald called Shih Huang-ti one of the great destroyers of history, and many other writers have fallen into the trap of emphasising the negative side of his reign. Communist scholars, on the other hand, emphasise the revolutionary side of the Emperor's approach in bringing a breadth of vision to problems which allowed him to tackle projects of a previously unimaginable scale. Although his dynasty was the shortest in Chinese imperial history, its effects were long-lasting. The fact that Shih Huang-ti was able to cope with colossal matters of state while suffering from paranoia is paradoxically consistent with that disease.

The revolution was carried into the class structure. Men in the conquered states that now formed part of the Empire, and whose families had enjoyed privileges for generations, suddenly found themselves faced with a loss of power and much of their wealth. Local aristocrats who had held authority before the unification were replaced by Ch'in bureaucrats directly responsible to the Imperial Court. Only those who were in agreement with the new system had any hope of getting any position of responsibility. Although the Emperor kept a nominal advisory panel of seventy learned scholars, they were virtually never consulted.

Consequently the nobility and scholars of the old feudal states were opposed to the reforms almost to a man. Shih Huang-ti and his circle of ministers were fully conscious of this dangerous body of opposition and soon after the unification of the Empire, 120,000 noble familes from all over China had been forcibly transported to what is now Shensi province, thereby totally undermining the hereditary clans' influence on the territory. Some of the Emperor's counsellors were worried that the regions would be harder to govern when deprived of their traditional symbols of discipline, but the Emperor disagreed, saying:

> The fact that the Empire has been the scene of wars and rivalry which has denied peace is because of the existence of nobles and kings. Thanks to the help of my ancestors, the Empire has been re-established. If new rulers were set up, war would break out again and the present calm would be smashed. Wouldn't that be disastrous?[9]

9 Ssu-ma Ch'ien, *Records of the Grand Historian.*

The most vociferous opposition to the social revolution came from the Confucianists, who believed that the duties and obligations of their theoretical ancient society were essential in a perfect world. The scholars quoted the works of Confucius and other writers as written evidence of the incorrect road along which Shih Huang-ti was leading China. Of all the Emperor's advisers, Li Ssu was the best qualified to know what was in the Confucianists' minds because of his early philosophical training. He was also aware of the prime importance of education, for the permanence of the new order would depend largely on the support of the new generations. Li Ssu appreciated the dangers of a situation where the education of the Empire's children rested in the hands of men of learning who were hostile to the régime, and who used texts which preached doctrines that were at variance with Legalist policy. The battle of arms had been won, but the battle for the minds must go on.

Li Ssu's drastically simple solution to the problem was the notorious 'Burning of the Books' of 213 BC, right at the height of building activity on the Great Wall. The action was the final nail in the coffin of the Ch'in Dynasty's fearful reputation for centuries to follow.

Some of the conservative forces in the Empire had been pressing yet again for the re-institution of feudal rights for aristocratic families. Li Ssu responded with a petition to the Emperor:

> The Five [legendary] Emperors did not copy each other, nor did the three dynasties [Hsia, Shang and Chou] imitate their predecessors. Each had their own form of government. It was not so much that they were opposed to the methods of those who had gone before, but that times had changed.
>
> Your majesty has been the first to accomplish a great achievement in founding a glorious structure that will last for ages to come. That is what the narrow-minded scholars fail to understand . . . They cause doubt and anxiety among the people . . . These men oppose the new regulations and discuss the new edicts according to their own principles as soon as they are issued. When they are at Court they hide their resentment, but when they are away from here they debate the issues in the streets and encourage the people to believe lies.
>
> This being the case, unless action is taken now the Imperial authority will be under-mined and the dissenting factions grow in power. We must prevent this. I propose that the state histories, with the exception of those of Ch'in, be burnt. Everyone who possesses copies of the classics apart from the [seventy] Scholars of Great Learning must take these books to the magistrates to be burned. Those who dare to discuss the classics shall be put to death and have their bodies exposed in the market places.
>
> Thirty days after the publication of the [proposed] decree, all those who have not burned their books will be branded and sent off to do forced labour on the Great Wall.[10]

Only books on medicine, divination, agriculture and related sciences were to be spared. In theory there should have been seventy copies at least of all other books left, but this was

10 Ibid.

68

not the case. The decree led to the total destruction of some works and the distortion of others, later incorrectly remembered and rewritten by scholars who had memorised them when young.

No fewer than 460 scholars perished for not handing in their books, though others did manage to hide volumes or fragments in walls or under ground. How many men of learning were actually shipped off to the cold north to hammer rocks for the Great Wall is not recorded, but they undoubtedly contributed to the total of thousands of men who died during its construction.

Lord Shang is said to have been the originator of the idea of disposing of the evil influence of non-Legalist literature, but he had felt that this could be done only when the Empire had been unified. He had seen the move towards conformity of ideas as a crucial stage in the breakdown of feudal control, as indeed it was. In the event, though, its immediate effect was to strengthen the opposition of the intelligentsia. Added to this was the discontent rife among the peasantry who grew weary of paying exorbitant taxes and of being liable to service on the massive building projects. The Emperor himself remained remote from all the suffering, relying increasingly on the sorcerers and those with similar vested interests who pandered to his passion for mysterious cults and the search for the elixir of life.

The Emperor lived such a guarded life by the end of his reign, that when he died in 210 BC during a tour of the eastern provinces, only a handful of people, including Li Ssu, knew what had happened. Just before he breathed his last, Shih Huang-ti asked the chief eunuch, Chao Kao, to write a letter to his eldest son, Fu Su, who had frequently remonstrated with his father in the past, and had therefore been sent off to the Great Wall to help Meng T'ien in the hope that this would cool his youthful folly. The letter said briefly: 'Accompany my funeral cortège to [the capital] Hsien Yang, escorted by Meng T'ien's soldiers, and bury me there.'

The letter had received the imperial seal but had not been dispatched, when Shih Huang-ti died. Because the Emperor had died outside the capital and had not specified whether he had really forgiven Fu Su and wanted him to succeed to the throne, Li Sssu decided that the best thing was to conceal the Emperor's death and get the body back to Hsien Yang, where the succession question would be settled. He therefore said that Shih Huang-ti was keeping to his sleeping chariot because of a slight indisposition, and a pretence was kept up that the Emperor ate as before and received documents from officials who presented them to eunuchs looking after the carriage. As the Imperial procession continued its journey however, the corpse began to rot, so the eunuchs tied a cart of stinking dried fish (known to be one of Shih Huang-ti's favourite delicacies) to the back to cover up the smell.

The Chief Eunuch Chao Kao kept the Emperor's letter in his possession, and went to speak to one of Shih Huang-ti's sons, Hu Hai, who was accompanying the party. Chao Kao pointed out that if Fu Su received the letter, he would come to the capital and inevitably be chosen as the Second Emperor of the Ch'in Dynasty. Hu Hai understood full well what the eunuch was hinting at, namely an alliance between the two of them to get Hu Hai on the throne and Chao Kao more power and wealth than he already enjoyed. But at first Hu Hai said that for a younger brother to usurp the position of an elder brother was completely contrary to the canons of conduct. Chao Kao retaliated by quoting examples from high antiquity of virtuous leaders who had been forced to seize power from wicked senior relatives, but who had none the less won heaven's approval. Hu Hai sighed, and agreed to go to speak to Li Ssu about the matter.

Li Ssu's instant reaction was to condemn the proposed liaison as being unfit even for discussion. The eloquent eunuch was not so easily put off however and explained to Li Ssu that if Fu Su did become emperor, General Meng T'ien would inevitably be recalled from the Great Wall to play an important role in the running of state affairs. Meng T'ien would be bound to be appointed Grand Counsellor, the eunuch said, which meant demotion or dismissal for Li Ssu. The Minister continued to stand by his principles for a while, but the eunuch's insistent arguments eventually convinced him, and Li Ssu looked up to Heaven and groaned: 'Alas! That I alone of my family line should encounter this unsettled age! If I cannot bring myself to die, on what should I rely for life?'

Chao Kao, Hu Hai and Li Ssu then worked together in composing a false letter allegedly from the Emperor to be sent to Fu Su at the Great Wall:

> We [Ch'in Shih Huang-ti] have traversed the Empire and sacrificed to the divinities of the famous mountains in an attempt to prolong our life. At the present time you Fu Su are staying with the General Meng T'ien, who has been in charge of several hundred thousand troops along the frontier posts for more than ten years. You have been unable to come to report to us on the state of Meng T'ien's advances, and indeed many soldiers have been lost without the gain of a single inch of territory, yet you have repeatedly sent blunt letters criticising what we have been doing . . . As a son you have been unfilial, and herewith is presented a sword with which to end your existence.[11]

General Meng T'ien was also instructed in the letter to take his own life.

Fu Su wept when he received the document, and took it to Meng T'ien, who warned him that it might be a forgery. But Fu Su was a man of enormous filial virtue, and, after saying there was no question of querying the order, he fell on his sword. Meng T'ien was not prepared to believe the letter, however, so the emissary who had brought it had him imprisoned and went back to report to the three plotters. Hu Hai was enstated as the Second Emperor of China, and so the old prophecy that Hu would be the downfall of the Ch'in Dynasty was on the way to becoming true. The Emperor Hu started a policy of wiping out those opposed to his rule, including General Meng T'ien's highly placed brother, Meng Yi. Meng T'ien languished in prison for some time, trying to work out why heaven had brought such unjust retribution on him, when suddenly the reason came to his mind. Remembering how the peasants and workmen had said that earthquakes and other disasters

11   Ibid.

70

that had slowed the building of the Wall were protests from the spirits of the earth against its construction, he said to himself,

> I have indeed committed a crime, for which I must answer. Starting at Lint'ao and so on to Liaotung I have constructed ramparts and dug ditches stretching more than three thousand miles [sic]. Over all that distance I must have cut across the veins of the earth somewhere. Therein lies my crime.[12]

And so saying, he picked up the vial of poison that had been left in his cell and swallowed the deadly liquid.

The Chief Eunuch Chao Kao was not content to let matters rest there, however. He knew that Hu Hai was inexperienced, weak in decision-making and more interested in pleasures of the flesh than state business, all of which could aid the eunuch's lust for power. The one man who would stand between him and his goal was Li Ssu. He therefore told the Emperor that Li Ssu had ambitions to become king of a region of China by encouraging partition, and that Li Ssu's son, Li Yu, Administrator of the area of San-Chuan, was co-operating with bandits. The Emperor sent a team of investigators to look into the San-Chuan affair.

Li Ssu got wind of Chao Kao's machinations, and asked to see the Emperor, but Hu Hai refused to give him an audience. Li Ssu therefore sent a memorial to the young and foolish ruler, exposing Chao Kao's plans for self-advancement, Chao Kao in turn received this memorial from the Emperor, who had far more confidence in the eunuch than in the Grand Counsellor. Li Ssu was arrested and thrown into prison. Chao Kao brought charges of treason against him, saying that Li Ssu and his son were plotting revolt. He ordered Li Ssu to be flogged more than one thousand times, and under this torture Li Ssu falsely confessed to escape the pain. To try to escape execution, Li Ssu sent up a memorial to the Emperor enumerating his 'crimes', which included helping the state of Ch'in rise to power over the Empire, the reform of harmful policies, and the building of imperial highways. The Emperor was startled to receive a memorial from a self-confessed 'traitor', and Chao Kao ordered the interrogation to be done again. Finally, Li Ssu was condemned to the Five Punishments, which were branding of the forehead, cutting off the nose, severing the feet, death by flogging and exposure of the head and corpse in the market place, though in his case he was killed by being cut in two at the waist. With his barbarous death, the order that had reigned in the Empire began to crumble. One of the northern garrisons had already revolted, and peasants were organising to protest against Hu Hai's vicious rule and ever-increasing taxes.

Chao Kao now wished to demonstrate his power over the Emperor himself, and one day had a deer brought to court, then he asked the Emperor to admire his 'horse'. Hu Hai protested that it was a deer, but all his courtiers said no, it was a horse. Hu Hai summoned the Great Diviner and asked him fearfully what all this meant. The Great Diviner replied

12 Ibid.

that the Emperor was being punished by heaven for not attending properly to the Spring and Autumn Sacrifices, so the Emperor left the capital to start a fast to atone for his negligence. He stayed in the beautiful game park of Shang-lin, and every day went out hunting. One day by accident one of his arrows hit a passing traveller and killed him, and Chao Kao informed the Emperor that this was sure to bring down the final wrath of heaven. The Chief Eunuch succeeded in reducing the Emperor to a complete nervous wreck, and persuaded him to commit suicide. Chao Kao took the imperial seal for himself, but no one would rally round him, and he realised that the Empire could not after all be his.

Meanwhile rebel forces were gathering in strength, and in desperation Chao Kao summoned one of Hu Hai's elder brothers, and had him enthroned. One of the first things the new ruler did was to order the death of Chao Kao, but it was too late. The rot was too far advanced, and only three months later (spring, 206 BC) rebel armies arrived in the capital, and the ruler presented himself to the commander, a silk cord hanging round his neck, signifying his readiness to commit suicide, but the commander had him decapitated. And so Ch'in lost the Empire, and China was thrown into civil war. It must have seemed that all the work and revolutionary zeal of the Ch'in régime had been in vain, yet its influence has lasted until the present day, and the snaking line of the Great Wall stood against the northern horizon as a gigantic monument to Shih Huang-ti and his dreams.

4

The Han Emperors and the Western Wall

CHAPTER FOUR

The Han Emperors and the Western Wall

WITH the surrender of the Ch'in capital, Hsien Yang, to the rebel forces, the internal structure and communications of the Empire collapsed. The link between the capital and the garrisons on the Great Wall was broken, but the mass of people were not concerned with what was happening on the northern frontiers as all attention was focused on the rebel leaders. Everyone wanted to know what sort of society would emerge, whether the Empire would be subdivided again into kingdoms and how the new rulers would set about solving economic problems such as the widespread poverty and currency instability that had resulted from the last decadent years of Ch'in misrule. The scholar class was particularly anxious to discover whether it would be in greater favour than during Shih Huang-ti's time. Meanwhile, scholars lost no time in explaining why the first imperial experiment had failed. A certain Chia Yi, writing at the beginning of the Han Dynasty (206 BC–AD 220), recorded that,

> The King of Ch'in was by nature base and greedy. He relied entirely on his own judgement without having faith in ministers of known worth, and would make no attempt to conciliate with the nobility or the common people. Torture was increased and punishments made even more terrible than they were before. The taxes and levies were intolerable, and the people of the Empire were crushed by forced labour [on the Great Wall and transport systems]. The officials were unable to keep the situation under control, and the common people were driven into the most extreme state of misery, but the sovereign had no pity for them and gave them no help ... The roads were lined with those who had been tortured and mutilated; from the royal princes and government ministers down to the humblest citizens, everyone lived in terror of their lives. When a man has the rank of Son of Heaven, and his personal wealth is that of an Empire, yet he cannot escape from being butchered himself, then it is because he has failed to make clear distinction between the means by which power is safeguarded and the road to disaster.[1]

1   Chia Yi, quoted in a Taiwanese anthology of Han essays.

The two principal rebel leaders who were in charge of the transfer of power when Ch'in collapsed were of strikingly contrasted character. Their subsequent rivalry and the war between their respective supporters became one of the favourite themes of writers of romantic histories. The city of Hsien Yang actually surrendered to a young man of lowly origins called Liu Pang in the last month of 207 BC. Liu immediately swept aside the complicated Ch'in legal system and installed three simple commandments against murder, bodily injury and theft. However, a more senior leader called Hsiang Yü soon arrived in the capital, having defeated the great army that was Ch'in's last hope of survival. Hsiang Yü exerted his position of authority, took over the direction of policy and ordered the death of the last Ch'in ruler. It is impossible not to sympathise with the position of the final Emperor of Ch'in who had to pay with his life for the mistakes of his relatives after only forty-three days on the throne.

Hsiang Yü was an aristocrat who combined a worthy command of traditional education and poetry with physical strength and cruel arrogance. He had a fiery temper and alienated many of his allies by his behaviour and overriding ambition. Liu Pang, on the other hand, was shrewd and cautious and although untutored in the niceties of social conduct and the histories of the (allegedly) chivalrous past, he was a fine judge of men and situations, and tempered his astuteness with a good nature and joie de vivre. Liu always retained a consciousness of his own lowly origins. The house where he was born, according to Ssu-ma Ch'ien, had a window made from the neck of a broken pitcher, and a door with a hinge made from a piece of rope. He was a kind, generous man, who attracted sound friends and advisers, whom he heeded. Although he never actually worked on the Great Wall, one of his first jobs in life had been as an overseer of a labour gang working on Ch'in Shih Huang-ti's mausoleum. He was so horrified by the number of men under his care who ran away, that he feared there would soon be none left, so released the rest, many of whom no doubt later rallied to his standard and formed part of his eventually victorious army. He went off to join the rebel forces in the mountains, and later became ruler of his own town before rapidly rising up the rebel hierarchy.

Initially the rebels, under Hsiang Yü, thought of retaining an Imperial structure, and conferred the title of Emperor on the grandson of the old king of Ch'u. But they were anxious that the generals should not lose their newly-won power, so Hsiang Yü decided to revoke this move and impose a new political system whereby China would be split up once again into fiefdoms, many of which would be given as rewards to rebel generals, the others being much-reduced versions of the old kingdoms. Liu Pang, the rebel leader, was temporarily disposed of with the title 'Prince of Han' and was given an area around the Han River Valley. He thoroughly disagreed with the methods of Hsiang Yü, which included the sacking of the capital, during which the Imperial Library was completely destroyed, a far more devastating event for the records of early Chinese civilisation than Li Ssu's burning of the books seven years before.

Hsiang Yü divided the old state of Ch'in into three parts, and appointed three new kings of Ch'in from the Ch'in generals who had surrendered. He assumed the title Pa Wang (Hegemonic King) for himself, and vainly tried to reconstitute the feudal system. Havoc was wrought by rebel leaders who felt they had not been awarded a large enough share of the spoils, and Liu Pang demonstrated his dissatisfaction by dispossessing the three new kings of Ch'in and declaring himself ruler of that north-western part of China. The situation deteriorated into total war between Liu Pang and Hsiang Yü, which took five years finally to resolve.

Ultimately, Hsiang Yü found himself surrounded by Liu Pang's forces. One of Liu Pang's followers, Lu Chia, described the scene:

> One night Hsiang Yü heard men's voices all around singing songs from Ch'u. He was greatly alarmed, and said out loud, 'Has Liu Pang managed to gain the support of the people of Ch'u [Hsiang Yü's native region]?' He got up and went to spend the night in his tent drinking. He had a beautiful wife called Yu and a superb horse called Ch'ui, which he rode in preference to all others. Expressing his sorrow, he sang the following lines: 'My strength has uprooted mountains, and my force dominated the world. But fortune no longer favours me. Ch'ui can gallop no more, and as Ch'ui can gallop no more, what could I hope to accomplish? Yu, Yu, what does fate hold for you?'[2]

Hsiang Yü fought his way out of the besieged camp, but committed suicide on the banks of the river Wu (in Anhwei province). Liu Pang was finally undisputed master of China, and the first peasant ruler of the Middle Kingdom.

Such was the dismal state of affairs in the Empire when Liu Pang came to power that he could not even find four horses of the same colour to harness to his chariot. Even the highest officials tended to use oxen to pull their vehicles, as horses had become prohibitively expensive. It is easy to imagine the state of the Great Wall after several years of negligence. The Wall demanded constant attention and garrisoning if it was to retain its usefulness, and in times of neglect it suffered badly due to extreme climatic conditions.

Liu Pang, who became known as Kao Tsu, first Emperor of Han, suspected the merchant classes of hoarding and speculation and brought in stringent legislation against the tradesmen, forbidding them to wear silk, hold office or even ride in carriages. The merchants had always been considered lower than the peasants in the traditional social scale, but they were now becoming extremely powerful and must be taught their place. Liu Pang also resented their wealth for the new Han imperial administration needed money if it was to retain its army and reorganise society yet again, without even considering extravagant luxuries such as keeping up the Great Wall.

A Han historian, Pan Ku, recorded that Liu Pang went home to his native village soon after quashing Hsiang Yü's forces 'and invited all those people he had known in the past both young and old and passed the wine among them. He drank and danced with them. Old men, wives and friends from the past let the days slip by in drinking and revelry.'[3]

Such light-hearted celebration could not go on for long however. There was work to be

2   Ssu-ma Ch'ien, *Records of the Grand Historian*.
3   Pan Ku, *Han Shu*.

done, an empire to reconstruct. He built a new capital called Ch'ang-an, not far from the ruins of Hsien Yang, and set about reorganising the economy. He realised he had little chance of patching up the sores of war by immediate centralised control, and therefore compromised his fundamentally imperial principles by initially dividing the territory into regions administered by his relatives and friends. He always intended to bring the Empire under his own control though, and was able to dispose of all the petty rulers before he ended his brief seven-year reign in 195 BC.

If the administration of central China was just cause for concern, the situation at the extremities of the empire was far worse. The defence mechanism had broken down, and there were ominous signs of a nomad revival in the north. The most worrying group for the Chinese were the Hsiung-nu, for they had rallied round a chieftain called T'u-man who seemed to inspire new strength and confidence into the tribe. T'u-man had not enjoyed a very brilliant start to his military career, for it was he who had led the Hsiung-nu when General Meng T'ien of Ch'in, commander of the forces who had supervised the building of the Great Wall, had pushed the barbarians out of the Ordos. Since then, however, T'u-man had grown in experience and stature, and had taken advantage of China's internal disarray at the very end of the Ch'in Dynasty to move his people once more as far as the Yellow River.

T'u-man was reputedly afraid of only one thing – his son. This son was called Baghdur (or Mo-tun), and was of such visibly unscrupulous ambitions that his father sent him off as a hostage to the Yüeh-chih, the western barbarians, in the hope of keeping him out of harm's way. T'u-man then attacked the Yüeh-chih on the supposition that they would kill Baghdur in reprisal. Unfortunately for the old chief, Baghdur was much too shrewed to be a victim of such a situation, and escaped on one of the Yüeh-chih's best horses. After T'u-man had recovered from the shock of seeing Baghdur enter his tent intact, he acknowledged that the only way of keeping his son under control would be to give him some responsibility, and therefore put him in charge of a cavalry division.

Baghdur trained his followers according to the harsh rules of the old tribe, demanding that they emulate without question any action that he made. He had some special arrows constructed which whistled in flight, and used them to drill his troops in shooting from horseback. 'Shoot wherever you see my whistling arrow strike!' he shouted to his men. 'Anyone who fails to shoot will be cut to pieces!'

Baghdur led his band on hunting trips, instructing them to shoot at the same targets as he. Then, to test his men, he shot a whistling arrow at one of his favourite horses, a nomad's most precious possession. Several men hesitated to pull their bows and, true to his threats, they were killed. Later he pointed his arrow at one of his wives, and again some of his men shrank back, which brought death to them as well as the target wife. After that he took his men out into the steppes again, and aimed at one of his father's favourite horses; without hesitation his followers discharged their arrows at the beast, and Baghdur knew that the time was ripe to execute the plan that had been in his mind since the beginning of the training. When T'u-man and Baghdur were out hunting one day with all the men, Baghdur suddenly swivelled round on his horse and aimed at his father. Before the chieftain realised what was happening, his corpse lay on the ground impaled with the arrows of all Baghdur's troops. By shooting their arrows, all the men shared the guilt of the old chieftain's murder and therefore had no alternative but to follow Baghdur, who proclaimed himself the new chieftain of the Hsiung-nu.

Some neighbouring eastern tribes sought to profit from this unprecedented change of leadership by making demands on the new Hsiung-nu ruler. They asked for a horse as homage from Baghdur, and promptly received it. They then demanded one of his wives, and received her as well. Baghdur's followers remonstrated with him, but he said there was no point going to war over a woman. Finally the eastern barbarians demanded part of the Hsiung-nu territory. 'Land is the basis of the nation!' Baghdur cried, and led his cavalry in a surprise attack on his eastern tormentors, routing their army and killing their leader. Having thus disposed of his eastern rivals, he swept west and attacked the Yüeh–chih, annexing part of their land, so that he had recovered possession of all the lands which the Ch'in General Meng T'ien had taken away from the Hsiung-nu. Not content with killing the Yüeh–chih chieftain, Baghdur had a drinking cup made out of the man's skull, lined with silver, which he would bring out to show any visitors who might not be thoroughly convinced of his power. Baghdur's forces had occupied all the territory as far south as the old defence lines, and for the first time since Ch'in Shih Huang-ti had conceived the almighty folly of the Great Wall, one alien group held sway over the north, and the line of stone took on a new and profound significance.

In the palace gardens of the new city of Ch'ang-an the Han Emperor Kao Tsu (Liu Pang) was perturbed. Had he struggled for power against his rival compatriots only to face the possible indignity of humiliation at the hand of some ruffian upstart to the north? The internal problems of the reconstructed empire meant that the possibility could not be ruled out. The Emperor's concern was heightened when he was told that the forces of Baghdur now actually controlled parts of the Wall designed to keep them out. Although the Great Wall was an effective break to cavalry forces galloping down from the steppes, it was little use unless constantly garrisoned, which was proving nearly impossible when soldiers and finance were occupied with internal matters. There was little defensive advantage in the Wall if the nomads were able to take over even one of the gates let into the Wall at the main passes.

In 201 BC Baghdur's men surrounded the Chinese city of Ma Yi. The feudal ruler, enstated there by Emperor Kao Tsu, surrendered to the Hsiung-nu who then continued their march south, well into Chinese territory. Kao Tsu personally led an army against the invaders, but it was winter and he encountered such extreme cold and heavy snow that between 20 and 30 per cent of his men lost their fingers from frostbite.

Baghdur feigned a retreat in the hope that the Han army would follow, the nomad leader showing a far better grasp of military tactics than his imperial opposition, who fell for the ruse. Baghdur concealed his best men and horses so that only a bedraggled force was spotted by advance scouts of the Chinese army. Kao Tsu led his troops north as far as the city of P'ing Ch'eng to await reinforcements. Before these could arrive, Baghdur brought out his hidden strength, surrounding the city with 400,000 cavalry, 'with white horses on the west side, greenish coloured horses on the east side, black to the north and red to the south' (Ssu-ma Ch'ien). For seven days the Chinese Emperor and his men were encircled, but the historians say that Kao Tsu was able to smuggle out an envoy who went to see one of Baghdur's wives bearing precious gifts which persuaded her to take the nomad chief aside, saying, 'What is the point of two rulers making trouble for each other? Even if you do manage to take over the territory of Han you could never keep them under control. And the Han Emperor might have powerful gods looking after his lands just as you have! I implore you to think twice about the matter.[4]

Baghdur saw the sense of her argument, though a highly fanciful account unearthed by Peter Lum and recorded in The Purple Barrier gives the story an entirely different aspect. According to this legend, one of the Han advisers shut up with the Emperor inside the beleaguered city had puppets made in the form of women. These realistic wooden figures were moved along the battlements, and appeared to the surrounding nomads to be beautiful Chinese women beckoning to them. The news of this was taken to Baghdur's chief wife whose jealousy was aroused at the thought of her husband being tempted by these refined and lovely creatures. For this reason she allowed the Emperor to escape rather than have the women come into her husband's hands. Knowing as we do that Baghdur was extremely unlikely to pay any attention to a woman's jealousy considering, as he did, that women were possessions of only moderate value, it is plain that the story is a charming fabrication. Unfortunately it is impossible to be so sure about other stories that appear in both popular and official Chinese histories.

Whatever the exact course of events, the outcome was that both Baghdur and Kao Tsu realised that neither could ever hope to rule over the territory of the other, so they chose to live in peaceful co-existence. Kao Tsu showered Baghdur with gifts such as silk floss and grain, and the succeeding years of the Han Dynasty were full of treaties and records of tribute between the two sides. Baghdur's men still occasionally carried out raids in the frontier zone, which brought politely worded reproaches from the Imperial capital, but in general the Great Wall and its passes became the scene of great exchanges between the two cultures.

The most significant item of tribute from the Han Chinese to the Hsiung-nu was a Chinese princess. The negotiators had decided that a girl of royal blood should be sent to Baghdur as a sign of good faith, and that she should marry the nomad chieftain to form a blood tie between the two peoples. This formed a precedent followed by other Han Emperors for it was an effective deterrent to war; nevertheless, the practice caused horror and revulsion among Chinese officials and poets for centuries to come. Originally Kao Tsu intended to present one of his own daughters to Baghdur, but the Empress was so outraged by the idea that he chose another girl from the inner court, provided her with the title of princess, and sent her instead.

The events and strains of the early years of the Han Empire proved too much for Kao Tsu and although popular belief credited him with superhuman powers for allegedly being

4 Ssu-ma Ch'ien, *Records of the Grand Historian*.

the son of a union between a dragon and his mother, he died a mortal death in 195 BC. The Heir Apparent was aged only ten at the time, so effective control passed into the hands of the Empress Lü who embarked on fifteen years of tyrannical and brutal regency. One of the most noticeable contrasts between the two cultures that were separated by the Great Wall was their attitude to women, for in Han China women had asserted their right to express their opinions, particularly in the matter of bringing up their children.

Empress Lü was one of a series of women who were to gain power during China's history through unshaking ambition, steel-like nerves and sadistic cruelty. This latter trait also became a characteristic of many Chinese mothers-in-law, who focused their aggression on their sons' wives. The Empress Lü seized the opportunity of Kao Tsu's death to relieve her bitter jealousy of her husband's favourite concubine. She ordered palace guards to cut off the girl's feet and hands, pluck out her eyes, burn her ears, force her to drink a solution that made her dumb, and then had this pathetic creature thrown into the pit that housed the pigs who ate the filth from the royal toilets. The Empress then took the boy ruler to see this 'human pig', whom he eventually recognised as the formerly beautiful concubine. He was so traumatised by the experience that he became insane. Shortly afterwards he died, and a second boy Emperor followed along a similar route to his grave. Empress Lü then considered making one of her own relatives the third puppet ruler, but her machinations were brought to a halt by her own death in 180 BC, which was followed by an uprising. Another son of Kao Tsu was placed on the throne and reigned successfully and benevolently for the next twenty years (180–157 BC) as the (posthumously named) Wen Ti, or the Cultured Emperor.

Wen Ti set about humanising the Imperial Court and instituted economies to ease the financial burden on the treasury. He was able to concentrate on home policies because the nomad leader Baghdur had mellowed with age, and the Great Wall had lost much of its defensive purpose. However the situation changed after Baghdur's death in 174 BC and Wen Ti sent off an envoy to investigate the state of the Hsiung-nu. He reported back that the basic problem was that their habits and desires were entirely different from those of the Chinese. 'If only they acquired the taste for our things, and if they had only one-fifth of our needs, they would become our tributaries,' the envoy said sadly. Between the lines one could see that the Chinese were softening because of their sophisticated civilisation, and were no match for the Hsiung-nu in steppe-land warfare. The Chinese Minister of War acknowledged this inferiority by dissuading Wen Ti from trying to lead a campaign north of the Wall.

The Hsiung-nu scale and descend even the most precipitous mountains with astonishing speed. They swim the deepest torrents, tolerate wind and rain, hunger and thirst. They can set off on forced marches unhindered even by precipices. They train their horses to cope with the narrowest trails, and are so expert with their bows that in a surprise attack they can fire their arrows at full gallop. Such are the Hsiung-nu! They attack, recoil and rally again, and if ever they do suffer a setback they simply disappear without a trace like a cloud.[5]

5 Ibid.

Wen Ti and his ministers suffered from a common problem for early Chinese Emperors, namely how to keep the Great Wall properly supplied in view of the rudimentary transport facilities. The Yellow River and other natural water routes of course ran downhill to the China plain, so that barges carrying men or material had to go against the current. Horses were not at that time bred in quantity in the Middle Kingdom, and usually had to be bought or captured from the nomads, further limiting transport possibilities.

The frontier defences were a considerable drain on the government's budget. The Treasury found itself unable to meet the entire cost out of their reserves and taxes, so thought up some ingenious ways of lowering the cost or acquiring additional revenue, such as giving grandiose titles to businessmen who could devise cheap and efficient ways of getting food to the garrisons on the Great Wall, or else simply selling noble rank for hard cash.

Wen Ti believed that part of the economic problem stemmed from a physical shortage of money, and rashly permitted private production of copper coinage in 175 BC. The results were predictable. Those people who had large copper deposits on their land soon found themselves richer than the Emperor himself, and the currency was debased, causing rapid inflation.

Nomad raids were becoming frequent again, and in 166 BC the Hsiung-nu came within sight of the capital, Ch'ang-an. This occurred again in 162 BC and yet again in 158 BC, causing Wen Ti to sigh, 'It is because of my imperfection that I am unable to spread my virtue far and wide. That is why the territories outside my domain have sometimes not had rest, and those who live outside the Four Desert Zones have not lived a tranquil life.' In 157 BC, he expired from grief.

The new Emperor, Hsiao Ching, (157–141 BC) was faced with the same problems as Wen Ti and found little that was new in the way of solutions, other than lowering the price of bought titles to attract a wider market, and arranging for criminals to have a reduction of their sentences if they would help get grain to the frontier posts along the Wall. It was therefore left to Wen Ti's grandson, the Emperor Wu (140–87 BC), to restore peace and a secure frontier to the Empire. The Emperor Wu has often been described as the Louis XIV of China by Western historians, reigning for fifty-four years over a brilliant court where artists and musicians were as welcome as military strategists. His economic reforms led to a prosperity so great that 'the treasury was piled high with strings of cash, so long accumulated that the cords rotted with age'.[6] The currency was stabilised, and a unique form of currency bond was created – foot square pieces of white deer skin, from a special breed that existed only in the Imperial Park and which were therefore impossible to counterfeit. As is often the case, there are several conflicting versions as to how the system worked, but one authority has it that there was just one white deer in existence, which was killed to make a necessarily limited number of hide notes, which were sold at the value of 400,000 copper cash to princes who came to the Han court to pay their respects. This was followed by the issue of coinage made of a silver-tin alloy, and heavy penalties were instituted against counterfeiters.

Throughout the first twenty years of Emperor Wu's reign, the Hsiung-nu plagued the

6 *Hou han shu* (the record of the later Han period).

northern frontier. Numerous military expeditions were sent north on the Emperor's orders, often suffering heavy defeat, but gradually the Chinese generals learnt how to deal with Hsiung-nu warriors. An important stage in this military development was their new grasp of horse breeding and riding, but another, perhaps more significant factor, was that several of the imperial generals were of mixed or even entirely barbarian origin. General Ho Ch'u-p'ing, for example, had started out as a shepherd boy in the steppe lands before becoming one of the most famous Chinese warriors of all time, responsible for pushing the nomads almost into the Gobi in 119 BC. He came back to the Chinese capital victoriously leading nearly one hundred nomad chiefs as prisoners, and the Hsiung-nu never completely recovered from this major defeat, though they continued to be a great nuisance.

In an attempt to stabilise the northern border, Emperor Wu decided to try to colonise the steppe land, a policy that had failed miserably during Ch'in Shih Huang-ti's reign a hundred years before. In 120 BC, the Emperor dispatched over 100,000 men into the Ordos region to settle the area. New walls were built, behind which labourers marked out and planted farms and dug irrigation canals. The basic intention was that if Chinese territory and settlement could be extended for just a few miles north of the Wall, then the whole of Mongolia could theoretically be reached and governed. The plan was doomed to failure from the start because of the climatic unsuitability, and things got off to a very ominous beginning when the Yellow River flooded in the first year of the endeavour, killing thousands of settlers.

Emperor Wu's sallies into the inhospitable north had a very important purpose, other than just being part of the general attempt to keep the Hsiung-nu at bay. They were colonial ventures by an Emperor intent on territorial expansion. The Han régime of Emperor Wu brought the new dimension of imperialism into Chinese policy. China's leaders had previously worked towards the goal of getting all the Chinese people under one administration, but Emperor Wu wanted to go further and bring essentially non-Chinese peoples and regions under his sway. This aggressively outward-looking attitude brought about an important change in the way the Great Wall was regarded. It was no longer a limit of desirable expansion, a barrier to keep out the barbarians while the Chinese sorted out their internal problems and found their own identity. Instead the Wall became a bridgehead, a departure point for further expansion of the Empire that would none the less retain its defensive function if the need arose.

Emperor Wu turned his attention to the four corners of the compass. To the east there seemed no possibilities of aggrandisement because of the sea. Armies set off south to colonise some of the humid, inhospitable regions that had been neglected since Ch'in Shih Huang-ti's day. In the north, there was a concerted push into Mongolia and Manchuria, and the imperial armies entered Korea, setting up a colonial administration centred in Pyongyang, the capital of the present-day Democratic Republic of Korea. But the most significant advances were made in the west, leading to contact between China and the great civilisations of central Asia, and bringing a great flood of foreign goods into the Chinese market.

The history of this great western expansion is largely the story of one man, an intrepid

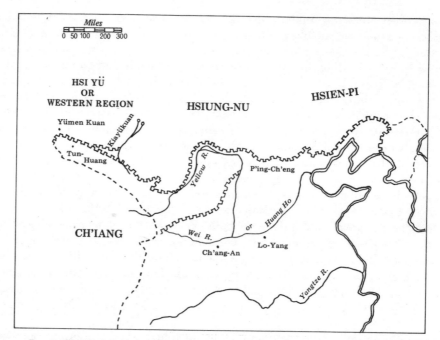

Fig. 7. The Wall during the Han Dynasty including Han Wu Ti's Western Extension.

member of the Imperial household named Chang Ch'ien. It may be recalled that during the time of Baghdur, the Hsiung-nu had defeated a tribe called Yüeh-chih and made a drinking cup from the Yüeh-chih chieftain's skull. The Yüeh-chih were totally demoralised by this sequence of events and abandoned their homeland to the Hsiung-nu, moving themselves further west beyond the Pamir mountains into the region of Sogdiana and Bactria.

Emperor Wu of Han had the idea that if only the Yüeh-chih could be persuaded to go back into their former lands, the Hsiung-nu might be restrained. Accordingly, he dispatched Chang Ch'ien on a mission to contact the Yüeh-chih and offer them an alliance against the Hsiung-nu. Chang Ch'ien was given a hundred followers and set off on his journey in 138 BC. Not surprisingly, no sooner had this party got to the other side of the Great Wall than they were rounded up by Hsiung-nu forces and taken to see their chief. The nomad leader, perhaps unaware of the exact nature of Chang Ch'ien's mission, showed great clemency, and instead of killing his captives he held them prisoner for ten years. At the end of this period, Chang Ch'ien succeeded in escaping, and with singular devotion to duty set off on his mission beyond the Pamirs as if nothing had happened. When he got to the valleys where the Yüeh–chih had been installed, he discovered that they had already moved on. Thereupon Chang Ch'ien embarked on a long expedition through Ferghana (now part of the USSR) before finally tracking them down in Bactria.

Chang Ch'ien put his Emperor's proposal for an alliance before the tribe leaders, and received the curt reply that the Yüeh–chih were very happy where they were and had no intention of uprooting themselves yet again to embark on a journey that could only lead to war with the Hsiung-nu over territory for which they felt little nostalgia. Chang Ch'ien loitered in Bactria for about a year, vainly trying to make them change their minds, but eventually acknowledged defeat and started the long trek back to report to Emperor Wu. He took another route in order to avoid meeting the Hsiung-nu, bypassing the Great Wall, but had underestimated the Hsiung-nu's patrol system, for he soon found himself once more their prisoner. This time he was held captive for only one year, eventually arriving in Ch'ang-an in 126 BC, after an absence of twelve years.

Emperor Wu had given up hope that Chang Ch'ien would return and seems not to have been particularly upset at the failure of the aim of the mission. Chang Ch'ien, with his one surviving companion out of the hundred who had set out, had brought with him specimens of goods, plants and animals from the west, and these captured the Emperor's imagination. Emperor Wu had a great taste for the exotic, as well as sharing Ch'in Shih Huang-ti's desire for the elixir of immortality. He was especially fascinated by tales of blood-sweating horses which Chang Ch'ien had seen in Ferghana. In fact, the phenomenon of the blood which the horses appeared to 'sweat' was caused by a tiny parasite in the animal's hide, but the description of these beasts made the Emperor determined to have some for himself.

Several years later, in 115 BC, Chang Ch'ien was sent back to the west with an entourage of three hundred men to broaden China's contacts with foreign kingdoms and to encourage trade. He sent some of his colleagues on to Ferghana to try to acquire some of the famous blood-sweating horses for the Emperor who believed that they would be useful in campaigns against the Hsiung-nu as well as for their curiosity value. The Chinese envoys took gold and treasure offerings, including a finely cast gold statuette of a horse, but the rulers of Ferghana refused to part with their special horses at any price. The Chinese envoy fell into a rage, and in a most un-Chinese display of emotion, he hammered the beautiful gold statuette into a shapeless mess, then attempted to take some of the horses by force, and was killed trying to flee the country.

Undaunted by this unpromising beginning, Emperor Wu sent several other missions to Ferghana, with equal lack of success. By 104 BC, he had become so infuriated by the intransigence of his western neighbours, which was as much an insult to the great Han Empire as a matter of horseflesh, that he sent off an army to deal with this stubborn people. The Han forces left Ch'ang-an in 104 BC, but the long journey across the Pamir mountains left them in no state to face a fresh opposition and they were badly beaten during an encounter with troops from Ferghana. Much disheartened, they turned back towards China, but the Emperor refused to allow them permission to return, so they camped down and awaited reinforcements. In 102 BC this strengthened force successfully penetrated the territory of Ferghana and brought the capital city to submission by cutting off its water supply. The beleaguered citizens turned against their king, who favoured no compromise with the Chinese, and presented the deposed monarch's head to the Chinese forces as a token of surrender. The Chinese commanders pressed their demands for some of the blood-sweating horses, and were given a few score of the fine steeds, as well as more than 3000 horses of more ordinary pedigree, which they herded back to the delighted and finally satisfied Emperor Wu.

The defeat of Ferghana pushed the limit of Chinese control several hundred miles to the west of previous frontiers. Much of this land was infertile tracts of deserts or mountain ranges, but was strategically very important in that it gave China control of the trade routes leading to the Middle East. Caravans bringing exotic spices, fruits and trinkets from the west to titillate the appetites of an increasingly sophisticated Han capital would return laden with Chinese silk and other prized goods. These caravans naturally became prey to roving bands of Hsiung-nu from the north, and Emperor Wu decided to bring a halt to such marauding by extending the Great Wall three hundred miles to the west of the old terminus of Kiayükwan making it now a total of over 2000 miles long. Local forces were used to build this extension, as witnessed by a Han document that instructed one of the region's governors to 'examine the configuration of the places. Utilising natural obstacles, a wall is to be constructed in order to exercise control at a distance.'

The Great Wall stretched as a gigantic finger pointing to the west, for once a symbol of hope, a sign of an expansionist Empire at its zenith. A new settlement was built at the western end, a town called Tun-huang, a highly fortified oasis that later housed the finest Buddhist art in China, based on influences from India. Isolated watch-towers were constructed outside the town to warn of the approach of invaders, and to help guard the traders who came along the two main Silk Roads that led to Parthia. Mithridates II (124–88 BC) was King of Parthia at the time, dying just one year before Emperor Wu, and he encouraged the trade in silk, which Parthian merchants were then able to send further west to the eagerly awaiting hands of ladies of the Roman Empire. In Emperor Wu's latter years, trade in rare and novel products thrived long the western borders. Merchants became rich, and thousands of settlers moved out of the central plains of China to seek their fortunes in the desert regions. Parthians, Sogdians and other foreigners visited the Middle Kingdom and entertained the Han Court with strange conjuring tricks, or provided skilled slaves who could make weird and beautiful ornaments. For the first time, the Chinese were coming into contact with 'civilised barbarians' and as this trade was not economically necessary, it can be deduced that the main reason for the exchange was sheer curiosity for things foreign, an attitude that very rarely surfaced during the subsequent history of China.

Although Emperor Wu was pleased with the new contacts with the West, he found the Hsiung-nu in the north a constant source of irritation. The nomads were not so highly organised as they had been in the glorious days of Baghdur, yet it seemed impossible to deliver a decisive blow against them. Emperor Wu himself led a force of 180,000 men north of the Wall in 110 BC in an attempt finally to subdue their forces, but failed to track down the elusive northern warriors. In 104 BC, the Chinese army did snatch a victory over the Hsiung-nu, but the situation was reversed in 103 BC, and four years later a large Chinese force was nearly wiped out by the Hsiung-nu, and the commanding general was taken prisoner. The general thought he would make the best of his enforced exile by collaborating with the Hsiung-nu, helping them to understand Chinese strategy. When the Emperor heard about this he ordered reprisals against the general's family and friends, including the famous historian, Ssu-ma Ch'ien, who was castrated for daring to speak up in favour of the treacherous general.

On the whole, relations between the Chinese and Hsiung-nu during the early Han period remained ambivalent. There were alternating periods of all-out war, settling of new treaties, exchange of gifts and considerable trading. The Emperor kept the Great Wall well garrisoned and in good repair just in case any new nomad leader should have the idea of making incursions south.

Emperor Wu intensified his interest in immortality cults towards the end of his reign, including the construction of a Dew Receiving Pillar, a contraption designed to collect life-giving essences from the heavens, and which can be seen looking like a colossal flag-pole on later paintings representing the glorious Han capital of Ch'ang-an. It is also quite possible that Emperor Wu believed that the blood-sweating horses of Ferghana, for which so much expense and energy had been spent, were the very legendary horses that could carry a soul to the land of immortality.

When the Emperor died in 87 BC, an era of growth and prosperity lay behind him. He had expanded the Empire, strengthened and extended the Great Wall, dug new canals and laid hundreds of miles of roads. It was to be roughtly seven hundred years before China again enjoyed such tranquil affluence. A high Court official composed a report on the state of the land, six years after Emperor Wu's death, that shows an optimism and self-satisfaction that was soon to be shattered.

A piece of ordinary Chinese silk can be traded with the Hsiung-nu for articles worth several pieces of gold, and thus we are able to whittle down the resources of the enemy. Unbroken chains of mules, donkeys and camels cross the frontier, and all sorts of horses come into our possession. The Imperial Treasury is filled with the furs of sables, marmots, foxes and badgers, patterned rugs and carpets, while jade, charmed stones, corals and crystals are added to the national wealth. All this means that foreign produce flows in at no disadvantage to our national budget . . . Chinese money not being spent abroad, the people enjoy abundance.[7]

7   Pan Ku, *Han Shu.*

5

Exile beyond
the Wall and
the Empire's Decline

CHAPTER FIVE

Exile beyond the Wall
and the Empire's Decline

THE garrisons that manned the Great Wall during the Han Dynasty were made up almost entirely of conscript soldiers. These men were usually from the fertile Chinese plains, sometimes as much as two months' march away from the northern defences. The extreme weather conditions and frugal way of life of the frontier zone were very different from the soldiers' previous experience, but the Han conscripts had the advantage of being warned about the situation before they went, and therefore rarely arrived totally unprepared as their Ch'in predecessors had done. During Emperor Wu's reign the Great Wall had acquired an efficient bureaucratic administration to support its military personnel, as witnessed by numerous contemporary documents which have mainly been discovered over the past fifty years.

According to research done by the sinologist Michael Loewe,[1] most of the conscripts arriving at the Wall would be sent to small units guarding the watch-towers, helping out with the extremely boring task of keeping watch for any suspicious movements by the Hsiung-nu on the other side, or else to the farms that had been established to try to lessen the frontier's dependence on supplies from the south. Once the raw recruits had been assigned to their detail, they reported to the garrison stores to pick up appropriate uniforms and tools.

The towers were mainly constructed of brick, covered with a coating of plaster and whitewash. Some of them boasted several rooms, whose doors were fitted with bolts to secure privacy. Some towers rose to a height of five to ten metres, with a stairway or ladder that provided access to the top. This was laid out as a platform and surrounded by crenellated walls so as to afford maximum protection to the defence. Heavy cross-bows were hung on the walls, their quivers stiff with arrows, and there were sighting devices with which to direct the shooting accurately. Defensive armour and helmets were provided, and there were supplies of grease and glue for the care and maintenance

---

1   From Loewe, *Everyday Life in Early Imperial China*, 202 BC–AD 220 (Batsford; London, 1968).

of weapons. At some sites a pole was erected for hoisting signals, and each tower kept flags, or torches, for the purpose. For their daily needs the men stored their water in jars, and they may have been able to convey it in earthenware pipes. There was a brazier stoked with dung on which the section's cooking-pot simmered, and some of the posts were equipped with medicine chests.[2]

The soldiers in the towers signalled at regular intervals to their colleagues so that news of any suspicious movements down on the ground would put all the sections in the area on instant alert. Torches or beacons were used for communication by night, and finely raked sand laid out at the bottom of the Wall meant that traces of any after-dark intruders would show up clearly the next morning.

The conscripts detailed to the frontier farms found agricultural conditions far more trying than any they would have experienced in the plains. Food had to be coaxed out of the ground by complex irrigation systems; walls were built to protect the crops from the wind and dust-storms and the crops also required constant attention by a labour-intensive land-force. Special fortifications were built to protect the men engaged on the digging of water channels, and to prevent sabotage of the irrigation system by Hsiung-nu raiders.

The grain harvested by the conscript farmers was transported to storage centres that measured as much as 570 feet by 150 feet. Full-time officials kept an accurate record of the amounts coming in, and looked after the distribution of grain rations to the members of the frontier colonies. These rations varied in size according to rank, work, age and number of dependants of the man concerned.

Some of the frontier conscripts worked in the police and customs services that had been set up along the Wall. A large part of their job consisted of checking travellers who wished to cross the Wall. Sections manning the gates had lists of undesirable persons, wanted criminals and the like, and a thorough search was made of travellers and their luggage to make sure they were not smuggling contraband goods. A passport or official authorisation was needed by people wishing to cross the barrier, and the border police kept detailed records of those who passed through.

Chinese poets of several dynasties have written moving accounts of the continuing bitter conditions and loneliness of life on the northern frontier, but Han documents show that during periods of proper maintenance the existence of those who guarded the Great Wall could be quite pleasant. Not all the soldiers living there were conscripts, and many professional officers stayed for several years, acquiring their own land, houses, slaves and horses. Soldiers and officials who had families with them were entitled to extra rations, and in some cases children would grow up knowing no other way of life than that of the blustery north.

To the noble and intellectual classes of the capital, however, service on the Great Wall was looked on as a form of living death, a view no doubt encouraged by old tales of the brutal conditions along the frontier during Ch'in times. The average man of Han thought of the land and people north of the Wall with fear, horror and disgust, and in particular

2 Ibid.

focused his sympathy and sense of outrage on the fate of those Chinese princesses and court ladies who were sent north of the Wall to be concubines of nomad leaders. The history of one of these reluctant girls, called Chao Chün (53 BC–AD 18), has become one of the favourite stories in the Chinese repertoire.

In 48 BC, the Emperor Wu's great-grandson ascended the dragon throne in Ch'ang-an to become the Emperor Yüan. Yüan Ti was a quiet and studious monarch who had little time for the usual extravagant pleasures of court life. When his father died, the twenty-seven-year-old Yüan Ti followed his wishes that the Imperial concubines should be released from palace service to enjoy the remainder of their lives with their families. Yüan Ti saw no reason to replenish the Imperial harem as he considered the institution a waste of time and money, but a few years later Court officials protested that palace servants and craftsmen in the capital were suffering because of the lack of work that the harem had always provided. Yüan Ti gave into pressure to resuscitate the harem, and commissioned an official named Mao Yen-shou to take charge of restoring the quarters and filling them with beautiful women. Five hundred was considered a suitable number of inmates, and Mao Yen-shou was ordered to organise a nationwide search for suitable candidates.

Legend says that the Emperor had a dream in which he found himself wandering through a secluded garden of peonies. Suddenly he spotted a beautiful girl swaying gracefully as she approached him through the blossoming peach trees. She smiled enticingly at the Emperor, but when he tried to get near her, she disappeared. He let out a groan in his sleep, and awoke sweating. For days after this dream Yüan Ti could not banish the vision of the girl from his mind, and found no enjoyment in wandering round the lovely gardens of the palace or in listening to music. So great was his consternation that he summoned the Court Diviner to explain the meaning of his dream. The Diviner replied that it was a harbinger of future happiness and prosperity, and that if only the Emperor could find the girl and make her his concubine, the welfare of the Empire would benefit.

Mao Yen-shou set off on his quest for the fairest maidens of the Empire, accompanied by eight other officials, sixty retainers and an escort. Wherever the official party travelled, their arrival was met with excitement and enthusiasm by families who knew that the selection of one of their daughters could mean wealth and imperial favour for the whole family. Mao Yen-shou was cunning enough to take advantage of the situation by demanding gifts from parents of the chosen girls, clearing his conscience with the idea that he would try to persuade the Emperor that the girl who arrived with the most lavish gifts was in fact the Dream Maiden. Mao's travels took him to the town of Ch'ichow whose prefect was instructed to post notices throughout the area calling on families to submit the names of unmarried daughters over the age of fifteen. Severe punishment would be meted out to any who disobeyed the imperial summons. The prefect himself had a beautiful daughter, later called Chao Chün or Beautiful Lady, who liked to spend her days in her father's garden, which was planted with palms, orchids and other exotic plants. In the middle of the garden was a pool full of carp, and the poets say that the fish in the pool would dart to the bottom in shame when they caught sight of Chao Chün's enchanting reflection on the water. Needless to say, this vision of loveliness was selected by Mao Yen-shou to be among the five hundred Inner Court ladies, and the wily official continued on his way, accumulating a large personal fortune of gold, silver and other valuable gifts that were officially described as down-payments on shipments of tea and fruit.

Meanwhile, the women's quarters of the palace had been restored to former glory and were stocked with many new decorations, rare birds and other amusements which would help pass the time for the Court women, cut off from everyday life and their old friends. Barges and caravans brought delicacies and works of art to the capital from every corner of the Empire and beyond, and in Ch'ang-an itself, the ringing of hammers could be heard in the streets where silversmiths and other artisans were busy working on articles for the palace.

The Emperor had been sitting in his study thinking about the imminent arrival of so many lovely girls, and suddenly became rather daunted by the prospect. He began to doubt that he would be able to recognise his Dream Maiden in a sea of five hundred made-up faces, even if she were among them. He realised that his investigations would take a con-siderable time, so rather than have the bevy of women parade before him for hour after hour, he commissioned Mao Yen-shou – who was a painter of great fame as well as an official – to execute two portraits of each of the girls, which the Emperor could then peruse at his leisure. Mao Yen-shou saw in this latest development yet another opportunity to make money, and tactfully let it be known to the girls concerned that his ability to accentuate their good points would depend upon their generosity.

Mao had been especially looking forward to the task of painting Chao Chün, as he had been struck by the innocent charm of the radiant teenager. Chao Chün was summoned to his studio and arrived resplendent in pale lavender robes. The more he studied her features and alluring eyes the more admiring he became, and he took considerable pains to produce a magnificent likeness of the girl in standing position. The Emperor had asked him to send a graded catalogue with the finished portraits so that Yüan Ti would be able to turn straight to the most beautiful pictures, and as Mao added his final brush-strokes to the silk canvas, he was perfectly prepared to place Chao Chün at the top of the list. However, in the intervening time between the completion of the first portrait and the next sitting, he dispatched a servant to see Chao Chün to hint that a payment of four hundred ounces of gold would act as a suitable incentive to the accurate completion of the task. Shortly afterwards, Mao Yen-shou painted a sitting portrait of Chao Chün dressed in fine pink brocades, her hair ornamented with phoenix-shaped pins set with pearls. He showered her with adulation, assuring her that the Emperor would be sure to call for her very soon, but when she got up to leave she did not present him with any gift, for she had too much honesty and too little experience to realise that such an esteemed man could alter a portrait if not bribed.

Twice messengers came to Chao Chün to try to persuade her to give money to the artist, but she stood by her principles, and in disgust Mao Yen-shou took up his brushes and painted in a black mole, symbol of ill-omen, beneath the right eye in each of Chao Chün's portraits. When Yüan Ti looked through the portraits some days later, he hesitated over those of Chao Chün, seeming to sense an affinity with the maiden of his dream, but both he and his ministers spotted the deforming and ominous mole. He asked Mao Yen-shou how it was possible that a girl with such a blemish could have been chosen to be one of the five hundred, but the painter begged forgiveness, saying that obviously the girl must have succeeded in hiding the mark when he first saw her. The Emperor suspected nothing, and Mao had Chao Chün hidden away in a distant pavilion in the Imperial Compound lest the Emperor should ever stumble across the truth. In the silent rooms of the Cold Pavilion, Chao Chün sat waiting as the months went by, becoming paler and more despondent as the days passed without a summons from her Emperor.

At this time the Hsiung-nu north of the Great Wall were going through a leadership crisis. The main rivalry was between a man called Khujanga (or Hu Han-hsieh, as the Chinese called him) and his elder brother, Chih-chih, 'Prince of the Left'. To ensure his own position as chieftain of the Hsiung-nu, Khujanga decided to seek a firm alliance with the Chinese, bringing a welcome end to decades of border skirmishes, and making the Great Wall redundant as a defence mechanism. Negotiations led to a state visit to the court of Yüan Ti's father in 51 BC, when a Chinese escort of 2000 cavalry travelled with Khujanga and his entourage from the Great Wall to the capital. The Emperor graciously received the chieftain in the Palace of Sweet Spring, and Khujanga was completely enthralled by the beauty and luxury of Ch'ang-an, and not least by the delicate, willowy Chinese girls, so different from the robust women of the steppe lands. He made himself popular with the Chinese officials because of his ingenuous behaviour, and amused the Court by imitating one of the dancing girls, pirouetting round in his clumsy nomad gear until he collapsed in a pile on the floor.

After a month of talks, parties and sightseeing, the nomad leader decided it was time to return to his tribe, but before leaving, he offered to move his headquarters southwards into the Ordos district, just outside the Great Wall, from which he could help safeguard the neighbouring vassal states. A force of 16,000 Chinese troops accompanied Khujanga back to the stone barrier.

Over the succeeding years, Khujanga kept in friendly contact with the Chinese court despite opposition from some of the Hsiung-nu elders who felt his policy of appeasement with the Chinese was contrary to the traditional virility of the tribe. When Yüan Ti ascended the throne in 48 BC the two leaders exchanged gifts and compliments. Soon afterwards two Chinese ambassadors visited the Hsiung-nu territory and discovered that many Hsiung-nu leaders were pressing for their headquarters to be moved further north again, as most of the game around the Great Wall had been killed off. The ambassadors knew that any move to the north would make it far more difficult to keep the Hsiung-nu under control, so they pressed for a non-aggression pact, which was concluded at a ceremony on top of a hill where a white horse was sacrificed with a sacred sword. Khujanga used a gold spoon to mix a concoction of wine and horse's blood which the two sides then drank out of the very silver-lined skull that Baghdur had made from the head of the Yüeh-chih chief.

For the next fifteen years the Chinese and the northern barbarians lived in relative harmony, and in 33 BC Khujanga once again crossed the Great Wall, this time to claim the greatest token of friendship between the two peoples, a Chinese bride. He arrived in Ch'ang-an bearing generous gifts for Emperor Yüan, including a thousand ounces of gold, a hundred horses and fifty rare pelts of sable and fox. Yüan Ti supported the plan to present Khujanga with a Chinese bride from the palace, but as there were so many young women in the royal household, and as he had not taken the trouble to get to know all of them, he relied entirely on Mao Yen-shou's catalogue and portraits to select the unfortunate girl. When the Emperor's eyes alighted for a second time on the picture of Chao Chün, he decided she was the obvious choice. The girl was evidently extremely beautiful, apart from the all-important little mole, which presumably would not have the same significance for an uncivilised nomad. Yüan Ti made the order that Chao Chün should be given in marriage to the visitor without delay, and palace officials traced the girl to the Cold Pavilion. Chao Chün burst into tears when she heard what fate had in store for her, but then consoled herself with the thought that at last she would see her Emperor, however fleetingly, and that by participating in this politically significant marriage she would be helping not only Yüan Ti but all the Chinese people. The title Princess of Eternal Peace (Yung-an Kung-chu) was bestowed on her, as by tradition such brides had to be of imperial rank.

The Emperor's audience hall was specially decorated with huge richly embroidered red and yellow silk banners and umbrellas, the day Chao Chün came to bid farewell to Yüan Ti. Many of the finest pieces from the imperial Treasury had been brought out to enhance the already glorious scene. Princes, nobles, army officers and court officials gathered in their finest robes, bustling with excitement at the historic union which should guarantee peace and make the Great Wall and all its costly defences a relic of the past. The assembled dignitaries fell to their knees when Yüan Ti entered the Hall and mounted the Dragon Throne. The Hsiung-nu ambassador, who would be in charge of seeing Chao Chün safely to the northern steppes, arrived in the hall, dressed in chocolate-coloured silk. From his low conical-shaped hat two feathers hung. From his belt were suspended silver hunting knives, a tiny tinder box and tobacco pouches. The courtiers stared at the man with awe and fascination, but soon all attention was turned to the Phoenix Portal through which Chao Chün would appear. A group of court ladies arrived, and in the middle was Chao Chün, dressed in a dragon-embroidered bodice of crimson, the colour of matrimonial felicity in China, below which shimmered a tassled skirt barely hiding pearl-encrusted shoes. Her elaborate head-dress included pale kingfisher ornaments, and strings of tiny pearls fringed her forehead. She moved in modest, swaying steps, her eyes humbly fixed to the ground. She approached the throne, kowtowed, and gently lifted up her face to the Emperor, who gasped at her unblemished beauty. Here indeed was the girl of his dream! In a flash he realised Mao Yen-shou's perfidy, but dared not show his feelings for fear of causing grave insult to the Hsiung-nu ambassador, who was as transfixed by Chao Chün's beauty as was Yüan Ti. The Emperor sat glumly through the elaborate banquet that had been prepared waiting only for the moment when he could retire and summon Chao Chün for a private audience. This done, he poured out his feelings to the long-suffering girl who shared his anguish but reminded him of their duty to go through with the arrangement for the sake of the nation. The Emperor could only agree, and forthwith sent off troops to arrest Mao Yen-shou who was hacked to pieces, his head being displayed in one of Ch'ang-an's squares as a warning to any other potential traitors.

The following morning the Emperor sent camels laden with precious gifts to the Hsiung-nu ambassador in a vain attempt to persuade him to accept a substitute for Chao Chün, but the envoy replied that this was quite out of the question. Khujanga had not yet seen his future bride, having left for home before Chao Chün's presentation to Yüan Ti in order to prepare a fitting welcome for his Chinese princess. But messengers were already on their way with a description of the lovely girl, and any last minute change of mind on the Emperor's part would throw into doubt China's good faith over the non-aggression pact. The Emperor sadly acquiesced. The Empress and other high Court ladies helped prepare Chao Chün for her long and arduous journey. As she left Ch'ang-an, the sky darkened, thunder roared and a violent downpour of rain swept the royal chariot which was to carry her to the Great Wall. Escorted by both Chinese and Hsiung-nu guards, the carriage moved slowly through the Imperial Enclosure, past the P'eng Lai Palace dominated by Emperor Wu's 'Dew Receiving Pillar', out through the thickly populated suburbs and across country. A long baggage train of horses, mules and camels threw up dust behind, as the caravan wound its way further and further from the centre of the Chinese world.

After several days travelling, the convoy reached the Great Wall, where snow lay on the ground. Chao Chün's Chinese escort left her to return to Ch'ang-an, and she descended from her carriage and climbed a hill to have a final glimpse of her native land.

> The cruel Wall shuts out her homeland,
> Her family, loved relatives and every
>   beautiful scene.
> Every common soldier of her escort
> Had been a countryman, if not a friend.[3]

Some later romantic writers recorded that Chao Chün threw herself into the Yellow River rather than pass through the Great Wall, and that the grass along the river bank grew greener than elsewhere because of her purity. But in reality she sent a last message to the Emperor before the gates of the Wall closed behind her then mounted a white Hsiung-nu steed to recommence her journey. Chao Chün was severely fatigued by travelling and soon transferred to a camel-drawn carriage in which she could rest or play music to herself. For three months the caravan advanced into increasingly barren territory before arriving one night at the brightly lit nomad camp where Khujanga awaited his bride.

Chao Chün was ushered into a tent, a circular felt construction 30 feet in diameter. Inside were a curious mixture of traditional Hsuing-nu household goods, a dung fire and some Chinese lacquered cabinets and ornaments which Khujanga had ordered to make Chao Chün feel more at home. She was given several days to rest before meeting her husband for

3 Han Dynasty poem.

the first time at the wedding ceremony held in the chieftain's official yurt (felt tent). Musicians played loud and strange tunes, while the air was heavy with musk. Nomad ladies dressed in robes of many shades of red and lavender and heavy gold jewelry watched excitedly to get the first glimpse of the foreign creature their chief had chosen to marry. Chao Chün was taken to the nuptial chamber while the men fêted the chieftain's health in the main tent. Suddenly Khujanga was overcome with desire to see his new wife and strode into the nuptial chamber to confront Chao Chün, who must have felt that she had been thrown into a different age from the life she had known on the other side of the Great Wall. Khujanga saw that the girl was petrified by his passionate entry, and reassured her by taking an arrow from the wall of the yurt and breaking it over his knee as a sign of devotion to her and of loyalty to the Chinese Emperor.

Chinese sources suggest that Chao Chün never knew happiness from the moment she left the passes of the Great Wall, whereas in fact her life must surely have become more interesting and enjoyable than it was during her cruel isolation in the Palace of Ch'ang-an. Khujanga was a thoughtful and exciting husband and gently taught her the ways of the tribe. Chao Chün was declared Queen of the Hsiung-nu and even participated in royal hunts with her husband. He was so impressed by the girl that he wrote to Yüan Ti suggesting that the Hsiung-nu take over the responsibility of looking after the security of the Great Wall and the areas along the northern frontier. As a token of friendship in his letter, delivered to the Han court by his Chief Minister, he said that the Chinese garrisons along the Wall could now be withdrawn, as the Hsiung-nu would guarantee peace for perpetuity. Because of Khujanga's sincerity and the attractive possibility of relieving the imperial Treasury of the expensive and seemingly futile garrisoning programme, most of the Han officials supported this idea. But an old and venerable Counsellor spoke against the move saying,

> Since the time of Chou and Ch'in the encroachment of the Hsiung-nu upon our territories has been of frequent occurrence. Even at the height of our power, the Empire was not free from their depredations. Formerly, the conqueror Baghdur and his descendants held on to the frontier area as their stronghold where they hunted and collected raw materials for making their bows and arrows. Yet their rapacious nature meant that they were forever launching raids against China until Emperor Wu defeated them utterly, driving them north into the desert and reinforcing the whole length of the Great Wall.
>
> Besides serving as a bulwark against invaders, the frontier posts are kept on constant guard to stop the escape of traitors from our own country. Many of the subjects of northernmost China are descendants of barbarians, and therefore have to be watched extremely carefully if treachery is to be avoided. The Great Wall was built more than a century ago. It is not a mere mud rampart. Up hill and down dale it follows the natural contours of the earth. It is riddled with many secret underground passages, and watch-towers with slit windows provide strategically placed lookouts from which our archers can cover the surrounding hills.

If we dispense with these fortifications China's safety would depend entirely upon the goodwill of the Hsuing-nu chieftains, whose ambitions would surely lead to annexation of part of our land.[4]

Yüan Ti could see the sense in the old Counsellor's arguments, and sent back a politely worded refusal.

We, Emperor of the House of Han, Supreme Ruler of the Universe and Son of Heaven, are deeply moved by the Great Chieftain's renewed expressions of loyalty and devotion to the Throne. We are happy to learn that you would be prepared to take over from our forces the defence of our frontiers as a token of this loyalty.

However, the Flower Kingdom [a commonly used term for China], as supreme arbiter of the Universe, possesses frontiers other than those to the north, and Our armies not only have to resist aggression from outside, but hold back Our people from invading the territory of friendly neighbours.

Know then that the Great Wall was built not so much to protect the Empire against the outer world, as to protect the outer world from the over-enterprising Chinese.[5]

Chao Chün came to love the freedom and simplicity of life in the steppes, and admired the people's frankness, generosity and skill on horseback. She knew that she could ask for anything in the Hsiung-nu territory, but deliberately made as few demands as possible, being conscious of the resentment that a foreign Queen could nurture. She accustomed herself to the odd diet of roast mutton, cheese and brick tea stewed with mare or goat's milk. Khujanga in turn frequently presented her with Chinese delicacies and tried to make her adaptation of lifestyle as painless as possible. Between them they worked to keep Sino-barbarian relations as cordial as possible, and the Great Wall free of conflict.

During her second year in the northern steppes, Chao Chün gave birth to a baby boy, but her family bliss was shattered soon afterwards by the death of Khujanga in 31 BC, only two years after the Chinese Emperor had died in Ch'ang-an. The new chieftain was a son of Khujanga called Vughturoi, and as it was the Hsiung-nu custom for a new chieftain to marry all the wives of his predecessor except his own mother, he wedded Chao Chün, who subsequently bore him two daughters. Vughturoi himself died in 20 BC, but Chao Chün lived on through increasingly depressing years until AD 18, when she and her son seem to have been killed by a new leader. Her brutal death away from China symbolised in Chinese minds the awful consequences of crossing the Great Wall, never to return.

The Han Court's sensible rejection of the proposal that the Hsiung-nu should look after the Great Wall meant that China was able to keep independent control of her defences, but the economic strain of the frontier garrisons was as difficult as ever. An interesting account

4   Pan Ku, *Han Shu*; Ma Chih-yüan, *Han-kung Ch'iu*.
5   Ibid.

of lively economic arguments about how best to solve the budget problem was left by a Han scholar called Huan K'uan, who shows that much of the necessary money came from government profits from iron and salt monopolies. The imperial bureaucracy was inundated with complaints that salt was so expensive because of the monopoly that many people could not afford to buy it. Iron tools produced at state foundries were allegedly of inferior quality to those formerly made by private enterprise, as well as being more expensive. When a Han minister asked protesting Confucian scholars how they proposed to defend the frontier if the monopolies which supported the army were abolished, he received a Confucianist diatribe which said that if the Emperor sufficiently cultivated benevolence and righteousness and set an example to the people, then the enemy would be overawed by his goodness, and huge military expenditure would not be necessary. The minister was understandably not convinced that benevolence and righteousness were enough to keep the Hsiung-nu the other side of the Great Wall.

The sophistication of economic theory and bureaucratic administration developed by the end of the first century BC, bears witness to a highly advanced civilisation that had made enormous progress since the confused feudal wars barely two hundred years before. It is worth quoting one short and amusing extract from a Han Dynasty school text book as translated by Michael Loewe, which shows the sort of problems that Chinese children had to tackle two thousand years before our generation was presented with almost identical questions.

A fast horse and a slow horse set out together on the 3000 li [approx 900 km] journey from Ch'ang-an to Ch'i. The first day the fast horse travels 193 li, thereafter increasing his speed by 13 li each day. The slow horse covers 97 li on the first day, thereafter reducing his speed by $\frac{1}{2}$ li each day. After reaching Ch'i the fast horse starts his return journey and meets the slow horse. When does the meeting take place and how far has each horse travelled?[6]

The answers thoughtfully provided at the back of the book are, 1: $15\frac{135}{191}$ days; 2: fast horse $4534\frac{46}{191}$ li; slow horse $1465\frac{145}{191}$ li.

Important developments were made during the Han Dynasty in most sections of the sciences and arts. Astronomy was remarkably advanced, and a minister at court was able to calculate the length of the solar year to be $365\frac{385}{1539}$ days. Unfortunately however, the Empire again became prey to political instability and conspiracy, and the rot began to spread throughout society. A cyclical pattern of blossoming and decay was beginning to emerge, and remained a striking feature of Chinese history thereafter.

A fundamental change in attitude from that of the great Han emperors was visible when Yüan Ti's son, Ch'eng Ti, succeeded to the throne in 33 BC. An envoy arrived from a western state called Chi-pin, not far from Kashmir, offering to place his territory under Chinese suzerainty. Ch'eng Ti rejected the offer when a minister advised that it would be better to insist Chi-pin look after itself, for in that way they would not be tempted to make

6   From Loewe, *Everyday Life in Early Imperial China.*

trouble elsewhere. The great imperial dreams of Han Wu Ti had obviously disappeared.

Another unhealthy development was the influence of the Dowager Empress, who succeeded in getting many of her relatives placed in high office. Her nephew, Wang Mang (33 BC–AD 23), was in the background of many palace intrigues and in AD 5 he put a one-year-old child on the throne, then acquired experience in administration and court politics before deposing the juvenile Emperor in AD 9 and pronouncing himself Son of Heaven.

The usurper put forward a radical programme of reforms, both political and economic, which included the emancipation of slaves, redistribution of land among the peasants and the calling in of all gold. Although many of his ideas now seem sound, his actions brought vitriolic attacks from the officials and scholars, and Wang Mang himself admitted that he had tried to move things too quickly, and was therefore forced to repeal some measures. Largely to divert attention from domestic problems, Wang Mang stoked the fires of discontent between the Hsiung-nu and the Chinese by decreeing that Hsiung-nu lands must become part of the Chinese Empire. Reinforcements were sent to the Wall, but the 'Emperor' was not so foolish as to try to carry out his occupation threat. Instead, he found himself faced with growing resentment at home, and in AD 18 a peasant rebellion broke out, when workers from the land marched on the capital to protest against high taxes, economic disorder and oppression. Wang Mang's answer was to call out the army, thus weakening the forces defending the northern frontier. The northern provinces became the scene of general disorder, and the government introduced a form of conscription to try to calm the situation and guarantee the manning of the Great Wall. The Hsiung-nu took advantage of the situation to launch some rather half-hearted raids south of the Wall, but they had long since ceased to be a sleek nation capable of a major invasion.

Wang Mang's overthrowers came from inside China, when members of the old royal family of Han joined peasant dissidents, and Liu Hsiu, a descendant of Liu Pang the first Han Emperor, led a victorious army into the capital, where Wang Mang was killed in AD 23. Liu Hsiu gained proper control of China after two years of civil war, but decided to move his capital away to the east of Ch'ang-an, to a town called Loyang. Once again the painful business of reconstruction after war had to be organised.

During Wang Mang's turbulent reign and the subsequent civil war, the frontiers of China had shrunk considerably. The Han administration had lost control of much of the territory in the extreme west, and Han Wu Ti's western extension of the Wall appears to have been abandoned. Certainly it rapidly fell victim to the ravages of desert storms, and in time people even forgot about its existence. Nineteenth-century travellers and historians all believed that the Great Wall ended at Kiayükwan and the 300 mile western extension (what little remained) was only positively identified as part of the Great Wall in 1908 by the Hungarian-born archaeologist, Aurel Stein.

The loss of the western territories was caused by a combination of weakness and introspection in China and the emergence of competent leaders in western states who were able to maintain their own independence and security. Some, such as Yarkand, even raided the lands of the Hsiung-nu, who were rapidly losing all vestiges of former glory before collapsing entirely around AD 58. The Hsiung-nu living just north of the Great Wall abandoned their nomad existence and accepted de facto suzerainty from China, so that the northern line of the Wall no longer formed a meaningful frontier. These sinicised Hsiung-nu were encouraged to criticise their northern brethren, who attempted to maintain a traditional tribal lifestyle, and the resultant discord effectively neutralised any barbarian threat to China itself, emphasising the anachronistic nature of the Demon Barrier.

The history of the later Han period is a complex and rather sordid catalogue of political incompetence, intrigue, puppet boy emperors, poisonings and violence. Although there were periods of recovery, such as the reign of Ming Ti (58–77), when a renewed thrust was made towards the west, and Buddhism probably made its first tentative incursions into China, the general trend was downhill, and by 150 real power had passed into the hands of the military. Revolts broke out because of the oppression and corruption of local warlords, and central authority became increasingly weaker. The last Emperor of Han, a nine-year-old boy, mounted the dragon throne in 190, but opposition forces marched on the capital. The child Emperor's main 'adviser' evacuated Loyang and set fire to it, which resulted yet again in the destruction of official archives. The bewildered Emperor became a pawn in the generals' hands, and was moved around China from one warlord to the next, maintaining a meaningless nominal rule for thirty years. The military situation gradually evolved into a clear pattern whereby China was divided into three parts, Wei, Wu and Shu. The Great Wall had become the northern frontier of a new kingdom called Wei, ruled over by a fierce dictator named Ts'ao Ts'ao who had possession of the Emperor towards the end. Although the Han rule did not officially cease to exist until AD 220, the Empire was finished and China entered its Dark Ages.

6

From the
Dark Ages to the
Glory of T'ang

CHAPTER SIX

From the Dark Ages
to the Glory of T'ang

THE decline and fall of the Han Dynasty led to nearly four hundred years of strife in China, a period with parallels to the Dark Ages of Europe, though the outcome of the Empire's collapse and barbarian invasions was not quite so devastating in China as in the later situation in the West. However, the fragmentation of China, and its domination by a succession of foreign masters up to the reunification of AD 589, acted as a serious impediment to cultural and technological advancement in Asia's leading state, though many of the barbarian intruders adopted Chinese customs and language rather than trying to impose their own limited alternatives on an antagonistic populace. China was split into north and south, and then further broken down. In the northern region surrounding the Great Wall, non-Chinese influence was at its strongest. The picture there was one of constant change as petty warlords and self-styled emperors struggled to consolidate power won by brutal carnage.

One of the major factors in the collapse of Han had been the evil influence of palace eunuchs who were a relatively new feature of Chinese life, but a feature which was to become classic. The problem came about largely because of the isolation of the later Han emperors. Unlike their warrior forbears, late emperors, such as Han Shun Ti (126–144) never had normal contact with the people. The emperor rarely left the imperial enclosure and if he did travel, the roads were cleared of people so that security would be ensured and the emperor would be spared the inquisitive gaze of the ordinary people. Ministers and advisers at court were in a position where they could in theory keep the emperor well informed of conditions, but in practice they either preferred not to or else were prevented by the over-elaborate etiquette that was usual during imperial audiences. So the only men the emperor had much communication with were the eunuchs, the only 'males' allowed to live in the precincts of the palace. The eunuchs were largely responsible for bringing up the boy heir, and they learnt to pander to whatever his weaknesses were to gain his affection so that their own influence increased disproportionately beyond the functions of their job. More often than not their only aim in life was the accumulation of money. Scholars who were alarmed at the situation formed an association to try to curb the eunuchs' power, but most of the protesting men of learning soon found themselves the victims of torture or the death sentence.

Effective action against the eunuchs seemed so unlikely through official channels that a peasant rebellion broke out in 184, the revolting forces taking the name Yellow Turbans from their distinctive head dress. Their leader was a certain Chang Chüeh, a faith-healer who had helped wipe out a mysterious epidemic in central China. He claimed that his followers would win immortality on the battlefield after drinking a magic potion, and his weird mixture of social theory, military adventure and pseudo-Taoist mysticism became a formula for many similar uprisings every time a Chinese dynasty began to look somewhat shaky.

The Yellow Turban Rebellion threw the capital into pandemonium, and many of the important Chinese families packed their bags and headed south. This trickle of émigrés into the southern regions became a torrent when the northern barbarians increased their raiding, so it can be justifiably argued that the centre of purely Chinese civilisation then moved away from the traditional heartland of the northern plains. Immigrants and people of mixed background replaced so many Chinese in the northern regions that generations of the new southern Chinese who had never seen the Great Wall, began to think of it as a very distant and rather foreboding phenomenon.

Of all the warlords that jousted for power at the turn of the third century, the most colourful and probably the most able was Ts'ao Ts'ao who had won fame by being one of the very small number of provincial military governors who had kept his area free of the Yellow Turbans. He was the adopted son of a eunuch, but relied on his own wits and military prowess to attempt to bring unity back to China. He has gone down in history as a highly romantic and ruthless adventurer, largely due to a classic Chinese novel entitled *The Romance of the Three Kingdoms* which stirred the hearts and imaginations of generations of Chinese boys and youths, making heroic and respectable one of the most ignominious periods of China's long and bloody history. Ts'ao Ts'ao himself was a man of admirable versatility. He was a fine military leader, and a capable poet. He had a flair for producing memorable epigrams, such as his damning couplet of the fallen Han.

> The monkeys who wore caps and girdles,
> Full of schemes but lacking in knowledge.

He imposed harsh discipline upon his followers, but won their admiration by making the rules applicable to all. Thus he once sentenced himself to death for not being vigilant in the care of his horse, which wandered into a field and destroyed some crops. His startled aides managed to persuade him to cut his hair instead, as a token of atonement.

By 208, Ts'ao Ts'ao had brought all of northern China up to the Great Wall under his control. He turned his armies against the southern regions but was routed when the opposition manoeuvred him into fighting a river battle in boats on the Yangste. Ts'ao Ts'ao returned north and contented himself with the domain of Wei. He died in 220 and his son officially deposed the last Emperor of Han, declaring the dynasty of Wei. Similarly, a man called Liu Pei in the south-west of China declared a new dynasty named Shu, and a third set up in the Wu régime in the south-east. The leaders of the Shu and Wu dynasties co-operated to keep out the forces of aggressive Wei, but in 283 a major Wei clan called Ssu-ma swept into Shu. Encouraged by this success, they overthrew the Ts'ao clan from the throne of Wei, and briefly succeeded in reuniting China in 280 when the Ssu-mas conquered Wu. The most important general of the Ssu-ma family adopted the title Tsin Wu Ti, inaugurating the Tsin Dynasty (265–316), but he made the fatal error of dividing responsibility for different regions among his twenty-five sons. The Chinese histories of the succeeding years become an unwieldy string of names of one-day wonders, plots, counterplots and upstarts who took on names of old dynasties in order to try to give themselves an aura of respectibility. However two points of major interest emerge from the chaos. Firstly, new and powerful nomad groups had taken the place of the Hsiung-nu and were turning their attention south, and secondly, Tsin Wu Ti decided to resuscitate the Great Wall, which had temporarily sunk into oblivion. The two facts were, of course, related.

In restoring the Great Wall, Tsin Wu Ti was acting against the advice of a very worthy minister who had made a name for himself in 280 by writing an inscription on a wall which read, 'Trust in Virtue, not in Walls!' The minister in question had won a high post as a direct result of this action, but Tsin Wu Ti clung to the idea that the Great Wall was an effective defence and ordered the building of new watch-towers west of the city of Suchow. Building squads were sent to patch up sections of the Wall that had suffered during previous years. Contrary to the widespread opinion in the West that the Wall stood proud and alone for thousands of years, the great barrier was as impermanent as any other human construction, and crumbled with alarming speed if not properly maintained.

It remains a matter of speculation whether Tsin Wu Ti was entirely sane when he ordered this undoubtedly costly renovation work. It was utterly futile to rely for defence on the Great Wall for the simple reason that the barbarians were already well entrenched on the southern side. For the past two hundred years growing numbers of political defectors from the northern tribes had been allowed to settle south of the Wall. Despite warnings, the Tsin Dynasty continued to allow nomad settlement within Chinese provinces. Although the policy had been inaugurated for basically altruistic motives, it suddenly became obvious that these barbarians felt no particular loyalty to China at all. On the contrary, they began to assume power in their areas, and Tsin Wu Ti was forced to try to buy their allegiance by means of the bestowing of titles.

Tsin Wu Ti finally ensured disaster by encouraging a revival of feudalism, with many of the new aristocracy living in the capital as absentee rulers. By the time of Tsin Wu Ti's death in 290, there were no fewer than eight princedoms in northern China. Any hopes of an amelioration of the situation after Tsin Wu Ti's death were shattered by the nature of the new ruler, who, when he was once told that the people were in a desperate state with no rice to eat, retorted, 'Why don't they eat meat?', antedating Marie Antoinette by 1500 years!

In 304 one of the princes of Tsin committed the final error by appealing to the nomads for help against one of his rivals. A second prince reacted by calling in an opposing group of barbarians, the Hsien Pei. The nomads were only too happy to bring their armies south of the Wall, and carried on marching until they reached the capital Loyang, taking the Tsin emperor prisoner in 311. Five years later they captured his successor, who had taken refuge in Ch'ang-an. Loyang was burnt to the ground, the official records and library going up in flames yet again, and Ch'ang-an was reduced to such a miserable shadow of its former self that a contemporary writer recorded,

> there were not more than one hundred families. Weeds and thorns grew thickly as if in a forest. Only four carts were to be found in the city, and officials had neither ceremonial robes nor seals of office, so that they had to use tablets made of mulberry wood on which their name and rank were inscribed.

Realising that the situation in the north was hopeless, the Tsin court en bloc fled south in 316 and settled in Nanking, just south of the Yangtse. A new Tsin emperor was enthroned and the Tsin descendants ruled for just over one hundred years in the south. The security of the south was guaranteed by the constant infighting further north. As many as eighteen different 'dynasties' came and went in the north, some existing simultaneously. Control of various parts of the Great Wall varied from year to year, but the edifice had entered yet another of its meaningless periods, and northern nomads travelled as they pleased through its passes.

The barbarian chiefs who held sway over the ravished cradle of Chinese civilisation were nearly all notable for their destructive perversions. Foremost among these uncouth leaders was Shih the Tiger who allegedly conscripted 260,000 farmers to build his palaces in which he kept a harem of 30,000 concubines. He was especially feared for his sadistic tortures, and when his ten-year reign was mercifully brought to a halt by his death, his own generals ordered the closing of the gates of his capital, after which everyone even remotely related to the Tiger was murdered, to wipe out the stain of his memory.

Those scholars who had remained behind during the great southern exodus were dismayed by such behaviour, yet following old precedents, a large proportion collaborated with the occupying generals in the hope that they would convert the barbarians to Chinese ways. This hope was largely fulfilled, for the nomad rulers realised that they needed the co-operation of Chinese officials and institutions if any semblance of economic viability was to be maintained in a basically agricultural country, whose problems were outside the nomads' experience. Warlords who ranted that there was not enough money in their coffers were advised that it would be sensible not to kill off taxpayers at such a high rate. Sinicisation of the barbarians took place at all levels, personal as well as official. Nomads found that the Chinese could not pronounce foreign names, so they adopted Chinese ones. They began to speak Chinese, recognising its linguistic richness, and intermarriage was common.

The first really sinicised leader of note was a man named Fu Chien, of basically Tibetan origins, who succeeded in getting most of northern China under his control around 370. He dreamed of being the first non-Chinese emperor to rule all China and accordingly led an expedition of one million men to face the armies of Tsin in an attempt to win over the south. Fu Chien's huge force must have comprised a high percentage of the able-bodied men of the kingdom, most of them untrained for warfare; the Tsin force was only one-tenth the size, but was a professionally led army, and the result was a military fiasco. Thousands of Fu Chien's raw soldiers were trampled underfoot by panicking colleagues, and Fu Chien himself returned home wounded only to find his northern kingdom on the verge of collapse.

Fu Chien was toppled by a tribe called the Toba, who proclaimed a new Wei Dynasty in 398. The Toba first appeared in the Chinese records towards the end of the third century, when a Toba prince visited the court of the old Wei Dynasty and was put to death by his own people for returning with too favourable a report. Yet despite their eagerness to cling to nomad habits, the Toba learnt to respect the Chinese and their sinicised nomad rulers. They maintained their traditional prowess in cavalry warfare, but absorbed the most desirable aspects of Chinese culture. They were also converted to Buddhism, which until then had existed in China as a fringe religion practised by foreigners and a few eccentrics. The first Toba emperor built up a fine Chinese library, though he could not understand the books it contained, and he inaugurated a university. This same emperor claimed descent from the legendary Chinese Yellow Emperor, and, following old traditions, he made sacrifices and built temples. His empire included most of north China east of the loop of the Yellow River, but his successors extended control as far as the old western terminal of the Great Wall at Tun-huang.

From the earliest days of their power, the Toba experienced trouble from another tribe, called the Jou-juan. The Jou-juan were wholly barbarian, with no developed culture, and counted with pieces of horse-dung which even the nomad Toba found disgusting. The Jou-juan despised the Toba for having abandoned the noble ways of the steppes, and plagued them with sudden raids, after which they would vanish without trace. The reaction of the second ruler, Toba Ssu, shows how far the Chinese mentality had infiltrated his people – he set to work on the Great Wall. In 423 he restored much of the old Wall, and built six hundred miles of new fortifications, some of which probably replaced parts of Ch'in Shih Huang-ti's Wall, which had almost disappeared in places. However, lack of contemporary documentation makes it impossible to trace the exact line of Toba Ssu's construction, and almost any of the odd bits of the Wall of indefinite age that are still found dotted round northern China could be part of this barrier.

Toba Ssu's son, who came to the throne a year after his father ordered workforces to the Wall, carried on his father's policy, and his engineers spent sixteen years patching up the defences and building a new loop running north of Kalgan. He began to have serious doubts about the Wall's effectiveness during this construction work, however, and decided to lead an assault on the Jou-juan to put an end to their raids. He marched up to the edge of the Gobi with a large army and then dispatched a crack cavalry corps who swept down on the Jou-juan, taking them by surprise. The Toba troops made short shrift of the Jou-juan camp, and it was several years before the nomad marauders were again in a fit state to pose any threat.

The Toba emperor sent expeditions to fight the northern barbarians many times during the next few years. Soon he felt confident enough to attack the small states to the west, and victory there led to a reopening of contact and trade with the states of South Asia and the Middle East. The Toba began to acquire the same taste for the exotic as the Han had done five hundred years before.

The man most responsible for consolidating the Toba hold on northern China was the sixth Emperor, Hsiao Wen, who succeeded to the throne in 471. He built on the military successes of his predecessors with all-important domestic reforms. Having streamlined the administration of his realm, he reformed the tax system allowing farmers more money to improve their land and yields. His boldest move came in 485 when land was nationalised. Under the new land laws, every male subject over the age of fourteen was entitled to approximately seven acres of land which would be returned to the state on his death, or when he was incapable of farming it, though he would also be given 3.5 acres of additional land to secure an income during his old age. Tax was largely paid in kind and was distributed between the central administration and the local authority who looked after law and order and the social services. How widespread was the implementation of these revolutionary measures, it is impossible to tell, but the years of peace in an era of disruption proved the validity of Hsiao Wen Ti's belief that contentment among the peasants was essential for the security of northern China.

In 492 Hsaio Wen Ti moved his capital south from the city of P'ing Ch'eng to the traditional Chinese siting at Loyang. Many of his advisers were sceptical about the wisdom of the move, but the Emperor silenced them with favourable reports from the court oracles. His practical reasons for moving the capital were twofold, namely, that the climate at P'ing Ch'eng was extremely bad and the roads often cut by snow, and that Loyang was a more central location from which to govern his people. Symbolically, the move was of enormous importance, as it was a recognition of an exchange of lifestyle, a rejection of the customs of the Toba herders in favour of Chinese civilisation. Hsiao Wen Ti went so far as to forbid the use of the Toba language and units of measure within his new court, and received instruction from Chinese officials in traditional protocol and sacrificial rites.

Opposition to Hsiao Wen Ti's policies centred around his son, the Heir Apparent, who made several appeals to the Emperor to reconsider the move to Loyang. The prince found the city oppressive and Chinese ceremonial repellent, but his main objection was that by abandoning the ways of the steppes and the Great Wall region, the Emperor was betraying his own people. The prince's protests went unheeded so he tried to take matters into his own hands by gathering together like-minded men with whom he marched north to P'ing Ch'eng. Such action constituted treason, and he was executed.

Hsiao Wen Ti turned his back on the northern lands and planned an invasion of southern China, which had recently changed rulers. The campaign was to be the means by which Hsiao Wen Ti would come nearer to his goal of becoming Emperor of all China, and would imbue feelings of patriotism and challenge into the minds of disgruntled Toba generals who bemoaned the loss of their nomad heritage. In the event, the attempted invasion of the south by Hsiao Wen Ti's armies was a military disaster, and the Emperor is said to have died of shame. His son ordered a second invasion in 501, resulting in the annexation of several hundred square miles of land. Before the Toba could build on this victory to gain control of all the Middle Kingdom, the rulers of the south were overthrown by an internal revolt, and a new southern dynasty was proclaimed under the name of Liang. The Liang Emperor and his strategists proved too capable for the Toba, who limped back to Loyang in 507 with heavy losses. This humiliation triggered off a breakaway movement among the Toba who lived along the Great Wall. They were tired of their sinicised brethren's pre-occupation with the re-establishment of a Chinese Empire, and felt that the honour of the Toba race was at stake. They refused to tolerate the posturings of the Toba Emperor in Loyang, and concentrated on teaching their young men the old values and habits of the tribe. While the Imperial Court laughed at these reactionary herdsmen along the Wall, northern activists fomented dissent and trained the young in horseback fighting. In 530 the movement's leaders felt ready to attack, and swept down on Loyang, massacring many of the Toba nobility in the capital. The rebels set up a new northern-orientated administration with its headquarters in the city of Ch'ang-an, while the remnants of the Toba Wei Dynasty fled east, maintaining a Court at Yeh that was a pale shadow of the Toba imperial structure of the preceding century. Within a few years northern China had disintegrated yet again into political disarray.

The most interesting occurrence along the line of the Great Wall during the troublesome fourth and fifth centuries was the flowering of Buddhist culture at Tun Huang, the old terminus of Han Wu Ti's decaying Wall. Stone sculpture is a rare art form in China, but Tun Huang houses some magnificent stone Buddhas, as well as wall paintings in nearby caves. Tun Huang became the departure point for Chinese pilgrims to India, who prayed at the end of the Wall for a safe journey. Shrines were built, and a lively community grew up.

Buddhism was the only major foreign philosophical or religious influence on the Chinese people before Communism. Teachers of Christianity made several concerted attempts at converting the Chinese, but were never completely successful except on the island of Taiwan, owing to the failure of the missionaries to compromise their beliefs to fit in with the Chinese tradition. Neither the Communists nor the Buddhists had such puritanical scruples. The early Buddhists liberally translated Indian texts using Chinese terms borrowed from Taoist writings, so that many people during the Toba rule thought that Buddhism was a sect of Taoism. The Buddhists had realised that the only way to make an impression on the people living within the boundary of the Great Wall was by accepting the Chinese belief in their own cultural superiority, and advancing slowly by infiltration. Buddhists won the patronage of most of the Toba emperors, which gave the stamp of authority to their conversion programme.

Of all the Chinese Buddhist pilgrims who made the long journey to the motherland of their religion, India, in the 500 years up to AD 790, only forty-two were recorded as having safely returned to China. Some probably decided to stay in India, having suffered the trek there by foot over thousands of miles of inhospitable territory, but others undoubtedly perished en route. One literate devotee named Fa Hsien left a record of his departure from Tun Huang in 399.

> Li Hao, the Governor of Tun Huang, supplied us with the requisite provisions for crossing the desert. There are a great many evil spirits in the desert, as well as hot winds, and none who meets them survives. There are neither birds up in the sky nor animals down on the ground. If one looks around to try to make out the road, the only pointer is the line of dead men's rotting bones.[1]

Fa Hsien and his companion took six years to reach India, stopping frequently to arrange provisions, travel authorisations and routes. He spent a further six years once he had arrived in India collecting sacred manuscripts and furthering his studies. Overawed by the prospect of battling his way back across the desert states to Tun Huang, he made the return journey by ship. After landing in China Fa Hsien made his way to the Toba capital in 414, then decided he would have better facilities for carrying on his life's work in the south. The account he produced was an interesting and colourful description of his own experiences, and of conditions in a great civilisation west of the Wall. Maybe because of his lurid rendition of the difficulties of travel beyond Tun Huang, the book seems to have done little to shatter the popular belief that the terminus of the Great Wall marked the limit of bearable existence.

Just as the Great Wall varied in usefulness from year to year, so Buddhism came into and went out of favour with the pendulum of events during China's Dark Ages. Its main rival was Taoism, for although the Taoists at first welcomed the Buddhists as colleagues in the religious war against the Confucian pragmatists, they soon realised that the Buddhists were a major threat to their own influence both among the people and at Court. The Toba Emperor, Tao, was converted to Taoism in 439 while supervising the final stages of reconstruction of the Great Wall, and obliged his fellow Taoist sympathisers by persecuting the Buddhists. After his death in 452, Buddhism once more enjoyed official approval and the Toba rulers celebrated their successful campaign to regain the Tun Huang area by endorsing work on the remarkable Thousand Buddha Caves at Tun Huang. Hundreds of sculptors and workmen fashioned likenesses of Buddha in varying moods inside nearly five hundred caves in a cliff face just over one mile long. By 500 Buddhism was the principal religion of China, but succeeding generations of religious conflict and cross-fertilisation led to the general situation in which a Chinese, when asked if he were a Buddhist, a Taoist or a Confucianist, would reply 'Yes'.

The sixth century saw a new host of petty empires, royal plots, drunken empresses and corrupt monks, yet amid the unrest several leaders built new stretches of Wall. The sinicised Toba, who had escaped their northern relatives' massacre by fleeing east, tried to defend their new domain with a Wall running far south of the old line of the Great Wall before being swallowed up. In 555 the king of a régime called Northern Ch'i built nearly three hundred

1 Fa Hsien, *Journey to the West.*

112

Nineteenth-century German cartoon of Western armies massing for the attack on the soft Chinese Giant, hiding behind the Great Wall. The caption reads, 'Best Wishes from the Chinese Wall!'

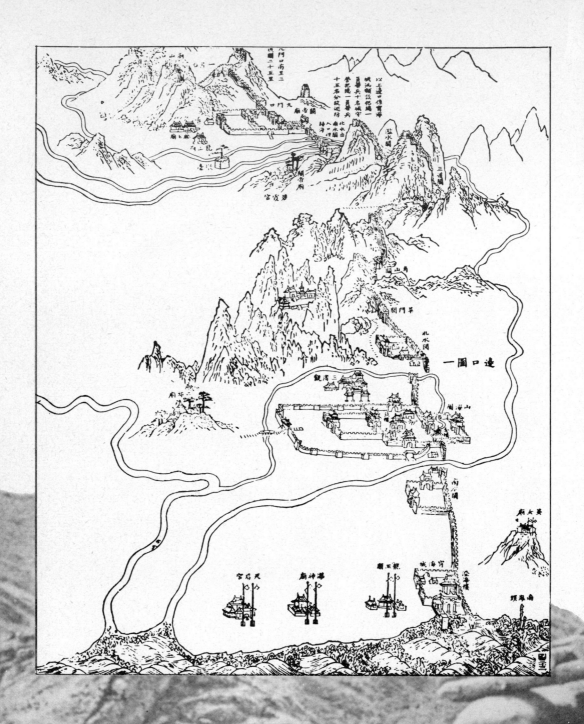

Inset: Chinese pictorial map showing the eastern end of the Wall where it meets the sea (foreground). The large fortified settlement depicted is Shanhaikuan.

Kuomintang sentries posted along the Great Wall during the Sino-Japanese war of 1937-1945. They were soon replaced by Japanese soldiers when the Imperial Armies completed their occupation of northern China.

Opposite: Chinese poster of the 1950s showing Chairman Mao symbolically viewing the Middle Kingdom from a vantage point on the Great Wall.

Above: Chinese troops marching along the Great Wall.

View of Wall in foothills behind Peking.

Inset: President Nixon being shown the Great Wall of China during his historic visit to China in early 1972.

Right: Ruined watch-tower north of the Tun Wang oasis, seen from the south-west.

Below: The remains of the ancient border wall between low dunes east of the tower.

miles of rampart from Peking to Tat'ung. Allegedly 1,800,000 men were employed on this last-mentioned endeavour, but it is more than likely that some over-zealous historian added a nought or two somewhere in order to make his account more exciting. It is inconceivable that any of the northern states could have organised such a workforce considering that the entire population of China at that time, both north and south, has been estimated at no more than fifty million.

While the men of Ch'i were busy on this latest addition to the conglomerate defences that we call the Great Wall, a new nomad tribe was pushing the Jou-juan out of the northern reaches and into Europe. The ascendant star was that of the Turks, who rapidly became masters of a wide belt of land stretching from Turkestan and Afghanistan to Mongolia. Their conquest proved too rapid and their Empire too unwieldy, but to the latest infant dynasties of north China they presented a ferocious appearance, and Chinese patrols on the Wall kept anxious eyes turned towards the steppes, constantly expecting an invasion. The ruler of the current Chinese régime based in Ch'ang-an (the Northern Chou) received envoys from the Turks and was only too pleased to enter into an alliance with them against the north-east Chinese state of Northern Ch'i. But his joy was shortlived for when his armies marched into Northern Ch'i in 563, no Turkish help materialised and the Northern Chou army was defeated. It was fourteen years before Northern Ch'i was finally occupied by the forces of Northern Chou, who took advantage of simultaneous attacks on the Northern Ch'i by the Turks and a southern state called Ch'en to move in their own divisions. The end result of this tortured sequence of events was that the Great Wall had once again become a frontier between two nations, the Turks to the north and the Northern Chou to the south. The two sides communicated in superficially friendly terms, but many experienced Chinese felt that conflict was inevitable. They could not believe that the Turks were impervious to the temptation offered by Chinese territory and goods, but what they did not realise was that the Turks were having problems with the size of their domain, and that in 582 the western Turks would break away from the mammoth state.

The man who had organised the overthrow of the Northern Ch'i and unified north China under the Northern Chou banner would not have carved an impressive niche for himself in the long gallery of Dark Ages' emperors had he not been the coolest imperial assassin of all time. He was the third emperor of the Northern Chou and ruled from 557–81. His two predecessors were his brothers, both of whom were disposed of by a powerful uncle who acted as regent. The Emperor summoned this uncle and asked him to remonstrate with the alcoholic Dowager Empress about her behaviour. While the uncle lectured the woman on the evils of wine the Emperor crept up behind and killed him with an almighty sweep of his ceremonial jade sceptre. Unfortunately this strong-minded Emperor was not able to enjoy his power for long because of his own premature death in 578, only months after his victory against the Northern Ch'i. His son and successor followed him to the grave after a mere two years, leaving effective power in the hands of the ambitious Prime Minister, Yang Chien, who was destined to bring the Dark Ages to an end by reuniting north and south China.

Yang Chien witnessed a boy emperor ascend the throne in 580, becoming the fifth ruler of

113

the Northern Chou in only twenty-three years of the state's existence, but he deposed the child the following year, taking the imperial insignia into his own hands. Immediately he occupied himself with the task of strengthening northern China, so that when the long-expected Turkish attack eventually came in 585 he was able to repel the invaders. When the fighting was over, he sent 30,000 men up to the Great Wall to build a new section that ran diagonally across the loop of the Yellow River, continuing for two hundred miles further west. In 586, other work squads were mobilised to build new watch-towers and fortify old ones. Even so, Yang Chien maintained relations with the Turks, to the extent of sending Chinese brides to the rulers of both halves of the Turkish Empire. He played off the western and northern Turks against each other, a dangerous policy which nevertheless worked in his lifetime.

At home Yang Chien won support by overhauling the system of food pricing and distribution. Every Chinese emperor had to cope with the problem of famine during years of poor harvests or natural disasters which occurred with sickening regularity. Violently fluctuating food prices were one of the major causes of dissent among the people of China, often leading to outright rebellion. Yang Chien put into practice a system of national grain stockpiles, imposing light but compulsory grain contributions from all farmers in normal or good years, thus accumulating reserves which could be sold off in bad years at nominal prices. Before Yang Chien died his administration was said to hold as much as fifty years' supply of grain in its warehouses.

Encouraged by his successful handling of basic problems in north China, Yang Chien sent his armies south of his borders in 587 and within two years had removed the southern rulers, sometimes without resistance, thereby becoming the first emperor of a unified China for nearly 370 years. He called his dynasty the Sui, and for the next fifteen years standardised the laws and practices of the Empire and purged the land of corruption and waste. Wherever possible he made economies even down to the imperial wardrobe, and he tried to keep tax demands and other obligations to a minimum. Despite this, he was able to embark on an ambitious programme of building befitting a new Empire. He ordered the construction of a 100-mile-long canal from T'ung-kuan to Ch'ang-an, and improved road communications leading from the capital. He not only renovated the Great Wall and built new sections, but also brought the Wall garrisons back to the same state of self-sufficiency they had enjoyed during early Han times by insisting that the soldiers grow most of their own food.

The one serious blight in Yang Chien's new dynasty was the conflict between members of his own family. Because of this discord a younger son was appointed Heir Apparent over one of his brothers and succeeded in 604 as the Emperor Sui Yang. Sui Yang Ti became the archvillain of all Chinese emperors, exceeding the notoriety of Ch'in Shih Huang-ti, with whom he shared many similarities. He was accused by historians of many moral crimes, including the rape of Yang Chien's favourite wife while her husband lay dying, and of marrying her the day after his father's death. The accounts of Sui Yang Ti's excesses are too numerous and too consistent to be complete invention, but they make it easy to forget that he was also one of the great constructors of history. His finest achievement was the Grand Canal which made possible direct water transport between China's two principal rivers, the Yellow River (Huang Ho) and the Yangtse, and which survived through the 1300 years of wars and barbarian occupations up to the present century. Yang Ti should also be remembered, however, as one of the principal emperors involved in the building of the Great Wall.

Because of the natural configuration of China, which slopes down from the mountains in the west to the eastern ocean, most of the navigable rivers run in the same direction. North–south transport by water was therefore virtually impossible, unless a boat made a detour down a river to the sea, and up another river at the required latitude. In ancient China the difficulty of transporting material around the country was a nuisance but not particularly serious as most areas were self sufficient, apart from the artificial anomaly of the Great Wall zone which usually depended on outside supplies. The situation had however changed radically by the time the Sui Dynasty came to power as the south of China had developed into a thriving agricultural area with an annual surplus which was often needed in the less fortunate northern regions, particularly during climatic upsets. The Grand Canal was to revolutionise the transport situation in China and help to unite the two halves of the country north and south. It was forty paces wide, with state highways running on each side, lined with willows. In 608 a northern section was built from the town of Panchu, on the Yellow River, up to Cho (not far from modern Peking). More than one million men were conscripted for this northern spur, and in 610 another huge labour force extended the Grand Canal south as far as Hangchow. When the whole project had been completed, boats could travel for one thousand miles in the previously impossible direction from north to south. The Grand Canal was as formidable

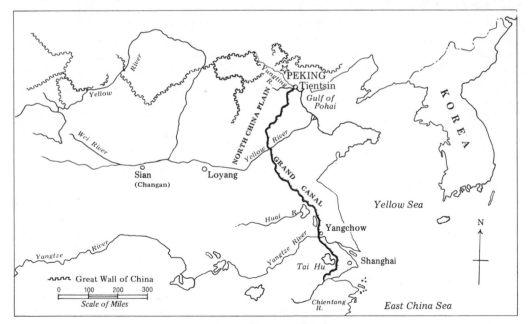

FIG. 8. The Grand Canal.

115

an achievement as the Great Wall, and unlike the Demon Barrier, never lost its usefulness.

Contemporary sources recorded that a total of 5,500,000 men worked on the Grand Canal, which meant that at times the entire able-bodied population of a region through which the Canal was being dug must have been engaged on the work. This sort of enforced voluntary labour by the civilian population has been a common occurrence in Chinese history. Many features of the Chinese landscape, from canals to terraced fields, are the result of co-operative action by villagers who would give certain days of each month to the common good. It is fair to assume that the workforces on the Grand Canal were also largely made up of this sort of volunteer brigade. As happens in China today, whole villages would 'spontaneously' march off to join the diggers, keeping their spirits up with enthusiastic songs. Although the labour force was far bigger than that used in the construction of the Great Wall, conditions were nowhere near so bad, though later historians wishing to besmirch Sui Yang Ti's reputation said that the great public works of the brief Sui Dynasty 'tortured the people and wasted financial resources'. There is no accurate record of how many people died while working on this project, and wild claims in later histories that two million men were lost should be taken as unreliable if not inaccurate.

While the Grand Canal was being dug, another large body of men were engaged on building a new section of the Great Wall east of the northern loop of the Yellow River, as well as completing the extension to the west begun by Yang Chien. A stereotyped fanciful report said that this construction was completed in ten days one summer (607) by one million men, half of whom died on the spot or ran away. It is significant that these preposterous statistics are in multiples of ten, as it was an early established habit in the Chinese language to make liberal use of round figures to give emphasis to a statement. Thus one of the most common words for 'many' is *wan*, literally ten thousand, used in such expressions as Mao Tse-t'ung Wan Sui (Long Live Mao Tse-t'ung! literally, Mao Tse-t'ung Ten Thousand Years!); or Wan Li Ch'ang Ch'eng (The Great Wall, or literally, the Ten Thousand Li Wall).

The burden of taxes imposed to finance the Grand Canal and the extension of the Great Wall was a far greater cause of suffering to the common people than actual labour on the projects. Frequently these taxes were paid in kind by the farmers, especially in the south where rice growers had to witness a large part of their produce being shipped up the Grand Canal for which this would help to pay.

Despite the heavy demands made upon the population, Sui Yang Ti would not have been so hated by his people had it not been for his irrevocably depraved nature. Everyone expected to make sacrifices to help get the new Empire on its feet, but while they were proud to follow the lead of a sincere ruler like Yang Chien, they balked at supporting the debauchery of Yang Ti. Not content with such useful building projects as the Canal, the Emperor constructed a vast palace at Loyang on the shores of an artificial lake. In the middle of the lake were three artificial islands, representing the P'eng Lai, the mountains of Immortality in the Eastern Sea which had obsessed Ch'in Shih Huang-ti's imagination eight hundred years before. Sixteen villas around the lake housed Yang Ti's favourite wives, each endowed with rarer and more beautiful treasures than the next. Even after this palace was completed, Yang Ti continued to visit the former capital of Ch'ang-an, and ordered forty palaces to be built along the way so he would always have somewhere to stay which would suit his extravagant tastes. The item which captured the imagination of later dynasties was Yang Ti's pleasure park. The Emperor loved the trees in autumn, but hated to see the leaves fall. No doubt the sight of the bare branches offended his sumptuous preferences, as well as being an unpleasant reminder of the passing of time and his own inevitable death. He therefore ordered the court suppliers to make thousands of silk and paper leaves and flowers which were then attached to the trees to shame nature. The Emperor would sail out onto the lake at night, singing verses which he himself had written, admiring the artificial water lilies and the dancing fireflies, which were released from boxes by attendants hidden in the trees.

To celebrate the completion of the Grand Canal, Yang Ti organised a triumphant water procession that would have outshone Cleopatra's talent for excessive displays. A line of boats and barges stretching for seventy miles carried the Emperor, his Court, foreign ambassadors and a whole army of retainers. The Emperor's barge was nearly 50 feet high, shaped like a dragon with four decks, two for the eunuchs and servants, the third for the favourite concubines of the moment, and the top deck for the Emperor himself. The barges were all pulled by huge teams of exquisitely dressed servants and boatmen, 80,000 in number, while the Emperor's own craft was drawn by hundreds of beautiful women in diaphanous robes that fluttered in the gentle breeze, perfumed by special runners who ensured that no unpleasant smell could reach Yang Ti's nostrils. Officials of towns and villages along the way were in charge of provisioning this monstrous flotilla, calling on the peasants and townspeople yet again for money and goods, while the people watched at some distance as the procession passed like some mythical man-eating beast.

Historians have tended to dwell on Yang Ti's faults, many of which are no doubt exaggerations or inventions of the T'ang Dynasty who had later to justify overthrowing Yang Ti's régime. The Sui Emperor in fact made a far greater contribution to Chinese civilisation than his detractors would admit, not least of which was to institute an educational code and examination system that lasted for 1300 years. Despite comparisons with Ch'in Shih Huang-ti (including the oft-quoted comment that had Shih Huang-ti not built the Great Wall, Sui Yang-ti no doubt would have done!) Yang Ti really consciously modelled himself on the wise and versatile Han Emperor, Wu·Ti, who had built the long western extension of the Wall. Yang Ti shared Han Wu Ti's view that it was best to follow a policy of 'walking on two feet' when dealing with the barbarians; in other words, to have two policies side by side, the first to wall them off and the second to maintain good relations with the tribes on the other side of the protective screen. To further this end, Yang Ti made the unusual step in the summer of 607 of going north of the Great Wall to meet the Turkish leader, Ki-min.

Court envoys went on ahead of the main Imperial party to warn the Turks of the Emperor's imminent arrival and were horrified to discover that the Turkish leader was living in a tent, albeit a luxurious one, pitched on the rough prairie grass, a marked contrast to the elegant grounds surrounding Chinese palaces. Obviously the Chinese envoys made known their fears about Yang Ti's reaction to the nomad camp, for hardly had they left than Ki-min and his men got down to digging up the offending grass around his tent with their hunting knives.

As there was no suitable town or palace for the Emperor to stay during his visit to the southern fringe of the Turks' domain, the Chinese brought with them an extremely elaborate mobile encampment, which included huge expanses of canvas on which were painted representations of the main palaces of Loyang. The Chinese did not spare themselves in their efforts to impress the Turks with their strength and advancement and when the Emperor himself arrived, he was reportedly accompanied by 500,000 horsemen. The exercise was aimed at impressing upon the Turks what solid resistance they would meet if they dared to invade the land south of the Great Wall, though T'ang chroniclers recording the scene implied that it was all a show on Yang Ti's part to impress the Turks of his own majesty. The Chinese distributed 200,000 bolts of silk to the Turkish chieftains, and issued an invitation to Ki-min to go to Loyang the following year, a visit which helped to secure peace along the Great Wall.

Yang Ti received many other deputations and embassies over the next few years, including kings from minor states to the west who acknowledged Chinese superiority without losing their independence. The armies of Sui pushed south into South-East Asia, bringing colourful hill peoples under Chinese rule. In the extreme north-east they were far less successful, and Yang Ti's stubbornness in that direction cost him his throne and his dynasty.

Yang Ti was determined to revive Chinese control of Korea which had accepted Chinese occupation during the reign of Han Wu Ti, but had otherwise remained remote from the affairs of the Middle Kingdom and was fiercely proud of its independence. Three times the Emperor sent costly expeditions way beyond the north-east section of the Great Wall, but the Koreans were brave fighters and the Chinese army too far from its home bases to support long drawn-out campaigns, particularly when the freezing winters arrived. The Koreans were expert at making conditions as difficult as possible for the invaders, harrying the forces and burning crops rather than allowing them to fall into Chinese hands. Heavy Chinese casualties in Korea depressed morale at home, and the campaigns exhausted the already over-extended Imperial Treasury. The domination of the Korean peninsula became a point of honour for Yang Ti, who severely damaged his own prestige by taking part in one of the unsuccessful campaigns.

The Emperor revisited the frontier zone around the Great Wall in 615, hoping to reaffirm co-operation between the Sons of Han (as the Chinese often called themselves) and the Turks. Ki-min had been succeeded by his son who, far from welcoming the Emperor's overtures, ordered a surprise attack so that Yang Ti and his men were forced to beat a hasty and undignified retreat, seeking refuge in the Great Wall fort of Yen Men. Chinese reinforcements rushed to the Wall but the Emperor was besieged for several weeks at Yen Men while his armies fought with Turkish troops. Fortunately, the dowager queen of the Turks, a Chinese princess married to Ki-min in the tradition of Chao Chün and many like her, heard about the Emperor's plight and fabricated a story that the Uighur barbarians (forefathers of the Islamic tribes who today continue a nomadic way of existence in the extreme west of the People's

Republic) were massing for a major attack on the Turks. The Turkish commanders feared that the steppe land was not properly defended against such an invasion while so many Turkish warriors were fighting the Chinese on the Great Wall, yet the Emperor of China seemed too great a prize to throw away on the strength of unconfirmed rumours. Their indecision over their next move was ended by the arrival of a new Chinese army led by a sixteen-year-old boy called Li Shih-min, later to become the second Emperor of China's most glorious dynasty, the T'ang. The number of troops in Li Shih-min's force was in fact quite modest, but he made his strength seem much more significant by fanning out his troops and ordering them to make as much noise as possible. The Turks decided that this new army could turn the siege of the Great Wall into a long affair, during which time the imaginary Uighur invaders would be able to make inroads into Turkish territory. They therefore withdrew.

Yang Ti was thoroughly disheartened by the Yen Men incident, coming so soon as it did after the humiliation at the hands of the Koreans. He developed such a dislike for the Great Wall and the northern regions in general that he moved his capital south to Chiang-tu, where he could forget the troubles of the Empire and enjoy a milder climate. Uprisings broke out in several parts of China but the Emperor refused to respond to urgent appeals from Court ministers to take swift action to put down the rebels and solve the people's grievances. Instead he shut himself away with his women, passing his hours with poetry and love-making. His courtiers despaired of ever making him see reason, and he fell to an assassin's hand in 618.

The city of Ch'ang-an had already been taken over by rebel forces led by Li Yüan, father of the boy solider who had gone to Yang Ti's defence at Yen Men. He quickly took over the rest of the country and deposed the boy puppet emperor who had been set on the throne by Yang Ti's assassins. A new dynasty was declared, and christened T'ang. Li Yüan became its first emperor, though in 626 he abdicated in favour of his able son, Li Shih-min, who reigned for twenty-four years and is generally acknowledged to have been the finest of China's emperors.

Li Shih-min's attitude to the Great Wall was negative in the extreme. He considered the vast construction a waste of time and money. The Wall presented a policy totally contrary to his own thinking as he believed that the secret for China's safety from the barbarians was to be found in expansion, not sedentary defence. He withdrew the inspection service of men who travelled along the Wall during the Sui Dynasty keeping an eye on its maintenance, and allowed the barrier to fall into disrepair. The T'ang was a brilliant period, three hundred years during which China was the foremost civilisation of the world, but in the history of the Great Wall it has little place. To the rulers the Wall was a monument to an inferior age, but to the poets it was a symbol of the human emotions of parting and sorrow, and therefore became a favourite theme of T'ang poetry. The poets' impressions of the Great Wall, and their romanticised version of its building, were absorbed by later generations who erred by accepting the accounts as fact.

The poems of such immortal T'ang writers as Li Po or Tu Fu are the finely wrought work of lyrical patriots. Even if the poets often found themselves at variance with the government of the day, they treasured their Chinese heritage and had little respect for foreign lands or the

Huns of the north. Many of the verses express the hope that the barbarians will leave the Chinese alone, while others sing of the sadness of a Chinese soul at or beyond the Great Wall. Li Po's 'Fighting South of the Rampart', based on an old Han Dynasty song, is typical in its mood.

> The Emperor's armies have grown old and grey,
> Fighting hundreds of miles from home.
> The barbarians know no trade but battle and
>   bloodshed,
> And have no fields or ploughed lands,
> Just wastelands where whitened bones lie among
>   the yellow sand.
> Where Ch'in built the Great Wall to keep
>   the barbarians at bay,
> The Han in turn light beacons of war.
> The beacons are forever burning, fighting and
>   marching never stop.
> Men die on the battlefield to the sound of
>   clashing swords,
> While the horses of the vanquished neigh
>   piteously to Heaven.
> Crows and hawks peck around for human guts,
> Carry them off in their beaks, and hang them
>   on the branches of withered trees.
> Captains and privates are smeared across the
>   bushes and grass.
> The generals schemed for nothing.
> The sword is but a cursed thing
> That a wise man employs only when he must.

The sensitive mind rejected the empty heroism of warfare, and seized on the decaying state of the Wall during the T'ang Dynasty as a symbol of the temporary nature of man's existence and the futility of his exploits, as in Wang Ch'ang-ling's poem 'Under a Border Fortress'.

> Of old the battles along the Great Wall
> Were spoken of with lofty praise,
> But antiquity has now been transformed to
>   yellow dust
> White bones jumbled amongst the grass.

Although the Great Wall was inextricably associated with death and despair, it could also inspire courage and determination in the hearts of men. Tsu Yung demonstrates this in a poem entitled 'Looking towards an Inner Gate of the Wall'.

> My heart sank when I set out from Yen
> For the Han camps where bugles and drums sound.
> For hundreds of miles a cold light gives
>   life to the packed snow.
> Flags fly on three borders like a rising dawn . . .
> The clouds and mountains carry the Great Wall
>   away from the sea . . .
> I throw aside my writing brush
> Challenging destiny like a student who
>   discards his cap.

The T'ang put the Great Wall into a sleep lasting hundreds of years, but Li Shih-min's belief that it would never be more than a museum piece was to be shattered. The T'ang hoped for the impossible, eternal peace, but not even the most pessimistic Chinese could have foreseen the monster that was hatched in the steppes north of the Wall, a barbarian régime so powerful that it would shake the very foundations of China and its Wall, and which would make the name of Genghis Khan a byword for fear from Europe to the China Sea.

7

Nomad
Domination and
the Mongols

CHAPTER SEVEN

Nomad Domination and the Mongols

THE story of the Great Wall is also the history of relations between the Chinese and a succession of barbarian tribes and kingdoms which originally came to power in the western deserts or northern steppes, then expanded to threaten the tranquillity of the Middle Kingdom. The T'ang Dynasty had enjoyed an unusually long period free from significant nomad incursions, but as central authority weakened during the ninth century, border areas were lost by the Chinese to other rulers. Uighurs and other Turkish groups occupied the far west, and gradually the whole line of the Great Wall fell into barbarian hands. Most of China was reunited in 960 by a fresh dynasty called Sung, militarily one of the weakest of Chinese régimes but culturally very important, but no Sung emperor ever succeded in regaining control of the Wall, which was not retaken by the Chinese until over five hundred years later.

The strongest of the northern nomads during the tenth and eleventh centuries were the Khitan, who ruled over a large kingdom in the north under the dynastic name of Liao (907–1125). Although they were foreigners the Khitan gave the West one of its first common terms for China – Cathay. The Russians still refer to the Middle Kingdom as Kitai. The Khitan originated from an area along the banks of the Liao River in Manchuria, and had Mongolian racial characteristics. In 907 a Khitan tribal leader named Apaochi conquered neighbouring tribes and brought Inner Mongolia and part of South Manchuria under his control. He skilfully used bands of highly trained mounted archers, called ordos, which the Mongols later made familiar to Europe as 'hordes', terrifying not because of their number, which was small, but because of their lightning speed and callous butchery. Eventually there were twelve ordos in the Khitan army, totalling 70,000 men.

Apaochi knew that while a country could be conquered on horseback, it could not be effectively governed from the saddle. He believed that agriculture would help give a strong economic foundation to his state and therefore invited Chinese settlers to come north of the Great Wall to farm land given on very generous terms. Natural resources such as salt and iron ore were developed, large townships grew up and trading stations were organised to conduct business with China. Unemployed Chinese bureaucrats and scholars were invited to take part

125

in a new government administration where their experience would be of great value, and they were conceded the right to be tried by their own laws. To defend this blossoming young nation from the Chinese (*sic*), the Khitan built an extension of the Great Wall from Shan Hai Kuan to the mouth of the Liao River.

Apaochi died in 927, but his successor carried on his expansionist policy. In 928, Khitan forces plunged south of the Wall, and in 936 sixteen prefectures in northern Shansi and Hopeh, including Peking, were put under Khitan rule.

Emperor T'ai-tsung (976–997) of Sung tried to win back this region for China on three separate occasions, each time suffering defeat. The Khitan took the offensive in 1004 and pressed south towards the Sung capital of K'aifeng on the Yellow River. The new Sung Emperor, Chen-tsung (998–1022), led his armies to meet the invaders, but a battle on the River Shan came to no decisive conclusion. Rather than continue the fighting at great cost of life, the two sides drew up a peace agreement, under which the Sung bought a measure of security along their northern frontier.

> The Sung government agrees to deliver 200,000 rolls of silk and 100,000 taels of silver each year to the Khitan . . . Garrisons on either side of the frontier shall defend their respective territories, and trespassing by both civilians and military is expressly forbidden. Robbers and bandits who flee from one side shall not be granted asylum by the other. Farmers on both sides should be left alone to live in peace; neither they nor their farms should be molested. Towns and their fortifications are not to be altered. No additional walls or canals may be built by either side.[1]

In the event, neither side honoured the clause forbidding new walls and defences. In 1074 Sung planted a 300-mile-long palisade of elm and willow trees which they believed would halt any Khitan cavalry attacks. Khitan envoys were sent to K'aifeng to protest about this new barrier, and when the Chinese refused to destroy it, the Khitan themselves cut through it. However in 1077 the Khitan started constructing new walls of their own in the north as well as in the south of their territory. The walls were a sign of the decline of Khitan strength, but the Sung were far too weak to take advantage of the situation by attacking the northern regions.

In general however, the Sung and the Khitan lived in reasonable harmony during the eleventh century as the Khitan were more interested in cultural and economic advancement than in warfare. The prosperity and agricultural development of the Khitan régime meant that its rulers had none of the traditional reasons for nomad raiding into China, which was frequently a result of shortages of food or other products which the nomads could not produce themselves. The situation was not so favourable at the western end of the Great Wall, where a nomad tribe called the Tangut (or Western Hsia) had come to power.

Initially, the Tangut paid tribute to the Sung, but as the nomads strengthened the situation was reversed. Apart from a few desert oases, the Tangut had no agricultural land

1 Sung Dynastic History.

126

and were forced to import grain from the Chinese, as well as silk, cloth and tea. The Chinese in return bought horses and furs from the nomads. When demand from both sides was equal, the situation was mutually beneficial, but at times when the nomads' need for food or cloth exceeded the Chinese need or will for trade, the Tangut would take part in raids, obtaining their requirements by force. The Sung authorities would sometimes break off trade agreements with the Tangut in retaliation for such raids, but the effect was only to exacerbate the problem.

Matters reached a climax in 1032 when open warfare broke out between the Tangut and China. The Tangut had the advantage of a capable and imaginative leader who was fully conversant with Chinese culture and habits (especially Buddhism) but prevented his people slavishly following things Chinese, a tendency which inevitably led to the ultimate weakening of a nomad tribe, as was happening at the other end of the Great Wall with the Khitan. The Tangut were encouraged to look upon their way of life as noble and manly, and victory in battle was regarded as the height of honour. This attitude was the complete opposite to current beliefs in Sung China where young men were positively discouraged from following military careers. Early on in the war with the Tangut, the Chinese tried to attack the nomads using conventional military tactics, but it soon became clear that the Sung army could not beat the Tangut in battle, contending, as they were, with difficult terrain and the nomads' rapid cavalry. The Chinese generals became resigned to the idea of a defensive war and accordingly retreated, setting fire to the land as they went, then retired behind strongly built fortifications. The Tangut carried on the war for twelve years before reduced enthusiasm and the cost in men and money made them sue for peace.

A third major nomadic group, which was to topple the Khitan and push the Sung out of Kaifeng, was the Nuchen, a tribe that lived in Manchuria and the area behind present-day Vladivostok. The Nuchen living closest to the Great Wall (who accepted Khitan sovereignty), adopted many Chinese customs and a more sedentary way of existence than that of their ancestors, but their brethren to the north disapproved strongly. A charismatic leader arose from these people by the name of Akuta. He pointed out that the Khitan were going through the very process of degeneration that awaited the Nuchen, should they forget the skills of the steppes. Akuta contrasted favourably with the Khitan emperor, T'ien-tsu, who mimicked the lifestyle of the worst Chinese emperors, passing his time in drunken revelry while the state was reduced to ruin and the people suffered grievously under the pressure of heavy taxation. At a feast in 1112, T'ien-tsu entertained all the tribal leaders of the Nuchen, and at the height of the festivities asked them to dance for him. Only Akuta refused, flouting the imperial will despite several requests. Three years later, Akuta was to exploit the grievances of the people of the Khitan empire to start a rebellion.

From the start, Akuta's Nuchen troops enjoyed victory. Town after town fell into rebel hands and the Khitan's ability to govern their realm broke down completely. Neglect of the irrigation system in the wheat-growing areas led to a severe famine in 1118, so that desperate peasants were forced to turn to cannibalism in attempts to stay alive. The Chinese Emperor, so far south in his capital of K'aifeng, was watching the sequence of events with great interest, and rashly decided to try to profit from the situation.

In 1122, Sung and Nuchen (who adopted the name Kin, or Golden, and called theirs the Kin Dynasty) entered into an alliance whereby the Nuchen would concern themselves with Khitan territory north of the Great Wall, while the Chinese Sung armies would take Peking and the sixteen prefectures south of the Wall. The Nuchen fulfilled their side of the bargain without much difficulty, sending the Khitan Emperor into flight. The Sung performance, however, was miserable, and they were unable to capture Peking until the Nuchen came to their aid. In view of this weak performance by their Chinese allies, the Nuchen considered it generous to suggest the Chinese could have Peking if they gave the normal annual revenue from the city to the Nuchen, in addition to a tribute. The Sung Emperor, Hui-tsung, was a painter and poet of enormous talent, immortalised by Chinese literature because of a romantic affair with a K'aifeng prostitute, but his military and political knowledge was sadly lacking. The Sung authorities protested that the Nuchen had reneged on the original pact, and further differences between the former allies led to an invasion of Sung by the Nuchen in 1125.

The artistic Emperor of China abdicated in favour of his son when defeat seemed inevitable, and when the Sung armies surrendered, the new Emperor and his Court were presented by the Nuchen with a huge demand for war indemnities which included 5 million taels of gold, 50 million taels of silver, 1 million bolts of silk and 10,000 head of horses and cattle. The prime minister and many members of the royal family were to be held hostage until the indemnity had been paid. The Sung Emperor agreed to the terms, but when another demand for money came from a Nuchen commander in the west, the Sung government refused to implement the peace terms. The Nuchen attacked K'aifeng again, and despite the Sung army's primitive bombs made possible by the recent discovery of military uses for gunpowder, the capital found itself hopelessly besieged. The Nuchen were now demanding an even higher indemnity, including 20 million taels of gold. In desperation the Sung leaders had every corner of the capital searched for gold, from the royal palaces to the brothels, but the amount could not be raised. The city fell to the invaders, and was sacked. The Emperor, his father and 3000 members of the Imperial Court were herded into carts and taken north into captivity. The Chinese Emperor was cruelly awarded the title 'Marquis of Recurring Confusion' by the Nuchen ruler, and was forced to parade with his father in the new Nuchen capital of Yenching (near Peking), both dressed as servants.

One of the Imperial princes had managed to escape the defeat, however, and fled south. When it became obvious that the royal prisoners in Yenching would never be re-enthroned, he declared himself Emperor of the Southern Sung, and set up his capital in Hangchow, which Marco Polo was later to describe as 'beyond doubt the finest and most noble city in the world'.

The Great Wall now formed a belt across the middle of the Nuchen Empire. It was of no direct military importance whatsoever, but the Nuchen cautiously maintained it as an outer defence for their capital Yenching, a precaution that proved fully justified. They built a 500-mile long extension in the north, reaching as far as the 48th parallel in places. They also build numerous smaller walls or earth ramparts in the north as protection against other barbarian tribes and to prevent a repetition of what they themselves had done to the old Khitan régime. Additionally, they renovated a section of wall that the Khitan had originally built as a defence against them, and in the west they built a new wall parallel to the Great Wall. The location of these walls shows that the Nuchen remained conscious of their vulnerability in relation to other nomad groups, long after they had discarded the Chinese as a meaningful threat. Along with the wall construction came powerful legislation to stop Nuchen citizens adopting too many Chinese customs, and in 1187 punishments were set out for people who had taken Chinese surnames or wore Chinese clothes. Some people carried their enthusiasm so far as to demand that the Chinese learn the Nuchen language and wear Nuchen hairstyles.

When the Nuchen first came to power their defensive watchfulness was unspecific; they could not have known who their enemy would be but were sure that some new nomad tribe would arise, just as they themselves had burst into maturity under Akuta's leadership after several hundred years of obscurity. The major requirement for any tribe to improve its position was a strong leader who could win the allegeance of the different clans and instil in his men the confidence needed for victory. Just such a man arose in the second half of the twelfth century, an intrepid youth called Temujin, who was to lead his Mongol brethren to the greatest empire the world has ever known.

Until the twelfth century, the Mongols were one of the least noteworthy of the nomad tribes that eked out a living in the barren lands of north and central Asia. Some of the Mongols lives as hunters and fishermen in the region of Lake Baikal, but the majority were herders who drove their flocks across the arid wastes of Mongolia looking for pasture for their animals. Their habits were almost entirely determined by climate; in summer they would move north to profit from the brief growth of vegetation, only to be driven back south with the migrating birds with the onset of the long winters. Vegetation was saved for the animals, while the Mongols themselves had a singularly carnivorous diet supplemented with milk products. In the harshest periods of winter, when food was scarce, the Mongols were prepared to satisfy their appetite with horse flesh or dog meat, and slake their thirst with horses' blood drawn off from a cut vein. Mongol society was based on the survival of the fittest; the men of the tribe had the first pick of the food, sat nearest the fire and looked after the most demanding tasks such as hunting or warfare. The women supervised the maintenance of the felt yurts (tents), did the cooking, helped with the flocks and looked after the children. The children were expected to be self-sufficient at a very early age, and would often find themselves chasing after their own food, even desert rats, because the adults had left only scraps for them.

The Mongols had very few material possessions for unnecessary encumbrance would hinder the speed of their movement. Wealth was measured in terms of the number of animals in a man's flock, the number of his wives (polygamy being widespread), or the number and quality of his sons. The Mongol's most precious chattel was his horse. From the earliest age a boy was taught how to use his horse to its maximum capacity. The Mongols could ride at full speed while firing arrows, as the peasants of Russia were soon to discover to their terror, and could survive for months on end with just their horses and weapons. Death and violence were an essential feature of everyday life so that they went to war without fear and with the excitement of a hunt in their minds. Battles were inevitable as the deserts and steppe lands could only support a limited number of people, and tribes fought over pasture lands. Those adversaries who had not been practised in Mongol fighting ways could not resist the impact of a Mongol attack. Numbers of fighting men were not of great importance against opponents who rode so fast and shot with such deadly accuracy that they killed and disappeared before the enemy had time to take aim. This is how a race of no more than 2,500,000 managed to subjugate hundreds of millions of people across Eurasia with an army of around 250,000.

Temujin, the future Genghis Khan, was born around 1167, son of Yesukai, an important chieftain. Legend says the baby was born with a clot of blood clenched in his right fist, a symbol of his bloody future. He was named Temujin in celebration of the fact that his father had just vanquished a rival chieftain of that name. Temujin's father died when he was young, which made the boy even more independent than he might otherwise have been. At the age of thirteen he was seated on a white horseskin as the rightful khan of his group, and immediately had to fight against older rivals to keep his position. He led his men in a surprise attack against the Karaïts, an important tribe who had settlements of mud and straw as well as mobile camps. This attack succeeded and gradually he brought all of the Gobi under his rule. Each new victory brought Temujin more support and intensified his desire to widen his control. In 1206, the Year of the Leopard, Temujin called together a *kurultai*, a council of the khans representing the different tribes of the steppe lands, and asked that they choose a leader who would be Emperor of High Asia. Temujin himself was of course elected to this position, and following the recommendations of a soothsayer, he was given the title Genghis Kha Khan, or the Greatest of All Rulers, Emperor of All Men.

Later in the same year an official from the Nuchen Court, called the Warden of the Western Marches, crossed the Great Wall to collect tribute from the outer barbarians and reported that 'absolute quiet prevails in the far kingdoms'. The unusual calm probably acted as a warning of future trouble to the more astute members of the Nuchen régime, particularly when they heard that the Mongols were gathering around a man of magnetic personality. Stories and legends already surrounded Genghis Khan's name, and shamanists declared that he was a *bogdo*, or a visitation from heaven, destined to bring glory to his race. The red-haired, green-eyed Khan gave his people a civil law code that aimed at keeping a strict moral standard as well as encouraging loyalty to himself. Penalties were stiff, and the death sentence was given for theft, spying, false witness, black magic, adultery and sodomy. The Mongol warriors were entreated to get drunk only three times a month. 'It would be better not to get drunk at all, but who can abstain altogether?'

The conquest of lands south of the Wall was a constant dream of Genghis, and he is recorded as saying, 'The greatest joy a man can have is victory: to conquer one's enemies, to pursue them, to deprive them of their possessions, to reduce their families to tears, to ride on their horses and to make love to their wives and daughters.'

The first major foreign campaign was against the Tangut or Hsia, at the extreme western end of the Wall. In 1209 Genghis captured their capital and launched repeated raids, convincing the tribal leaders of the west that a peace agreement was desirable. Some tribes living along the Wall succumbed to Genghis without fighting, and joined alliances with him. Encouraged by his success in the west, the Khan turned his interest to a much greater prize, the Nuchen empire of northern China.

By coincidence the Nuchen Emperor had just died, and an officer was sent from Yenching over the Great Wall to ask for tribute from the Mongols for the new Emperor. Genghis refused, saying,

> Our dominion is now so well ordered that we can visit Cathay. Is the dominion of the Golden Khan [the Nuchen Emperor] so well ordered that he can meet us? We will go with an army that is like a roaring ocean. It matters not whether we are met with friendship or war. If the Golden Khan chooses to be our friend, we will allow him the government under us of his dominion; if he chooses war, it will last until one of us is victor, one defeated.[2]

The Nuchen rulers had largely ignored Mongol horsemen who rode up and down the northern frontier waving Genghis' standard, but this latest provocation was much too serious to go unnoticed. The Nuchen launched a punitive expedition against nomads in the south of the Gobi, but Genghis massed his forces ready for the invasion of north China. The Nuchen Emperor asked for a report on the situation from the Warden of the Western Marches, whose duty is was to keep abreast of developments among the outer barbarians. When the unfortunate Warden replied the Mongols were busy making arrows and rounding up horses, the Emperor was so annoyed he put him in prison.

The Mongol invasion of Cathay began in 1211. There are widely contrasting accounts of what happened during the China campaign, but most authorities agree that the Mongols advanced quickly through the northern regions of the Empire to the Great Wall, without losing a man. The goal was the Nuchen capital of Yenching, and the Khan obviously had a very low opinion of the defensive strength of the Great Wall as he chose a direct route to Yenching which passed through the strongest points of the Wall. Initially his judgement seemed fair, and the Mongols swept through the outer loops of the Great Wall without any difficulty, gratifying the cynics of ages past who had said that the Great Wall was an anachronism. However, the hordes soon found themselves stopped by the heavily fortified Wall gate at Chü Yung Kuan. Historians disagree as to whether the fortress fell or not, but the end result was that the Mongols were discouraged by the delaying effect of Chü Yung Kuan's resisting forces, and the knowledge that more fortifications existed between them and their prize. Not least of these were the battlements of Yenching. In their wisdom the Nuchen had ringed the capital with 40-foot-high city walls, incorporating hundreds of watch-towers and heavy gates. The gate-towers were well stocked with missiles of all kinds, and news of the Mongol attacks on the Great Wall caused extra provisioning to be made of the capital's defences. Outside the city walls were three moats, and four huge stone forts containing impressive arsenals.

2 From Lamb, Harold, *Genghis Khan: Emperor of All Men* (Bantam Books; New York, 1953).

After many weeks of futile attacks on the inner defences of the Great Wall, the Mongols withdrew; but further west they had much greater success. The Nuchen had made an agreement with the Ongut tribe for the defence of part of the Wall, and the Ongut in turn made a pact with the Mongols, giving them transit permission. The Mongol troops flooded through into the Shansi area and a Nuchen army rushed to confront them, only to be slaughtered on the roads by the arrows of thousands of galloping horsemen.

Genghis and his men were used to warfare by raids and did not like to stay far away from home for too long. They needed to return north for new horses and supplies, as well as to rest. Genghis therefore ordered his men back across the Wall after the successful advance into Shansi, taking plundered goods with them. The Chinese of the northern regions had already learnt to fear the passage of the Mongols, who wore ferocious leather uniforms and pointed helmets, who smelt (bathing being forbidden by Mongol rules), and who daubed grease on their faces to protect themselves from the cold winds.

Genghis seems to have attached particular significance to bringing about the fall of Chü Yung Kuan as autumn 1213 saw his army outside its gates and again attacking the fort. Additional defences had been built during the previous months, and the big gate itself was said to have been sealed with iron to prevent its being opened, though this seems somewhat unlikely as Mongol forces were able to pass through it from the other side soon afterwards. In any case, the nomads were deterred by new earthworks and the prospect of a long and possibly fruitless siege, so a detachment of Mongols outflanked the fortress by leading a sudden attack on the gate at Tzu-ching Kuan, south-west of Yenching, which fell to their unexpected pressure. This force then over-ran Chü Yung Kuan from behind and opened the gate to their compatriots.

In the spring of 1214, three Mongol armies continued the invasion of north China. One moved in force across Shansi; another crossed the Khingan range to join up with local allies called the Liao (descendants of the old Khitan régime), and the third, under the command of Genghis, advanced on Yenching. The armies laid siege to towns along the way and often drove crowds of farmers before them when they made an attack. Frequently towns surrendered in the hope of gaining clemency from the invaders. Yenching, however, presented a much more difficult problem. Genghis ordered two assaults on the city's defences, both in vain, and then realised he had no chance of an early victory. His men were tired, many were diseased, and they were suffering from repeated bombardment from the battlements. The Khan did not want to spend a winter outside the gates of Yenching, so prepared to withdraw, but first asked the Nuchen Emperor for 'gifts', namely an imperial princess for himself, 500 boy slaves and 500 girl slaves, a herd of fine horses and large quantities of gold and silk.

Some of the Nuchen ministers protested to the Emperor that if the Khan was prepared to leave, it obviously indicated that he knew he could not take Yenching. Instead of merely giving him bribes, they therefore argued, the Emperor should send out troops to take advantage of the situation and conquer the Mongol forces. The Emperor was not convinced and, anxious to save his own skin at all costs, willingly paid the required amounts, displaying

132

great relief when the Mongols packed up their tents and returned north. He was clearly not hopeful that the lull in Mongol attacks would last for long, so to his Court's dismay he announced that he was going to settle in the southern capital, and left Yenching in the hands of his son. The Mongol army meanwhile returned slowly to the steppes, putting most of their civilian prisoners to the sword before they crossed the Great Wall.

In Yenching a revolt started. Some of the Emperor's own guard defected to the side of the revolutionaries, while others rallied round the Crown Prince. The Imperial authority still rested with Emperor Wan-yen Hsün, who summoned his son to join him in his new headquarters at K'aifeng. The Prince reluctantly obeyed his father's command, leaving the city of Yenching in the hands of faithful soldiers and eunuchs. Outraged Nuchen patriots led a surprise offensive against some Mongol outposts, and Genghis halted his march north to await news. When informed of the state of affairs in China he sent a crack division to chase Emperor Wan-yen Hsün, who was driven to take temporary refuge in Sung territory, the Sung regarding the Nuchens' undignified demise with a certain amount of pleasure.

Genghis remained encamped near the Great Wall, content to leave the dénouement to his trusted officers. A truly great leader, he knew just how to delegate authority to people who merited it. He was already about fifty years old, a grandfather (the future Kublai Khan had already been born at home in the Gobi), and now that defeat of the Nuchen seemed a mere formality, his enthusiasm for the invasion seems to have waned. Another Mongol leader soon appeared at the gates of Yenching with 5000 nomad warriors, supplemented by a host of Nuchen defectors, ready finally to take over the city. Panic reigned behind the battlements as women tried in vain to persuade disillusioned garrisons to carry on the fight. Looting was rife in the streets, and by the time the Mongols had entered the city, fire had spread through many quarters. The general in command of the city wrote, on the hem of his gown, a valedictory letter to his unworthy Emperor, before committing suicide. Genghis Khan greatly admired the Nuchen who had remained faithful to their nation even after their Emperor had fled.

The idea of conquest was much more appealing to Genghis than the reality, and he suddenly found himself confronted with the necessity of working out an administration for the occupied Nuchen territory, which could hardly be run in the same way as nomad lands. He even began to think of his new acquisition as something of a handicap, and asked a young Khitan who had worked for the Nuchen what advice he could give for the running of the territory. The Khitan replied:

Now that you have conquered the world and all the riches between the four seas, you have everything you could want, yet you have not organised it. You ought to tax land owners and merchants, and make money from wine, salt, iron and the products of the mountains and fenlands. In this way you could obtain 500,000 ounces of silver, 80,000 bolts of silk and 400,000 piculs of grain in a single year. How can you say that the Chinese are of no use to you?

133

Genghis followed the advice of those who suggested he allow the economy of north China to be run on fairly traditional lines. He had retained an unsophisticated outlook on life and the finer intricacies of Chinese taxation regulations were as uninteresting to him as they were incomprehensible. Leaving the organisation of the economy to others better qualified, he turned his attention to the western end of the Great Wall where trouble had again started with the Tangut nomads and a group called the Black Khitai, descendants of fugitive Khitan who had fled from the overthrow of the Khitan Dynasty a hundred years before. The Mongol armies first dealt with the Black Khitai, but instead of subduing the Tangut around the Wall, Genghis ordered his troops to carry on marching westward, so that in 1221 Bokhara and Samarkand were added to the Mongol Empire. A rather spurious story records that the Khan would have continued his incursion westward had a unicorn not come to him in a dream to ask him to desist. It is far more credible that he viewed the restless Tangut people as a pest which ought to be dealt with firmly. Their land formed an obvious gap in the Mongol control of north Asia, and in late 1224 the Khan directed his armies towards the Tangut to redress the situation. This campaign saw some of the most bitter fighting of the Mongol period, and 300,000 men are said to have been killed in the final battles. The Tangut were finally subdued in 1227, but not before Genghis Khan himself had died, without seeing the whole of the Great Wall of China in Mongol hands. He had, however, laid the foundations on which his descendants could build an empire that would make even the Great Wall seem puny in comparison.

Genghis' third son, Ogödai, succeeded to the Mongol throne and supervised the annihilation of the last pockets of Nuchen power. Despite the collapse of the Nuchen Empire several years before, the last emperor still held court in K'aifeng, but in 1234 Ogödai's troops surrounded the city and the ruler killed himself. In other parts of Asia and Europe, states were falling to the Mongol wave. Korea was conquered in 1231–2; Moscow after 1235; the Danube valley in 1240. The great push of the Golden Horde into Europe came to a halt in 1242 with the news of the death of Ogödai, for the horde's leader, Batu, rushed back to his homeland to participate in the election of a new Khan. During the reign of Mangu (1251–1259), the Mongol Empire spread south-westwards to Persia, Mesapotamia and Syria. This colossal Empire was, in theory, governed by the Great Khan, based in Peking, following Kublai Khan's sacking of the old Mongol capital Karakorum to assert his own dominant position.

Considering the weakness of the Sung Chinese down in the south, it is superficially surprising that the Mongols should have taken as long as they did to bring southern China into their Empire. While the Mongols swept across central and western Asia in only a few years, it was half a century after Genghis Khan's death before all of China was under the nomads' rule. The reasons were largely geographical, for Mongol methods of warfare were totally unsuited to the paddy fields of tropical China. The population density was far higher than anything the Mongols had come across in their trans-Asian experience, and the Chinese fought with great tenacity to preserve their proud independence and individual way of life. Even if the Great Wall had proved miserably inadequate to keep out the nomads, the Chinese were not going to succumb easily. Some cities withstood sieges for several years. Nevertheless, Chinese territory was consistently gnawed away by Mongol generals, and in 1276 Hangchow fell without a fight. The last claimant to the Sung throne drowned himself three years later.

In 1271, Kublai Khan adopted a Chinese dynastic name, Yüan, thereby recognising his dual role as Great Khan of all the Mongols and Emperor of China. He was also given a Chinese name, Yüan Shih-tsu, and his Chinese collaborators did everything they could to make him acceptable to the Chinese people. They failed. Kublai Khan was never regarded as anything but barbarian by the Chinese, and no matter how impressed visitors such as Marco Polo might be, the Chinese considered the eighty-nine years of Mongol rule as the blackest period of the history of the Middle Kingdom. The Great Wall had been built, extended and renovated over the past 1500 years to prevent just such an occurrence as the Mongol occupation of China. Large parts of China had been under foreign control before, but never until this time had the foreigners refused to sacrifice their barbaric ways for the wisdom of the Flowery Kingdom. The Mongols never assimilated, and the Emperor Yüan Shih-tsu persisted in such pleasures as hunting with falcons long after he ascended the Dragon Throne. The Chinese were particularly horrified by the mass slaughter carried out by Mongol troops at the slightest provocation – the entire population of Chinkiang on the south bank of the Yangtse was massacred in reprisal for the Chinese killing of a group of drunken Mongol soldiers, or so reported Marco Polo.

Marco Polo's account has often been queried because he failed to mention the existence of the Great Wall (as well as footbinding and Chinese writing), and ingenious reasons have been produced as to why he should have ignored this fantastic structure. Some people said outright that his book was a fabrication, and that he had never been to China at all, but if that were true he must have had some remarkable sources for his information, and it is unlikely that these sources would have neglected to mention China's – and the World's – largest monument. Sir George Staunton, a member of Macartney's embassy to China of 1793, worked out a fanciful route for Polo by which he could have avoided seeing the stone barrier. Even had the Venetian followed this highly improbable route in entering China, it is inconceivable that any man of intelligence could spend several years in China without being aware of the Great Wall's existence. A nineteenth-century scholar named Archimandrite Palladius argued that the Wall escaped Marco Polo's notice because it had fallen into such a state of disrepair. Even allowing for the Wall's rapid decline when neglected, it is unlikely that it would have een such an insignificant ruin in Kublai Khan's time considering its strength at the time of Genghis Khan's invasion. Like many irritating scholastic mysteries of little real importance, Marco Polo's omission of the Great Wall from his book was probably no more than forgetfulness, or else a wish not to clutter his volume with details of things which had no real function in Yüan China.

The Mongols accentuated the racial and cultural cleavage within China by introducing a caste system, aggravating the injury of subjugation. The Mongols belonged to the top caste; the other non-Chinese (such as Persians or Turks or Central Asians) to the second category; the former subjects of the Nuchen Empire to the third, and the Sung Chinese to the least respected. The Chinese were forbidden to walk the streets at night, were inferior in the eyes of the law, could not possess arms and if murdered by a Mongol, were worth only a donkey in compensation compared with the forty measures of gold for a Muslim. The Yüan rulers ensured undying hatred from the Chinese by openly despising their traditional culture, persecuting intellectuals and making a mockery of the bureaucracy, which had been evolved with such care during centuries of previous dynasties. When Ogödai first entered China, for example, he sold the right of collecting taxes to an Uighur merchant. Every new day brought fresh examples of Mongol incompetence and stupidity (in the eyes of the Chinese), not least of which was the turning of good agricultural land into fields of grass to ride around and hunt in.

Not all of Mongol rule was negative however. Although they had no reason to add a single brick to the Great Wall, the Yüan emperors did authorise several construction projects, notably in the transport sector. Roads spread out from Peking to the farthest flung corners of the vast Mongol Enpire, and a postal system of admirable efficiency was instituted. During Kublai Khan's time, 200,000 horses were kept in permanent service for the courier service. The Mongols built a long extension to the Grand Canal, which now stretched all the way from Hangchow to Peking (Khanbalik) a distance of approximately 1000 miles. Two-and-a-half million men reportedly worked on this project, which was terminated in 1289. In the cultural field, also, not all was bleak, for the Yüan period saw the writing of some of China's finest plays, including Wang Shih-fu's *Romance of the Western Chamber*.

The middle years of the fourteenth century brought numerous uprisings against the corrupted and declining Mongol régime. For the last ten years of the Yüan Dynasty the Mongols themselves had very little to do with the battle for power in China, as rival rebel leaders set up their own organisations. A young man called Chu Yüan-chang from Anhwei province fought his way to victory in south China; by 1367 most of the area south of the Yellow River was in his hands. He sent an army of 250,000 men north to Peking and the Mongols were incapable of putting up a serious resistance. The last Yüan emperor left the capital in the summer of 1368 and crossed the Great Wall into Mongolia, thereby symbolically bringing to an end barbarian control of China.

Chu Yüan-chang declared himself Emperor in Nanking, and so the Ming Dynasty was founded. The Ming rulers were among the most active wall builders in Chinese history, as if anxious to eliminate the possibility of any repetition of the Mongol disaster. It was they who created most of the Great Wall as we know it today. If any group had shown that the Great Wall could not stop what was inevitable, it was the Mongols, yet, superficially, the Ming did not acknowledge this. The Great Wall seems to have become a way of life, a necessary demonstration of the barrier between China and the world outside, unbreachable in spirit if not in fact.

8

The Empire in Autumn

CHAPTER EIGHT

The Empire in Autumn

IN the last thousand years of Chinese Imperial history, the Ming Dynasty (1368–1644) was the only Chinese régime to have control of the entire length of the Great Wall. The Wall, under Ming rule, took on a new lease of life, was almost entirely rebuilt and was kept in a better state of repair than it had been since ancient Han times. Although the Ming Empire stretched north of the Wall in north-east China, the central and western sections of the Dragon Screen formed the actual frontier with the barbarian regions. Despite the known fact that the Wall had never managed to keep out serious invaders for long, the Ming emperors believed that it justified the expense to maintain and properly garrison it if only to stop minor incursions and give the imperial armies time to rush north in the event of a major threat, while the Wall defenders kept the enemy back as long as possible.

In keeping with the by now traditional dynastic cycle, the Ming period began vigorously with strong, imaginative emperors occupying the Dragon Throne. The founder, Chu Yüan-chang, also called the 'Beggar Emperor', pursued the Mongols north of the Wall and kept a vigilant watch on the northern regions, at the same time streamlining the country's administration and intensifying the autocratic nature of the Emperor's position. His had been a strenuous childhood as the fourth son of an extremely poor family. He had witnessed the death of his parents and brothers in a severe famine that followed a drought and a plague of locusts in 1344. The young Yüan-chang was taken into a monastery, but when the revolt against the Mongols spread to his province of Anhwei in 1352, an oracle told him that the spirits wanted him to join the rebels. His new colleagues were deeply impressed by the young man, not least because he was considered one of the ugliest men on earth. He was later called the Beggar Emperor because of his time as a mendicant monk, but the children in the streets called him the Pig Emperor because of his grotesque features. Chu Yüan-chang was obviously deeply sensitive about his origins, for two Confucian scholars who used the word for birth (*sheng*) in their congratulatory memorials on his accession, were put to death because the word bore too close a relationship to the word for monk (*seng*)!

Chu Yüan-chang was a firm believer in the absolute power of the monarchy and thought

139

that the strong continuation of his Imperial line was just as important for the security of his new dynasty as was the Great Wall and a strong army. The Crown Prince was a weakling, but died young, so the Emperor appointed his grandson as the new heir apparent. Being well versed in the sordid in-fighting of imperial circles in former dynasties, the Emperor decided to ensure the boy's calm transition to power by eliminating his potential rivals. This was carried out during two bloodbaths in 1380 and 1393. Even the prime minister was disposed of allegedly for plotting with the Japanese to overthrow the Ming régime. Chu Yüan-chang died in 1398, little realising that he had secured his grandson's demise by his own arrangements for protecting north China from invasion.

Chu Yüan-chang had shared the widespread scepticism about the Great Wall being barrier enough to stem a resurgence of Mongol power, so had put three of his eldest sons (uncles to the heir apparent) in charge of three key military regions along the northern frontier. The three princes were charged with the task of guarding the area contiguous to the Wall, and of coming to the rescue of the capital, now Nanking, should this prove necessary.

Chu Yüan-chang's grandson, Ming Hui-ti, received the insignia of power in 1399, at the age of sixteen, and almost immediately fell victim to the personal ambition of his uncle, Chu Ti, who had been endowed with considerable autonomous power in the Peking region. Chu Ti declared that the boy Emperor was being used by unscrupulous persons in Court, and that it was therefore necessary to take matters into his own hands. He marched on Nanking with a large body of troops originally destined to maintain peace in the frontier zone. For three years Chu Ti's forces fought against the young Emperor's loyal supporters, eventually capturing Nanking in 1402. The royal palace was burned to the ground, and the Emperor disappeared, his fate unknown.

Fortunately for China the Mongols north of the Wall were in no state to take advantage of this internal dispute. Chu Ti took the throne of China for himself, and despite the manner of his usurpation, was one of the finest emperors China ever had, being granted during his reign the title of Yung-lo, or 'perpetual happiness'.

In an attempt to win the intellectuals over to his new government Chu Ti commissioned the compilation of a huge encyclopaedia intended to bring together the whole of Chinese knowledge from earliest times to 1400. The encyclopaedia was called *Yung-lo Ta-Tien* after Chu Ti's title, Yung-lo, and comprised 11,095 volumes totalling 917,480 pages written out by hand. Many years later two copies were made, but the original and one copy were destroyed during the collapse of Ming rule in 1644, and the last copy went up in flames during the Boxer rebellion of 1900.

While a staff of more than 2000 was engaged in compiling the great encyclopaedia, Chu Ti's armies went north of the Wall to deal with a sudden revival of Mongol strength. The Mongols had recovered from the beating they received at the hands of the first Ming Emperor, Chu Yüan-chang, and had found a vigorous new leader in a man called Alutai, who overthrew the ineffectual reigning khan in 1405 and replaced him with a pliant descendant of Kublai Khan. Alutai and his puppet ruler refused to send the customary acknowledgement of supremacy to the Ming emperor, and authorised raiding along the Great Wall by Mongol tribesmen. In retaliation, Chu Ti sent an army over the Wall in 1408, but the offensive was rebuffed. The following year Chu Ti himself led 100,000 men into the Mongol lands, and the khan fled before such an army. Alutai made a fast appraisal of the situation and escaped in the opposite direction from his ruler, taking a large force with him. Chu Ti was sufficiently aware of Mongol politics to know that Alutai was the more valuable prey, and therefore ignored the fleeing khan to pursue Alutai. The Mongol leader was surrounded by Ming troops and heavily defeated, though he himself survived. He duly acknowledged Chu Ti's supremacy, and was generously bestowed with a title. The Mongols became split into two factions following this Ming victory, and Chu Ti found it to his advantage to alternate favour from one to the other so as to confuse and weaken the nomads north of the Great Wall.

In 1421, Chu Ti moved his capital away from Nanking to Peking, building a new heavily defended city not far from the old Nuchen capital of Yenching. Chu Ti retained a great affection for the area that had been his domain before he usurped the Imperial throne, but another reason of special importance in choosing Peking was that he felt from this more northerly situation, more control could be exercised over the frontier region. The Mongol leader Alutai was again making threats, and the organisation of an adequate defence system

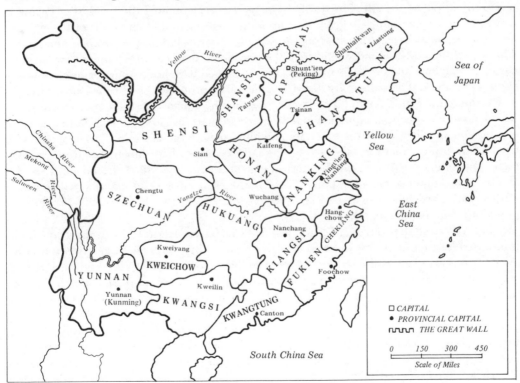

Fig. 9. China proper around AD 1400.

along the Great Wall became a major preoccupation of Chu Ti and his successors, as witnessed by a dynastic history:

> Once they had been driven out of China, the descendants of the Yüan dynasty [the Mongols] constantly endeavoured to regain their lost domain. When the Yung-lo emperor [Chu Ti] moved the capital up north, the Great Wall was close by on three sides [the capital being protected by spurs of the Wall except in the south] but the enemy became daily more troublesome. The defence of the Great Wall therefore became of leading importance as the Ming Dynasty wore on. Beginning at the Yalu River in the east and extending westwards as far as Kiayükwan for a distance of 10,000 li, the Wall was divided into numerous garrisons.
>
> At each transit pass capable of admitting carts and horsemen, guard posts manned by one hundred people were established. Ten men looked after the smaller gates that could let through fuel gatherers and herdsmen.

Chu Ti knew that the old Nuchen capital of Yenching had withstood the Mongols for several months with the aid of its sturdy battlements, so he ordered the builders of Peking to construct even more impressive ramparts around his new capital. The walls of Peking were nearly fifteen miles in length, on average 40 feet high, not including the parapets and towers. The core of the walls was more solid than the traditional tamped earth; alternating layers of earth, gravel, lime and bricks formed the kernel, encased with huge stones or bricks seven or eight layers thick. The walled city had nine gates, each protected by a walled enclosure.

Considering Chu Ti's careful policy of strengthening China's northern defences, it seems odd to modern strategists that he should have entrusted parts of the Wall to friendly barbarian or semi-nomad tribes who had entered into an alliance with the Chinese. This idea had been tried on several occasions in other dynasties, and experience had shown that it was a risky tactic depending for success on the unswerving loyalty of the allied defenders. The only feasible explanation is that Chu Ti felt his own armies insufficient to man the whole length of the Wall, particularly as he had set up large garrison camps in the north-east to help protect the hub of the Empire.

Persistent disquiet from the Mongols justified Chu Ti's concern. In 1421, the year Chu Ti transferred his capital, Alutai planned an invasion of China, but cancelled it when his own territory was attacked by the western Mongol faction, known as the Oirat. He was forced to take shelter in Manchuria, but in 1422 had recovered sufficiently to supervise new raids on the Chinese frontier. Chu Ti raised an army of 235,000 men to launch a major offensive against the Mongols, but as often happened, the Mongols evaporated in the face of this massive assault. More expeditions were led by Chu Ti over the next couple of years, and in 1425 the Emperor was taken ill and died on the way back from one of these campaigns. His body was transported back to Peking, where it lay in state for a year awaiting an auspicious day for the burial. The Court Astrologer eventually decided the time had arrived, and the Emperor was buried at a site he himself had chosen. This was the site of the Ming Tombs, now one of the most impressive monuments in northern China, about thirteen miles south of the Wall itself, located in a dip protected by hills on three sides, and guarded in the south by mounds shaped as a dragon and a tiger. The Great Wall was thought to protect the tombs from demon spirits from the cold north, while colossal and rather hideous stone animals line the road to the graves.

The Great Wall has often been cited as an indication of Chinese xenophobia, but however true this may have been in some dynasties, it was certainly not the case in early Ming China. Chu Ti wished to shut off the Mongols because they were a perpetual irritation and a danger, but his attitude to the great world outside was very different. Chu Ti and his two immediate successors patronised a remarkable series of maritime expeditions and adventures, so that the first half of the fifteenth century saw Chinese boats and explorers as far away as East Africa, the Persian Gulf, Ceylon and Indonesia. From 1405 to 1431, a court eunuch named Cheng Ho led Chinese vessels on seven different voyages to the Western Sea. The first expedition carried 27,800 men to India, as well as several states of South-East Asia, where local rulers were requested to announce their devotion to the Celestial Emperor in far-off Peking. Those who obliged their Chinese visitors with courteous words of humble submission were rewarded with gold, silk and other precious goods, while those who refused to put on an act for the Ming emissaries were sometimes subjected to violence. The vessels returning to China during these enterprising years brought many strange things to entertain the emperor, not least of which was a giraffe from Africa.

The motives for the great Ming maritime expeditions were very different from those which pressed the great Western explorers to take to the high seas. The fundamental reason seems to have been a wish to impress upon the people of distant lands the magnificence and advancement of the Ming Empire. Chinese historians also said that the Emperor wanted to try to find his deposed nephew, Ming Hui-Ti, who had disappeared in the smouldering ruins of Nanking when Chu Ti seized power, but that seems highly improbable. Certainly the incentive of commercial transactions and the thrill of discovery seem to have had little or no role to play in the Ming ventures. The Chinese emperors continued to regard themselves as the Sons of Heaven, and it was therefore fitting and right that as many people as possible in the world should come under the emperor's sway. Their acceptance of themselves as the centre of the world was complete. Kings and ambassadors from foreign countries were welcome at the Ming Court, providing that they accepted from the start their inferior position. It was the refusal of the first Western delegations to China to accept such a situation that led to the closing of China's doors to the outside world, and to the bitter conflicts of the nineteenth century.

While Chu Ti and his successors were intrigued by Cheng Ho's stories of his men's experiences in foreign lands, there were many men at Court who felt that the vast expenditure involved was not worthwhile. China's interest in the seas was in any case very shortlived, as the 1430s saw trouble yet again from the barbarians north of the Wall, and Imperial eyes were once more turned north.

The culmination of disturbing events not concerned with the Wall was partly brought about by palace eunuchs in Peking. A nine-year-old Emperor named Ying Tsung came to power in 1436, and placed considerable trust in a eunuch companion, Wang Chen, whose self-esteem was equalled only by his incompetence. Within a short period of time Wang Chen succeeded in alienating most of the Court officials, and worse still, in upsetting the forever volatile Mongols.

In 1439, the Oirat, or western Mongols, acquired a new forceful chieftain named Esen who was acknowledged as leader by tribes along the major parts of the Great Wall. To give a certain kudos to his position, Esen demanded a Chinese princess in marriage, following the tradition of the great nomad leaders of former times. The eunuch Wang Chen grossly overstepped his authority by agreeing to this request, then made his crime infinitely more serious by neglecting to tell the Emperor of what he had done. Esen sent horses, furs and other gifts in preparation for the marriage, but the foolish and greedy eunuch kept these for himself. When an Oirat envoy arrived to escort the Chinese bride back to Esen, he was informed by an outraged Emperor that no such agreement had been made. This rebuttal was a grave loss of face for the Oirat chief who drew up his forces along the Chinese frontier in 1449 ready for a war of honour.

Emperor Ying Tsung raised an army of half a million men, but like many hastily organised forces, it suffered from lack of co-ordination. Esen's troops broke through the Wall at Tat'ung and cut Ying Tsung's army to pieces, proving once more that the Great Wall was only useful as a delaying mechanism. Ying Tsung was taken prisoner and the remnants of the Ming fighting force fell back to Peking, which was successfully defended. Esen felt he had the trump card by holding the Emperor prisoner, and demanded a huge ransom for Ying Tsung's release. The Oirat received a curt reply that amounted to no less than an exposition of the view that incompetent emperors were expendable; Ying Tsung's brother was placed on the throne by the Minister of War, and the bemused Oirat leader returned to his homeland with the Imperial hostage in tow.

Ying Tsung remained with the Mongols for a year before being released. His brother had no intention of abdicating, so Ying Tsung was forced temporarily to relinquish his rights, though several members of the Court acknowledged their loyalty to him, thereby causing a split in official circles in Peking. Ying Tsung's brother (Ching Ti) fell ill in 1457, and a general named Shih Heng organised Ying Tsung's restoration. Ching Ti died soon afterwards and a purge of his supporters followed. This occurrence allegedly triggered off a confusing series of heavenly portents. A comet appeared in the sky, signifying disapproval on the part of the gods. Ying Tsung decided to appease them by clapping General Shih Heng in irons; when storms and floods broke out across the Empire immediately afterwards, the Emperor set him free again. Finally, an astrologer informed Ying Tsung that it was written in the stars that Shih Heng would found a new dynasty. Ying Tsung decided to take no chances, and ordered the arrest of Shih Heng and his son in the Great Wall border town of Tat'ung, where they were instructed to commit suicide. Ying Tsung's own inglorious life and reign came to an end in 1464.

The Oirat leader Esen reaped only scant benefits from his victory over the forces of Ying Tsung. He declared himself Khan of all the Mongols in 1454, but fell victim to tribal politics and was assassinated the following year.

In 1472, Ying Tsung's son, Ch'eng-hua, rebuilt part of the Wall after the Oirat had swept down through the less well-guarded western section of the barrier, occupying part of the land inside the bend of the Yellow River. Ch'eng-hua's own successor, Chu Yu-t'ang, constructed forts north of the Wall to try to maintain order in the frontier zone, and stocked these forts with cannon, which were given the grandiose title of Great General (Ta Chiang Chün). The cannon made a suitably terrifying noise, but were of little practical use against fast-moving nomad horsemen. Considering the Chinese had gunpowder several hundred years before the West, it is perhaps surprising that they did not adapt it for sophisticated military use until well into the nineteenth century, but neither cannon nor the Great Wall was enough to prevent the inevitable rise of yet another fierce nomad leader.

In the middle of the sixteenth century Altan Khan (Anda) carved out an empire for himself stretching from the sea to the borders of Tibet. He led his men in raids against the Chinese provinces of Shensi and Shansi, and by 1550 was confident enough to aim for Peking. In keeping with the time-worn sequence of events, the nomads broke through the Great Wall without much difficulty, but were unable to storm the fortifications of the capital. For the next twenty years Altan Khan continued to plague his Chinese neighbours, harrying the population of the border provinces, carrying off captured livestock and valuables and causing despair among the Ming rulers. At least one Ming emperor of the period was so depressed by the seemingly inescapable cycle of barbarian invasions that he turned to alchemy and magic, perhaps hastening his own death as a result. Court officials were summoned to express their views on the subject of defence, and the same arguments that had been thrashed out in Chinese courts for hundreds of years surfaced yet again. Some ministers argued for an increased budget for the Great Wall, but others retorted that the barrier wasn't worth the money already expended. Yet another view was that if the Great Wall didn't exist at all, China would be on the receiving end of nomad attacks every season instead of experiencing only a few major invasions every century. The Ming rulers gave vent to their frustrations by introducing draconian measures concerning court administration. Officials were often criticised for their conduct or lack of ability, and were subjected to severe floggings for alleged misdeeds or disloyalty. Several died during their corrective punishment, which was said to have helped cure the Ming administration of corruption, but which did precious little to find a solution for the barbarian problem.

The Chinese generally relied on three methods to maintain an acceptable level of security along the northern frontier. The simplest method was to rely entirely on the Great Wall and its defences, constantly looking for weak points in the 2000-mile structure and keeping the garrisons full and on the alert; this policy worked only when the nomads were weak. The second method was to launch offensives north of the Wall to subdue the nomads before they were able to launch another attack. This method too, rarely had constructive results, as the nomads when weak would disappear, and when strong had every likelihood of beating the Chinese; besides, offensives tended to be counter-productive as they only intensified nomad resentment against the Chinese. The third method of defence was to try to teach the nomads the 'advantages' of living in settlements, and thereby undermine the barbarians' instinctive aggressiveness, without which they could not survive. None of the methods was really productive but the Ming tried out all three in their attempts to cope with a nightmare situation.

Very occasionally an enterprising Chinese general would contrive an ingenious ruse or plan which would give temporary relief from Mongol attacks. One of these was the entertaining sabotage of the Mongols' horses as recorded by a Portuguese traveller in the late 1550s:

> At the boundary of the Kingdom of China, where it borders with the Tartars, there is a Wall of wondrous strength, of a month's journey in extent, where the king keeps a great military force in its bulwarks. Where this wall comes upon mountains, they cut them in such a manner that they remain and serve as a wall [a very common European misconception], for the Tartars are very brave and skilful in war. At the time we were prisoners [the writer being held captive for six years by the Chinese], they broke through a part of the wall and entered into the territory for a month and a half's journey; but as the king prepared great armies of men provided with artful contrivances – in which the Chinese are very crafty – he kept back the Tartars, who fight on horseback.
>
> As their [the Tartars'] horses had become weak and were dying of hunger, one of the Chinese officers commanded a large quantity of peas to be placed in the fields, and thus it was that the horses – being so hungry as they were – set themselves to eat against the will of their masters; and in this manner the army of the king of China put them in disorder and turned to drive them out. And now a strict watch is kept on the wall.[1]

An effective solution to the problem of Altan Khan and his raiders emerged by itself. As the nomad warrior matured, he began to weary of a life on horseback, and built himself a capital at Kuei-hua outside the Wall north-west of Tat'ung. He encouraged trade with the Chinese, and normalised relations between the two peoples. The government in Peking was delighted by this unexpected turn of events, and awarded Altan Khan with the preposterous but flattering title of 'Obedient and Righteous Prince'. Altan Khan was converted to Lamaism, a Buddhist sect with origins in Tibet, but which soon became the national religion of the Mongols and gave north China many of its starkly beautiful stupas (memorial shrines). Eventually every Mongol family was expected to send at least one male member into a Lamaist monastery, where they practised strict celebacy. The ancient historian Robert Silverberg believes that this changeover from a nomadic way of life to a sedentary, semi-religious society was a major factor in the Mongols' subsequent decline, which in turn reduced pressure on the Great Wall.

The Ming Emperor, Wan Li, (1572 – 1620) seized the advantage of relative quiet along the northern frontier to renovate huge sections of the Wall. So considerable was his contribution to the barrier that the Chinese often use a word-play in the expression *Wan Li Ch'ang Ch'eng*, which is normally written with the characters meaning Ten Thousand Li Long Wall (ie, the Great Wall), but which can be written with characters meaning The Long Wall of Emperor Wan Li. Much of the Great Wall as it is known today is that which Wan Li rebuilt or

1 From Mendoza, Juan G. de, *History of the Great and Mighty Kingdom of China* (The Hakluyt Society; London, 1854).

146

restored, including the tourist spot at the Nankou Pass behind Peking. The Emperor is said to have personally inscribed Twelve Resolutions following a solar eclipse in the third year of his reign, the last of which was to 'Beware of Lavish Expenditure'. The extent of his work on the Great Wall, together with his restoration of the Grand Canal, shows that he did not take such resolutions to heart.

Wan Li's engineers left hundreds of memorials and tablets along the line of the Great Wall, extolling their Emperor's virtue and wisdom, and providing interesting data about the work they had completed. A typical example reads,

> General of the Light Brigade Tsui Ching, commanding the yeomanry under the juris-diction of the governor by imperial appointment at Paoting, Ensign Shen Tzu Hsi of the above department, Ensign Sun Erh-Kuo, superintendent of works, Liu Ching, military contractor, and others to the number of one hundred and thirty names co-operated in building this extension of five hundred and ninety-one feet six inches of Third Class Wall, beginning on the north at the end of the Military Graduate Lung Kuang-hsien's portion of Tower Number Fifty-five of the Black letter 'Wu' series. The completion of the construction was reported by the Autumn Guard on the sixteenth day of the ninth moon, of the fourth year of Wan Li.
>
> Master Stone Mason Chao Yen Maei and others. Master Border Artisan Lu Huan and others.[2]

Wan Li's Wall was of sturdier nature than his predecessors' efforts, and many of the granite blocks used are as long as 14 feet. At 50-foot intervals along the roadway on the top, stone drains were installed which prevented water settling. In the past, water had been a major problem as it would seep into the structure of the Wall, freeze in winter and crack open some of the stones by its expansion.

The first years of Wan Li's reign saw prosperous activity in many quarters. Agriculture thrived and the population expanded. Trade increased, and the Chinese enjoyed some European curiosities brought by the Portuguese, such as 20-foot cannons, superior in design to anything the Chinese had, which were placed with great reverence on the top of the Wall, defiantly overlooking nomad territory.

By the 1850s, however, events were turning sour. Many of Wan Li's early successes had been due to his wise ministers, but several of these died and the Emperor drifted into a life of reckless extravagance and debauchery. Imperial expenditure included 9 million ounces of silver for the building of palaces and 12 million ounces for wedding ceremonies and gifts for princes. As the Emperor grew older, the proportion of money spent on worthless projects increased, while essential construction, such as dykes, was ignored. Natural disasters added to the chaos caused by economic recession at the end of the sixteenth century when floods devastated parts of the north and droughts in other areas upset crop production. Even the Great Wall, on which the government had spent so much time and money, was allowed to slip

2 From Geil, William Edgar, *The Great Wall of China*, (Sturgis and Walton; New York, 1909).

into disrepair again, and garrisons along the Wall deserted when pay and supplies failed to materialise.

Wan Li himself was probably unaware of the extent of the ills of his Empire as the palace eunuchs vetted every report that came into the palace and manipulated public funds. Some eunuchs even had their own private armies; they controlled the running of the Empire and the careers of men far more talented than they. The early Ming emperors had instituted censors to investigate and criticise just such abuses of power or malpractices, but as the censors often found it impossible to get their reports past the eunuchs to the Emperor, their value was largely annulled. Two of the censors were especially consigned to the Great Wall on a year-long appointment, to assess the state of the Wall, the preparedness of the garrisons and any necessary repairs. One censor looked after the western section of the Wall and the other the eastern, noting down the number and types of weapons at the soldiers' disposal, and bombarding Peking with complaints and recommendations. Each zone of the frontier area had its own regional inspector, who reported on conditions in the neighbourhood of the Wall.

On those occasions when campaigns were led across the Wall, special censorial commissions would report on the way the generals were handling the situation. The bigger the campaign, the more prestigious or numerous were the censors assigned to the job. The intention was to rule out inefficiency and corruption, but no doubt some army men found the interference of prying scholars highly irritating. The censors were disliked by many people in power, and their existence could be precarious as a result. A good example was a famous man of upright character named Fang Chen-ju (1585–1645) who was one of the censors charged with investigating the army. The north-east of China was being threatened by a new barbarian grouping known as the Manchus, and the Ming Court was involved in the usual interminable arguments as to what could be done about the threat. Fang Chen-ju showered the palace with recommendations (thirteen in one day alone!), and managed to get himself assigned to the frontier in 1621 on an ad hoc commission which was sent to distribute presents to the garrison soldiers to raise their flagging morale. Over the following months Fang kept up his stream of reports and communications on the deteriorating situation, including the Chinese retreat inside the Great Wall in 1622. He personally tried to take over command of one unit of the defending army after Kuang-ning was abandoned by its commander. Depressed and exhausted Fang Chen-ju successfully applied for sick leave but found himself hounded by partisans of a powerful palace eunuch whom he had offended. In 1626 Fang was sentenced to death by strangulation, but received a last-minute reprieve when the eunuch in question was himself toppled from power. The virtuous censor rejoined official life as Grand Co-ordinator' of Kwangsi province, but reportedly died of grief when Peking fell to the Manchus.

Fang Chen-ju was not entirely alone in his struggle to make the Peking government realise the danger of the state of affairs along the north-east frontier. Records show that in 1621 another member of the censorial service managed to persuade the Emperor to divert 100,000 taels of funds earmarked for building a palace to an operation to repair the Wall at Shan Hai Kuan, where the Great Wall meets the China sea. A colleague similarly obtained money to buy winter uniforms for the frontier garrisons. Their actions were contrary to the general trend however, which was to ignore the Manchus and hope they would go away. When the province of Liao-tung was invaded by the Manchus, it was relinquished without a fight. When the first Dutchmen appeared off the Chinese coast and seized the island of Taiwan (Formosa), the Ming again did not or could not offer strong resistance.

The Manchus were a group of tribes descended from the Nuchen who had ruled north China as the Kin Dynasty in the twelfth century. They lived in the woodlands of south and east Manchuria, east of the River Liao and west of the Manchurian-Korean border. Their economy was mixed pastoral and arable farming. The land of south Manchuria was fertile and coveted by the Chinese, who reasserted control over the area during the Ming Dynasty after hundreds of years of barbarian rule. Chinese settlers went north in droves to open up the virgin lands for farming, and came into conflict with the local tribes who wished to preserve the forests and grasslands for their hunting and herding. A tenuous truce was eventually worked out between the Chinese and the nomads, the latter accepting the situation so long as the Chinese were militarily in control and could offer goods that the tribes wanted. Chinese control of the area weakened during the sixteenth century, and their settlements came under increasing pressure from the nomads. The area was especially vulnerable as it was out on a limb from the rest of China, the principal link being the narrow pass through the Great Wall at Shan Hai Kuan. Early in the seventeenth century the Peking government felt it could no longer guarantee the safety of its subjects on the fringes of south Manchuria, and therefore issued a directive that some settlements should be abandoned. Chinese pioneers who refused to comply with the defeatist attitude were forcibly evicted by the Ming authorities and settled in more secure areas.

Whenever the Ming authorities retreated in Manchuria, the Manchus advanced. They traded horses, timber and ginseng (a herb medicine rumoured to lengthen life and now credited as a tranquilliser) with the Chinese, but with the decline of Ming power in the region, trade fell off and the Manchus took to raiding Chinese settlements to make up for the deficiencies in supplies. At first the raids were unconnected and for simple, economic motives, but under a Manchu leader named Nurhachi (1559–1626) the raids became part of a clearly defined overall strategy of military conquest. Nurhachi kept his intentions a dark secret, and successfully deceived the Ming Court by obeying all the ritual required of a vassal of the 'Celestial Empire'. He personally led a tribute delegation to Peking in 1590, and the Ming Emperor was so impressed by Nurhachi's dealing with bandits in the Liaotung area that he gave the Manchu leader the honorary title of 'Dragon-Tiger General' in 1595.

The first essential for Nurhachi was to organise the nomad tribes into a regimented society. The Manchus had proved their effectiveness in brief surprise attacks on small settlements but if they were to conquer large areas they needed to be welded into a military machine capable of sustaining long campaigns and following rigid discipline. Nurhachi set up a system of administrative units or banners into which all Manchus, including their slaves and captives, were assigned. The divisions were called banners because each unit had a distinctive colour for its flag. Originally there were four – red, yellow, blue and white – but by the time the Manchu had taken over China there were twenty-four, sixteen Manchu and eight Chinese. The banner leaders were men personally chosen by Nurhachi.

In 1616 Nurhachi considered his preparations complete, and declared a new dynasty, the Later Kin. Two years later he sent notification of 'Seven Grievances' to the Ming Court, and declared war. An auspicious happening augured well for Nurhachi's hopes of attaining the Chinese throne when a Manchu farmer by chance dug up a jade seal which Genghis Khan had received at his coronation four hundred years before, and which had been lost during the flight of the last Mongol ruler. The Ming government reacted to Nurhachi's revolt by sending an army of 200,000 men into Manchuria, only to receive eventual news of their heavy defeat. The Chinese generals changed their strategy, withdrawing their army behind strong fortifications, hoping that a long drawn out struggle would wear down the Manchu and drive Nurhachi to sue for peace. Nurhachi died of battle wounds in 1626, and was succeeded by his son Abahai who temporarily abandoned the attack on Ming fortifications to lead a successful campaign against Korea, which he brought under Manchu control. Returning triumphant from the Korean peninsula, Abahai once more directed his troops against the fortified Chinese settlements without success. Had the Great Wall ever been as effective as the fortified towns of Manchuria, or the walled city of Peking, the whole history of China might have been different. The situation of stalemate in Manchuria looked as if it could last for many years, but revolts south of the border altered matters considerably.

In 1628 the last emperor of the Ming Dynasty ascended the throne, inheriting a realm on the verge of collapse. Emperor Ch'ung-chen was a humane and conscientious man, but China needed more than a wise ruler. Nothing short of an overthrow of the whole administration would suffice to remove the cancer that had grown in the Ming Empire. Corruption, inefficiency and demoralisation were the keynotes of the latter part of the régime. Starvation in the provinces along the Great Wall provided the catalyst for popular uprisings. One of the first memorials Emperor Ch'ung-chen received graphically portrayed the degree of famine in Shensi province.

> People peeled off tree bark for food. Among tree bark the best was that of the elm. This was so precious that to consume as little as possible people mixed it with the bark of other trees to feed themselves. Somehow they were able to prolong their lives. Towards the end of the year the supply of tree bark was exhausted, and they had to go to the mountains to dig up stones as food. Stones were cold and tasted musty. A little taken in would fill up the stomach. Those who took stones found their stomachs swollen and they dropped and died in a few days. Others who did not wish to eat stones gathered as bandits. They robbed the few who had some savings, and when they robbed, they took everything and left nothing behind. Their idea was that since they had to die either one way or another it was preferable to die as a bandit than to die from hunger and that to die as a bandit would enable them to enter the next world with a full stomach.[3]

3   From Li, Dun J., *The Ageless Chinese* (J. M. Dent; London, 1965).

Disaffected peasants formed a large part of the rebels' ranks, swollen by soldiers who had deserted from south Manchuria or the Wall because they had not been paid for such a long time, and employees of the postal service who suddenly found themselves unemployed when the Ming government cut back on the mails to reduce expenditure. In 1629 the Manchu made a southward push into China in the direction of Peking. Government reinforcements came from Shansi, Suiyuan and Kansu to help the capital, but many of the soldiers mutinied along the way. The Manchu failed to bring off a serious invasion, but the Chinese rebel armies continued to grow until they numbered more than 400,000 in 1635.

There were two rebel armies, in fact, both led by men from Shensi. A brutal mercenary soldier named Chang Hsien-chung was in charge of a group which went on a rampage along the Yangtse valley, murdering anyone who seemed to bear the stamp of the establishment. In one famous incident he organised a civil-service examination, and had all the candidates butchered when they arrived. Some of his generals were sentenced to death for the sole reason that their men had not killed sufficient people. Chang Hsien-chung chose Szechuan province in the west as the base for his murderous hosts, and in the provincial capital of Chengtu he erected a tablet with the unsubtle inscription 'Kill, Kill, Kill, Kill, Kill, Kill, Kill!' Small wonder that some people greeted the eventual arrival of the Manchus with rejoicing.

The other main rebel leader was an ex-postman and Buddhist monk, Li Tzu-ch'eng, nicknamed the 'Dashing King', who joined the revolting peasants in the earliest days. At first he was little better than his rival, Chang Hsien-chung, and brought havoc to the provinces of Shensi, Shansi, Hupei and Honan. He had an awe-inspiring appearance with a striking aquiline nose and heavily pock-marked face, and exercised a strong magnetism over his men. Li implemented a simple but effective policy to encourage cities to surrender to his forces; if the inhabitants allowed his men in on the first day without a fight, they would all be spared. If they resisted, however, a percentage of the population would be massacred in proportion to the number of days it took to bring the city to its knees. In 1642 the important city of K'aifeng (old capital of the Sung) fell to Li Tzu-ch'eng's army after a four-month siege. A Ming general arrived to try to recapture the city, and in a display typical of government inhumanity, cut down the dykes above K'aifeng in the hope of dislodging the rebels. Li Tzu-ch'eng himself escaped the ensuing disaster, but more than 200,000 people died in the flood waters. Li returned soon afterwards in a boat to reclaim the city.

Li Tzu-ch'eng's methods softened when he decided that his mission in life was to remove the Ming despots from power and set himself on the throne as Emperor of China. He changed his practice of indiscriminate brigandry to a Chinese version of Robin Hood, robbing the rich to feed the poor. His popularity among the peasantry soared accordingly. Many presumably apocryphal stories are associated with his attempt to become the 'Son of Heaven', including one that he thrust an arrow into the ground one sunny afternoon, saying to his followers that if the arrow shaft was buried in snow the following morning, heaven approved his claim. Sure enough, a snowstorm blew up during the night and dawn revealed the arrow buried just to the top of its shaft in snow. Encouraged by such manifestations, Li Tzu-ch'eng proclaimed a new dynasty and conducted a mock Imperial enthronement

151

ceremony in the old capital of Ch'ang-an in 1644. All that was left for him to do was to capture Peking.

Li Tzu-ch'eng followed a circuitous route to the capital, crossing the Wall twice as if in defiance of this mighty barrier and the Ming Dynasty. He marched his army north through Shensi and Shansi, broke through a weak point in the Wall's inner loop north-west of Peking and marched on the supposedly impregnable fortress of Nankou which guarded the Nankou Pass through the Wall. Perhaps Li had intimations in advance that the commander of the fortress would desert and join his ranks, for his army would have suffered a great delay and heavy casualties had they been forced to fight through the pass. Most of the garrison's soldiers followed their commander's example, but those who remained loyal to the Ming standard journeyed eastward along the Wall to join an army under General Wu San-kuei at Shan Hai Kuan.

Li Tzu-Ch'eng's forces camped outside the walls of Peking waiting for the last Ming Emperor, Ch'ung-chen, to surrender. The Emperor believed that the only man who could save the Ming from downfall was Wu San-kuei, who had been in charge of the Great Wall defences during the Manchu raids. Several times Ch'ung-chen considered summoning General Wu to the capital, but had always checked himself because of the importance of having a first-class man at the frontier. With the rebels at his gates and a defending army of dubious loyalty, the Emperor felt he must have Wu San-kuei by his side. He sent messengers off to the Great Wall to fetch the general, but the same night Ch'ung-chen went to a temple to read his fortune. He consulted the Bamboo Stick Oracle, whose verdict was determined by the length of the stick drawn from a bunch held by the priest of the temple. Ch'ung-chen grasped a bamboo slither between his fingers and pulled – the shortest stick in the bunch, which meant death. Dolefully he returned to the palace where he was informed that the commander of the Peking garrison had himself opened one of the gates of the capital to the rebels. The Emperor cried to heaven that he was not entirely to blame for the end of the dynasty as his officials had hidden the true state of affairs from him.

The Emperor sent instructions to the Empress, his wives and concubines to commit suicide so that they would not fall into the hands of Li Tzu-ch'eng's soldiers. He had his three sons dressed in ordinary clothes and told them to attempt to escape through one of the city gates before the palace was occupied. Ch'ung-chen wished to kill his favourite daughter himself so that her spirit might accompany his into the next world, but in his emotional state he misdirected his blow, and suceeded only in amputating the princess's arm. The traditional histories then say he climbed up Coal Hill overlooking the palace and hanged himself from a tree, which was later bound with chains in symbolic punishment for being the agent of the Emperor's death. A faithful retainer changed clothes with the Emperor's body before killing himself in the hope that this would spare Ch'ung-chen's corpse from being defiled by the rebels. He need not have worried, for Li Tzu-ch'eng paid posthumous tribute to Ch'ung-chen, giving him a fittingly magnificent funeral in order to give his own new régime the stamp of respectability.

Once the Emperor's death became public, Li Tzu-ch'eng quickly effected the takeover of

Peking, then sent a messenger to General Wu San-kuei on the Great Wall to inform him of the change of dynasty and to ask him for his support. Wu San-kuei agreed to recognise Li's mandate over the south and west of China, but wished to keep control of the north-east for himself. As a condition for accepting Li's position, the general also asked for the release of the Ming heir, whom Li's troops had captured, and the release of a certain concubine, the 'Roundfaced Beauty', with whom Wu had fallen passionately in love on a visit to Peking. It seems barely creditable that Li Tzu-ch'eng should jeopardise his fledgling dynasty for the sake of a concubine, but that was precisely the result when he refused to hand over the girl to Wu San-kuei and, indeed, had her officially inducted into his own harem. General Wu's dramatic reaction was to renounce all intention of co-operation with the rebels, and to form an alliance with the Manchus, whom he had been trying to keep north of the Wall for many years. Consequently he sent word to the new Manchu leader, Dorgon, a nephew of Nurhachi, to let him know of his willingness to surrender the Great Wall gate at Shan Hai Kuan. Li Tzu-ch'eng was aware of General Wu's rejection of the pact with his rebels, but had no inkling of the arrangement between Wu and the Manchu. Accordingly, he marched north with his army as far as Shan Hai Kuan, expecting to have little trouble in defeating the General and his garrison. Wu San-kuei led his soldiers out of Shan Hai Kuan to meet Li's army, when suddenly hordes of Manchu horsemen, who had been secretly moved through the Wall by Wu, swept down on Li's forces. The rebel army panicked, and Li fled back to Peking. The combined strength of Wu and the Manchu forces marched on the capital, gaining easy entrance to the city when Li escaped westwards with as much treasure as he could carry.

The Ming officials remaining in Peking welcomed the new invaders, seemingly under the false impression that the Ming Dynasty would be restored. Instead, the Manchus took the throne of China for themselves, and General Wu led his army west to finish off Li Tzu-ch'eng, who was finally murdered by villagers in Hopei province. General Wu returned to the capital, where the Manchus stated clearly that they did not intend to relinquish the Dragon Throne to any Chinese. Wu negotiated with Dorgon for various concessions, such as the continuation of the Chinese practice of binding women's feet, before accepting their authority. Dorgon stepped down from power when Nurhachi's grandson was old enough to rule, the young man becoming the first Emperor of the Ch'ing dynasty.

Never again did the Great Wall play a significant role in the pattern of Chinese history. The Manchus controlled the territory on both sides of the Wall up to the end of the Imperial system, brought about by the revolution of 1911. Living conditions were kept different on the two sides of the Wall, the northern lands retaining more or less traditional Manchu habits, while the Manchu rulers south of the great barrier became almost completely sinicised. The Wall itself was allowed to fall into disrepair, only a few 'frontier' posts being maintained to check or aid travellers going north. China was increasingly the victim of hamfisted adventurism and exploitation from Westerners who humiliated the Ch'ing régime with their superior military prowess and even carved up parts of China among themselves. Ironically, these very Westerners were fascinated by the Great Wall, and were largely responsible for keeping up interest in what W. E. Geil has described as 'the world's largest fossil'.

9

Along the Wall: Westerners' Impressions

CHAPTER NINE

Along the Wall:
Westerners' Impressions

ANY Western books on China understandably give undue emphasis to the role of Europeans in the shaping of Chinese history. From an objective standpoint, China remains one of the least westernised of all the countries of Asia, and in this lies part of her fascination. The failure of the Western powers successfully to colonise the Chinese mind as well as the Chinese soil was not for lack of trying. China was assaulted from all sides during the nineteenth and early twentieth centuries, as British, French, German, Japanese and others ravaged the tottering Ch'ing Empire and carved up the map of China between them. The Communist régime in Peking constantly reminds its children of the grim Imperialist past, portraying in books, plays, operas and films endless variations on the same theme of long-nosed European colonialists and their evil collusion with tyranical Chinese landlords and greedy profiteers. Without such frequent recollections it would be easy to forget the past, for apart from the heavy Victorian architecture of Shanghai there is little in China that is not distinctively Chinese. In comparison to the situation of cultural desolation in Tokyo or downtown Manila, this is admirable. Much of the credit lies with the success and thoroughness of the People's Revolution which has wilfully excluded outside influences over the past twenty-five years, particularly since the Russians were moved down from their former pedestal.

But a large part of the conservation of China's original culture is due to what might be termed as the 'abstract Great Wall', a barrier separating ideas as well as habits, a defence against the outer world behind which a satisfied population developed its philosophy and more in line with ancient traditions. This abstract Great Wall has long been as appealing (and often as irritating!) to Europeans as has the Great Wall of stone, and indeed the two have coalesced in the minds of most people so that Ch'in Shih Huang-ti's Dragon Screen has been seen as the physical representation of an attitude to life. It is fair to repeat that up to the end of the seventeenth century, the history of the Great Wall was a record of the turbulent co-existence of the Chinese and their barbarian neighbours, usually nomadic tribes. From the eighteenth century onwards, the Wall played a new and significant role as the barrier between China and the West.

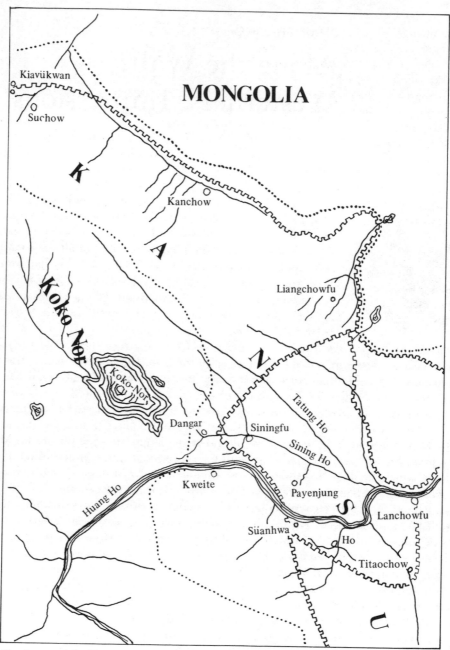

MONGOLIA

Kiavükwan
Suchow
KANSU
Koko Nor
Kanchow
Liangchowfu
Koko-Nor
Dangar
Siningfu
Tatung Ho
Sining Ho
Kweite
Payenjung
Huang Ho
Süanhwa
Ho
Lanchowfu
Titaochow

FIG. 10. Sketch-map of the Tibetan loop of the Great Wall as discovered and mapped by the American traveller William Edgar Oeil in 1908.

ALONG THE WALL: WESTERNERS' IMPRESSIONS

The change of emphasis concerning the Wall is reflected in Western accounts of China's great landmark. The earliest descriptions, often based on hearsay, concentrate on the physical magnificence of the structure – its length, its age and its beauty. Later reports frequently dwell on the nature of the people who would build such a colossal thing. Nineteenth-century travellers tend to be fairly scathing in their comments, though it is interesting to see the correlation between the section of the Wall that the traveller visited, and the conclusions he drew. Those who rode over the pitiable remains of the western Wall on a donkey were, for example, far less impressed with the Wall and the Chinese than those who saw the stupendous line of the Ming Wall rearing up near-perpendicular slopes in the mountains of the north-east.

News of the Wall's existence reached Europe long before the first European had set foot in the Middle Kingdom. The earliest mention of China in a Western text is generally acknowledged to be the account of an anonymous Graeco-Egyptian writing around AD 80 (during the Han Dynasty). He wrote:

> The sea comes to a termination somewhere in Thin [a corruption of Ch'in?], and in the interior of that country, quite to the north, there is a very great city called Thinae, from which raw silk and silk thread and silk stuff are brought overland through Bactria to Barygaza.... It is not easy, however, to get to this Thin, and few and far between are those who come from it.[1]

We know that the writer of the above passage was a merchant, and it is self-evident that he acquired his information about 'Thin' from colleagues, probably from the Middle East, who were involved in trading along the silk route. Silk, in fact, made China famous in the West, for it was highly prized by the peoples of the Roman and Byzantine Empires, and for several hundred years its method of manufacture remained a mystery known only to the Chinese who were very anxious that this situation should remain as the silk trade brought in enormous amounts of gold to the country, to the Westerners' distress. Legend says that the Chinese silk monopoly was finally broken in about AD 552 by two Indian monks who smuggled out some silkworm eggs in a bamboo tube past the watchful eyes of the customs guards stationed at the end of the Great Wall at Tun-huang. The secret was thus transported to the Byzantine Empire. Ptolemy and other classical writers referred to China as Seres and Serica because it was the land which produced silk (the names very probably derivated from the Chinese word for silk, now pronounced 'ssu'). It was a very long time, however, before Europeans realised that Thin, Serica, Cathay and Mangi (a term used by Marco Polo for southern China) were in fact the same country.

The silk merchants passing out of China could not fail to notice the existence of the 300-mile western section of the Great Wall built, as described, by Emperor Wu of the Han Dynasty. Thus the first mention of the Great Wall came via the silk route, and is mentioned in the book *Rerum Gestarum*, written by the Roman historian Marcellinus. Marcellinus talks of

1 Periplus of the Erythraen Sea, from Yule, Sir Henry and Cordier, Henri, *Cathay and the Way Thither* (The Haklyut Society; London, 1914–16).

159

Serica being a land surrounded by a continuous barrier, which kept the populace secure in their rich plains. *Rerum Gestarum* was written at the end of the fourth century AD, and many writers, including Sir Henry Yule, scoffed at the idea that the Roman was talking about the Great Wall. Sir Henry declared in his book *Cathay and the Way Thither* that Marcellinus was merely referring to a barrier of mountains, even though as Silverberg pointed out,[2] the Latin word used was clearly 'agger' or wall. There is every reason, however, why Marcellinus should have heard of the Wall's existence as he had been a soldier in Persia where Parthian rulers were engaged in diplomatic relations with Han China.

The exact meaning of Marcellinus' phrase about China's 'barrier' is a classic case of one of those niggling academic points that continue to worry scholars; the Chinese have their counterparts. What makes the controversy at all worthy of notice is the fact that a line in *Rerum Gestarum* is the only mention of the world's greatest construction in early Western literature. Unless of course the idea can be accepted that Alexander's wall against the Gog and Magog was in fact the Great Wall of China, a contention that makes the Marcellinus dispute fade into insignificance.

The names Gog and Magog first appear in the Bible, which includes an account written around 600 BC by Ezekiel, who prophesied for Gog,

> Thou shalt come from thy place out of the uttermost parts of the north, thou and many peoples with thee, all of them riding upon horses, a great company and a mighty army... Surely in that day there shall be a great shaking in the land of Israel...and the mountains shall be thrown down, and the steep places shall fall, and every wall shall fall to the ground.[3]

Ezekiel's Gog and Magog could refer to any of several barbarian tribes which troubled the Near East in the preceding centuries, and whose names remained for hundreds of years to describe later nomad warriors. As Silverberg has pointed out, citizens of the Byzantine Empire no doubt thought that Gog and Magog had arrived when the Huns swept down into the eastern Roman world in 395, possibly encouraged in that direction by the existence of the Great Wall. The situation reminds the present author of conversations in southern Siberia in 1969 when Russian peasants were fully convinced that the descendants of Genghis Khan were massing on the other side of the Chinese frontier to sweep across the Soviet Union.

Another signpost in the tortuous trail to Gog and Magog and the Great Wall appears in the Koran, where Alexander the Great (under the name Dhu'l-Qarneyn) is begged to build a wall between the civilised world and the horrendous Gog and Magog.

> [The people cried:] 'O Dhu'l-Qarneyn! Lo! Gog and Magog are spoiling the land. So may we pay thee tribute on condition that thou set a barrier between us and them?

2   In Silverberg, Robert. *The Great Wall of China* (Chilton Books; New York, 1965).
3   Ibid.

He said: That wherein my Lord hath established me is better [than your tribute]. Do but help me with strength [of men], I will set between you and them a bank.

Give me pieces of iron – till, when he had levelled up [the gap] between the cliffs, he said: Blow! – till, when he had made it a fire, he said: Bring me molten copper to pour thereon.

And [Gog and Magog] were not able to surmount, nor could they pierce [it].[4]

Alexander was (presumably falsely) alleged to have built this barrier around 330 BC. A real wall was in fact built 870 years later on the western shore of the Caspian Sea by the Persian king, Anushirvan, and this wall was christened the Iron Gate. Inevitably, when news of Anushirvan's wall reached Europe, it was confused with Alexander's fictitious Copper Gate. Marco Polo who, as stated, makes no mention of the Great Wall of China in his travel book, none the less refers to 'Alexander's Iron Gate, as does William of Rubruck, a Flemish Fransiscan monk who visited the Mongol capital of Karakorum in 1253 and who left a much neglected travel book regarded by Yule as 'of much higher claims than any one series of Polo's chapters'. Be that as it may, by the time the famous Catalan Map was printed in Barcelona in 1375, Alexander's wall and the Great Wall of China had become the same thing, as the 'Wall For Keeping Back the Gog and Magog' is clearly marked in north-east Asia. The European mind of the late fourteenth century would clearly have had a very inaccurate and colourful idea of the Great Wall, which would only have added to its mystery.

Ironically, a Moslem expedition sent out to try to discover Alexander's wall probably found the Great Wall of China instead. Wathiq-bi'llah, Caliph of Baghdad, dispatched a man named Sallam to find Alexander's wall in the middle of the ninth century. The Caliph was aware of the existence of Anushirvan's wall in the Caucasus, and was convinced that it was not the same as Alexander's. He was particularly anxious that Sallam find the barrier, as he had dreamt that it had fallen down. Sallam travelled eastward for a year and four months before reaching a wall which he described as being built,

...in a broad opening between two mountains, the breadth of which is two hundred cubits. That was the road through which [Gog and Magog] issued and spread over the earth.

And he dug the foundation of it to the depth of thirty cubits, and built it of iron and copper until it reached to the surface of the ground...The whole was built with iron bricks covered with copper, each a cubit and a half by a cubit and a half, and four finger breadths high.[5]

There is obviously a large element of fiction in the above account, but it nevertheless seems plausible that Sallam reached Tun-huang where he saw the Great Wall and coloured

4 From Pickthall, Mohammed Marmaduke, *The Meaning of the Glorious Koran* (New American Library; New York, 1953).
5 Ibn Khurdadbin, from Silverberg's *The Great Wall of China*.

the story to please the Caliph. Whatever the truth of the matter, Arab geographers of the thirteenth and fourteenth centuries were confidently placing Alexander's wall in China, and a prolific traveller named Ibn Battuta was able to report on a visit to China in 1347:

> Between [Canton] and the Rampart, or Great Wall of Gog and Magog, there is a space of sixty days' journey as I was told. This territory is occupied by wandering tribes of heathen, who eat such people as they can catch, and for this reason no one enters their country or attempts to travel there. I saw nobody in this city who had been to the Great Wall, or who knew anybody who had been there.[6]

It should rapidly be becoming clear why the Great Wall acquired a cloak of mystery long before the West knew the exact story behind it. One thousand six hundred years after it had first been built, nobody had conveyed to the Western world an accurate description of the Purple Barrier, as the Chinese themselves sometimes described it.

The early pioneer travellers who braved the journey to the Mongol Empire were rare. The only known route was overland, and many never completed the arduous journey. Bishops and friars were sent to China from Avignon, but were never heard of again. A new era was reached in the sixteenth century when the Portuguese discovered the sea route to China round the southern coast of Africa. They initiated rather tentative trade contacts and were soon followed by the Spanish and Dutch who were little better than pirates. Mention has already been made of the Dutch seizure of Formosa from Ming China, but it was the appalling behaviour of the European sailors and their commanders which was a major reason for the extremely low opinion the Chinese had of the first 'Western Barbarians'.

The earliest Portuguese arrivals landed in 1514, their brown and hirsute bodies causing amazement and disgust, and prompting the Chinese to call all Europeans the 'Hairy Barbarians'. The Portuguese were also a little taken aback: '[The Chinese] are a people of great skill, and on a par with ourselves, but of uglier aspect, with little bits of eyes'.[7]

The Chinese who greeted the Portuguese warily had changed considerably over the seventy years that separated the last great Ming sea expeditions and the arrival of the 'Hairy Barbarians'. The Ming had become introspective and uninterested in, even suspicious of, anything alien; evidence of the mental Great Wall which had been erected. It was indeed unfortunate for the Portuguese, with their aspirations for wondrous trade, that they had not arrived a hundred years sooner. After a few years the Chinese grew tired of their un-welcome guests and expelled them.

A second major Portuguese attempt to capture the interest of the Chinese Dragon took place in 1537. On board one vessel was a young adventurer by the name of F. Mendes Pinto (his enemies at home were later to make a pun on this to Mendax Pinto, or Lying Pinto, on account of an extravagant travel book which he wrote following his adventures in the Far East). Pinto was a jack-of-all-trades who used his versatility and wits to steer him successfully through

6   From Yule and Cordier's *Cathay and the Way Thither.*
7   Ibid.

a chain of awkward or unusual situations from Africa to the East Indies before being ship-wrecked off the Chinese coast near Nanking. The survivors clambered up onto a rocky promontory and headed for Nanking in the hope of finding a boat that would take them back to South-East Asia. No doubt they were aware of the antipathetic Chinese attitude to the Portuguese, and were therefore keen to leave. The Chinese they encountered presumably had never seen foreigners before, and, according to Pinto's account, readily accepted the ship-wrecked men's story that they were Siamese, and as such deserving of a kind of patronising help. They survived by the generosity of the local population, and neared Nanking, only to be picked up by a visiting official who was on a tour from Peking. The official questioned the Portuguese (one shudders to think in what language, but then so much of China's history does not bear close scrutiny) and came to the conclusion that they were clearly layabouts who were contravening Ming laws. Consequently, the Portuguese soon found themselves in a Chinese jail, where they were flogged and chained in a lice-infested cell, and one of the number died.

After four weeks in this local prison, Pinto and his unfortunate comrades were transferred to a larger detention centre in Nanking, where more floggings and more lice brought two more deaths. Eventually they were summoned for trial and seem to have received fairly generous treatment in comparison to native Chinese who would no doubt have been beaten or tortured in the open court-room until they 'confessed'. The European prisoners had their case referred to Peking, and were sent up the Grand Canal by boat. Chinese charity organisations provided them with food, money and clothing.

The Peking Court sentenced the Portuguese to a year's hard labour on the Great Wall, a singularly classical solution to a brand-new problem. Ever mindful of his future readership, Pinto made detailed observations of his surroundings. He was housed in a vast camp along with 300,000 (*sic*) other men sentenced to work on the Wall. Pinto's statistics bear little resemblance to the scale of works as executed by the Ming emperors, but exaggeration for dramatic effect is by no means a Chinese prerogative. The prisoners' camp was,

> Two leagues square, or a little less, both in length and breadth: it is enclosed with a very high wall without any battlements; the wall on the outside is environed with a great deep ditch full of water, over which are many drawbridges that are drawn up in the night with certain iron chains, and so hang suspended on huge cast pillars; in this prison is an arch of strong hewed stone abutting in two towers, in the tops whereof are six great sentinel bells, which are never rung but all the rest within the said enclosure do answer them, which the Chinese affirm to be over a hundred and indeed they make a most horrible din.[8]

Turning his attention and imagination to the Great Wall itself, Pinto writes,

> King Crisnagol [!] (which reigned as we may accord our computation with theirs about the year our Lord 528) builded the wall, the people contributing ten thousand

8   From Ley, C. D., *Portuguese Voyages 1498–1663* (J. M. Dent; London, 1960).

pikes of silver (which are fifteen millions of cruzados) and two hundred and fifty thousand men (thirty thousand officers and the rest labourers), which was continued seven and twenty years.[9]

Much of the information about the Wall that appears in Pinto's book is sheer fantasy, but it is impossible to draw the line between fact and fiction. Whether he actually worked on the Great Wall or not, he did manage to convey a few accurate notions about the Wall to the eager European public. He correctly estimated that the Wall was about 2000 miles long (excluding the spurs), and that it had five principal gates (Shan Hai Kuan, Kupeikou, Kalgan, Yenmen and Kiayükwan), but the majority of his stories are outrageous. Nevertheless, they had a profound effect upon the European view of China generally and the Great Wall particularly, as his book (published posthumously in 1614) was a wild success, appearing in nineteen editions in six languages. The serious scholars in Lisbon tended not to believe a word of it, and were pleasantly surprised when parts were corroborated by other travellers.

Pinto's book made a major, if sometimes dubious, contribution to Western knowledge about China, but much of its effect was diminished by the long delay before its publication (nearly seventy years after the events described). During this time, other books had appeared. It is fascinating to see how the sequence of publication of books on a totally new subject such as China could shape the general public's knowledge of that subject. Paradoxically, the best early account of China was written by a man who had never been there, João de Barros, the father of armchair sinologists, who include in their number such worthies as Arthur Waley, the great translator and fringe member of the Bloomsbury Group who never set foot in China for fear of shattering his illusions. Barros worked entirely from Chinese sources translated by an intelligent Chinese slave whom he had in service, and from letters written by Portuguese prisoners from the first Portuguese expeditions to China of 1514–21. Barros's imagination was stirred by the Great Wall; he too correctly gave it a length of roughly 2000 miles, and put it between 43 °N and 45 °N (in fact, it is nearer 40 °N). He was also perhaps the first person to state categorically that it was built to keep out the Tartars.

For some reason Barros and his book never received the wide acclaim that it deserved, and its readership was limited to the Iberian and Italian peninsulas. However it was a source for later books, not least the most popular book on China of its day *Historia de las cosas mas notables, ritos y costumbres del gran Reyno de la China*, published in Rome in 1585 by an Augustinian monk, Juan Gonzalez de Mendoza. By the end of the century Mendoza's book had been translated into almost every European language, and papal approval helped ensure its success. The first part of the book, in ten chapters, dealt with the geographical placement of China, its climate and peoples, products, early history and kings, cities, roads and architectural wonders. Of the Great Wall he wrote:

There is in this kingdom a defence or wall that is five hundred leagues long, and beginning at the city of Ochyou [Ho-chow in Shensi], which is upon the high mountains,

9   From *Purchas His Pilgrimes*, edited by Samuel Purchase and quoted in Silverberg's *The Great Wall of China*.

and runneth from west to east. The king of that country which made it was called Tzintzon [Ch'in Shih Huang-ti], and it was for his defence against the Tartaries, with whom he had wars; so that the wall doth shut up the frontier of Tartaria...This king, for to finish this wonderful work, did take of every three men one through his kingdom... They almost all did perish that followed that work.[10]

Mendoza's account, even though it contains many errors, gave Europe an even clearer idea of what China was like, and even if the mystery had been removed from the Middle Kingdom, the fascination was increased, not diminished. Traders built up glorious dreams of the commerce that could be initiated between the Mediterranean countries and China, and the jingaistic military longed to add China to Spanish and Portuguese Empires. Mendoza received much vitriolic criticism from some quarters for suggesting that China was a strong country. In particular, Don Juan Fernandez de Velasco, the Constable of Castile, abused Mendoza, saying that he grossly exaggerated the extent and power of China, and that all his details of Chinese habits were only a cover for his real intention of winning China over to Christianity. Fortunately no foolhardy Spanish expedition was sent to try to conquer the Ming Empire, perhaps because of Mendoza's warnings of the sort of reception they would receive. The preface to the English edition of Mendoza's book, however, appearing in the very year of the Armada, carried the publisher's warning that the contents were not entirely reliable as the Spanish, in keeping with their expansionist ambitions, tended to extol their own virtues, even to the extent of distorting the truth. China would remain enigmatic for the Anglo-Saxon world so long as the sources of information were England's enemies.

The first European to make a significant impression in Ming China, and who gave the West its most reliable information to date, was the Italian Jesuit Matteo Ricci, who showed that the only way to storm the Great Wall of China was to learn Chinese. By successfully mastering the language, Ricci earned the respect of the Ming Court, and had access to information no European before him had enjoyed.

Matteo Ricci was born in Macerata in 1552, the son of a well-placed family. As a youth he was drawn to a religious calling, and after an abortive beginning to a career in law, joined the Society of Jesus, a spiritual and intellectual crusade based in Spain, Portugal and Italy and far in advance of its time. His early years with the Jesuits were spent in prayer and preparation for a religious life, but it was always Ricci's hope to work in the Far East. Many young Jesuits were enamoured with the idea of missionary service in India or Japan, but competition was severe. The missionaries had to be of the highest calibre, with strong physical constitutions and intelligence as well as spiritual uprightness. Many times Ricci petitioned to be sent East before his request was granted in 1576, and he was summoned before Pope Gregory XIII. Ricci had to spend a time of transition in Portugal as the eastern Indies had been assigned to the Portuguese by papal decree. The only ships sailing with regularity to India were Portuguese, the long journey entailing six months at sea round the coast of Africa from Guinea to Abyssinia and across the Indian Ocean to Goa.

10   Haklyut Society edition translation.

In Goa Ricci was confronted with the harsh reality of 'conversion' of foreign peoples; all the Hindu temples on the island had been destroyed following Portuguese orders in 1540. Christians were forbidden to keep non-Christian servants in the house, which had the effect of making baptism almost compulsory. Slavery was widespread.

Ricci studied and worked in Goa and Cochin, 400 miles south, from 1578 to 1582, when orders came through for him to join a proposed mission to China. He sailed for Macao, a tiny peninsula south of Canton (near present-day Hong Kong), which the Portuguese had wrested from the Chinese nearly seventy years before. The experience of Macao convinced the Chinese that the Western Barbarians were as undesirable as the Northern Barbarians. As mentioned, the Chinese expelled the Portuguese from Canton at the beginning of the sixteenth century following numerous acts of piracy and other misconduct. The Portuguese later seized Malacca on the Malaysian peninsula, formerly a Chinese protectorate, and the Chinese retaliated by forbidding entry to Portuguese vessels in any Chinese port. Eventually, persuaded by the profitability of trading with the Portuguese and the eloquence of the 'Foreign Devils' seventy-pound guns, the Chinese ceded Macao to them, and promptly built a wall between Macao and China as a tiny southern counterpart to the Great Wall. Twice a year the Portuguese were permitted to sail up to Canton for several weeks' intensive trading, often acting as middle men for the Japanese, bartering Japanese silver for Chinese silk, pearls and porcelain.

The most distinguished missionary teacher in Macao at the time of Ricci's arrival was Alessandro Valignano, who had served in Japan, and was en route for Goa. Valignano was certain that China, by nature tolerant to diverse religious beliefs, would be responsive to Christianity if the missionaries sent into China could communicate with the officials and scholars in their own tongue, thereby showing that the Jesuits were men of learning with noble intentions and not spies for the Portuguese pirates. Ricci was put to learning Chinese, even though at that time permission was never granted to missionaries to visit the principal cities of China. In the summer of 1583, Ricci received a surprise invitation from the governor of Shiuhing, who had heard rumours of Ricci's skill in mathematics and his ability to draw maps, make clocks and other mechanical devices. In September, the Italian and one companion set out for the interior of the Middle Kingdom.

Ricci and his companion travelled in robes resembling those of Buddhist priests, so that their intent would be understood as religious and honourable. On arrival in Shiuhing, Ricci discovered that the Chinese he had learnt in Macao was only a local dialect, so he set about learning Mandarin, the language of the educated classes and the basis of *p'u-t'ung hua*, the common Chinese of today. The governor of Shiuhing explained to the missionaries the conditions under which they would be allowed to remain in China.

While the laws of the Middle Kingdom forbid foreigners to live in the country, nevertheless having regard to the brotherhood of man, any stranger who comes from a distant country and either cannot or does not wish to return, may remain in the Middle Kingdom, provided he is quiet, humble and useful to the country...

[You] must promise to fulfil certain conditions. You must not be joined by other

166

barbarians; you must continue to wear our dress; you must promise to conform to our habits; you must obey our magistrates; if you marry, you must choose a woman of our country. You will become, in all save your physical appearance, men of the Middle Kingdom.[11]

The missionaries accepted the conditions and were granted some land on which to build a house and a 'temple'. The foreigners were the victims of much opposition and abuse from the inhabitants of Shiuhing, but received sympathy and support from the upright governor. Initially Ricci made little effort to convert any Chinese – an action that would have been doomed to failure, and would almost certainly have resulted in his being expelled. Instead, he concentrated on familiarising himself with the Chinese language and way of life, and making himself acceptable to the local population. When his Mandarin studies had advanced sufficiently however, he did make a translation of the Ten Commandments.

Of all the missionaries' European gadgets and possessions, the most fascinating to the intellectuals of Shiuhing was a Flemish map of the world. This map bore absolutely no resemblance to Chinese maps of the period, which depicted 90 per cent of the world as the fifteen provinces of the Flowery Kingdom, the remaining 10 per cent being those countries of which the Chinese had reports. The Chinese who visited Ricci to see his extraordinary document were split into two camps, those who believed it to be some sort of Taoist charm and those who thought it the figment of the barbarians' imagination. The broadminded governor was prepared to believe that the map might have some relation to reality, so asked Ricci to draw up another using Chinese names. Ricci did just that, showing an excellent grasp of Chinese psychology by placing China in the centre. The Governor was deeply impressed by the result, and circulated it among his friends, so that now at least a few Chinese had a reasonable idea of the shape of the outside world. Ricci's relationship with the authorities suffered periodically when townsmen brought various imaginary charges against him, but in general he remained on good terms with the governor, and further won appreciation by adopting a Chinese name, Li Ma-tou, (Li being the Chinese surname nearest to Ri-cci). The governor was convinced that Ricci and his companion, Ruggieri, had brought him luck, so when the people of Shiuhing erected a statue in his honour, he had statues of the two Jesuits put up with it. Ricci made sundials and globes to give as presents to the Chinese, and had some illustrated books sent up from Macao to give his visitors some idea of Europe, its great cities and art.

By spring 1589, Ricci had baptised sixty-eight Chinese, but his worst fears were realised when a new viceroy in the Shiuhing area ordered his departure. After lengthy arguments and bargaining, this harsh decision was modified to a transfer which prompted Ricci's departure further north to Shiuchow. Ricci dreamed of reaching Peking, the imperial capital, as he thought conversion would only come about through the Emperor. Using his guile he managed to get as far as Nanking, where he was greatly impressed by the city walls, 50 feet high, and as much as 20 feet broad at the top, extending eighteen miles. Ricci was refused

11   Cronin, Vincent, *The Wise Man from the West* (Fontana Books; London, 1961).

permission to settle in the great city, so established himself just outside, earning a reputation as a man of enormous intellect. Among Ricci's new admirers and acquaintances was a Chinese prince, whom Ricci approached hoping for help in getting to the Court in Peking; he little realised that no prince would ever do such a thing, as the Emperor regarded male members of the royal family as a potential threat, and would be even more suspicious of a prince who seemed to be in league with foreigners.

In September 1598, Ricci did succeed in getting to Peking, but soon discovered that penetrating the barrier of eunuchs and officialdom around the Emperor was a major operation. The Court was preoccupied at the time with conflict with Japan over Korea, and had no time for a Hairy Barbarian, however ingenious his gifts may be. Ricci withdrew south, dejected and weary, and soon overcome by dysentery.

Eventually Ricci was allowed to return to Peking. Recovered in health, he sent sixteen presents to the Emperor, including a picture of the Virgin Mary, a rhinoceros tusk, a large chiming clock and an atlas. Some time later he received an urgent summons from the palace to say the clock had wound down and needed attention. When he went to solve this problem, Ricci became the first European to set foot in the Forbidden City. He instructed Court mathematicians to deal with the clock, and answered hundreds of questions about Europe, brought by messengers from the Emperor, Wan Li, who was responsible for rebuilding and repairing much of the Great Wall. Ricci was informed that the Son of Heaven had seen no one but eunuchs and concubines for sixteen years, making it impossible for him to receive the talented foreigner. The Jesuit became a familiar figure in the palace, however, where he was treated with great courtesy. The Chinese continued to consult him on numerous technical topics, and on aspects of Western society and its customs.

Matteo Ricci lived in China twenty-eight years before his death. During that period he was able to send detailed letters and reports about China to Europe, as well as writing books in Chinese about technological subjects and Christianity. He was able to observe the treasures and ritual of the Forbidden City, with its four imposing walls and sumptuous art collections. His description of the Great Wall, however, is surprisingly cursory, suggesting that he was not fully aware of its grandeur. He disposes of it in two sentences.

> To the north the country is defended against hostile Tartar raids by precipitous hills, which are joined into an unbroken line of defence with a tremendous wall four hundred and five miles long. To the northwest it is flanked by a great desert of many days' march, which either deters an advancing army from attacking the Chinese border or becomes the burial place of those who attempt the attack.[12]

While Ricci worked in Peking, a fellow Jesuit on the western frontier of China had more than ample opportunity to contemplate the Great Wall. Benedict de Goes was a lay associate of the Jesuit order who originated from the Azores. He went to India as a soldier in the 1570s, then decided to devote his life to the Jesuits. In 1602 he was selected for an expedition to

12   Silverberg, *The Great Wall of China.*

Cathay, financed by King Philip III of Spain. Ricci had, in the course of his geographical writings about the Middle Kingdom, conclusively shown that Cathay and China were the same place, but many Jesuits doubted his findings, and believed that Cathay was not only different from China, but Christian. An exploratory party was therefore assembled in the Indian town of Agra and in October 1602, Goes and his fellow travellers set out for Cathay. Goes disguised himself as an Armenian and acquired a genuine Armenian named Isaac as a servant.

The road east was a perilous trail at the beginning of the seventeenth century as the barren mountains provided excellent cover for highly organised bandits who lived off the merchants' caravans. Goes' route seems inordinately long to a modern reader, but was largely due to the necessity of skirting the highest ranges of the Himalayas. From Agra he went west to Lahore to join an annual caravan of 500 merchants making their way to Kabul. Discipline was strict on the caravan and night travelling was accompanied by the beating of drums. Goes was anxious that his Moslem fellow travellers should not find out either his nationality or his religion, but as he spoke Persian, called himself Abdullah and had Isaac the Armenian as a companion, he went unsuspected. The merchants passed Attock on the north-west frontier of the Grand Mogul's empire, which had its capital at Agra. The road followed the rising valleys between snow-covered mountains, then through the narrow and dramatic Khyber Pass where sturdy forts stood proud against the precipices. At Kabul, the caravan dispersed so Goes had to wait for another in midsummer before he dared continue his journey. He was fortunate enough to meet a sister of the Khan of Kashgar, a princess returning from a pilgrimage to Mecca, who had run out of money. Goes helped her by selling some of his stock of lapis lazuli, and accompanied her over the next and most difficult stage of the journey north through the mountains. The party could only travel at night, when the snow had frozen hard enough to bear the weight of the pack animals and the blinding glare of the daytime had subsided. As they passed into the Khanate of Samarkand and Bokhara, the caravan was attacked by rebels needing horses and money. Goes and Isaac managed to escape injury, and after many torments and casualties the caravan reached the town of Yarkand in November 1603. To his joy Goes discovered that the people knew where Cathay was, though he would have to wait another year before a caravan would make the journey.

During his enforced wait, Goes visited the palace of the princess whom he had helped in Kabul, who repaid her debt to him in jade, regarded as a most precious stone with almost religious qualities by the Chinese who had to import their supplies. Goes also met the merchant who had bought the right to lead the caravan, and paid him to include himself in the seventy-two merchants allowed to enter Cathay under the leader's authority. In November 1604, the caravan set out across the Takla Makan desert, pausing at oases to feed and water themselves and their animals. During one long halt Goes met some Muslims travelling from Peking who told him they had met a Jesuit missionary there who had gained great favour at court. Goes was by now convinced that China and Cathay must be the same place, and thought only of getting to Peking to meet Ricci. He evidently did not realise the problem posed by the Great Wall and its transit regulations.

169

Around Christmas 1605, Goes arrived at Kiayükwan, the fortress and pass in the Great Wall which separated the arid wastes and heathen ways of the desert from the Middle Kingdom. The caravan was halted for twenty-five days at the Wall while permission was sought to proceed to the Chinese city of Suchow. Suchow was a garrison town populated by frontier guards and foreign merchants. The caravan was obliged to wait at Suchow for permission to travel on to Peking. Goes wrote to Ricci, but he did not know the Jesuit's Chinese name, and the first letter did not reach its destination. A second letter took eight months to find Ricci, who delightedly sent a Chinese convert to try to find Goes who had become stuck in Suchow, unable to complete all the necessary formalities to pass into China proper. He could not speak Chinese, had no influential patron and was victimised by the Muslims. He became increasingly despondent and impoverished so that when Ricci's emissary finally arrived at the Great Wall garrison town, he found a dying man. He comforted Goes in Portuguese, and gave him letters from Ricci. Ten days later, Goes died, the first notable European victim of China's Great Wall policy. The Jesuits gave him the brief and touching epitaph 'In seeking Cathay, he found Heaven'.

The Jesuits maintained their mission in Peking long after Ricci's death, and survived the change of dynasty when the Manchus came to power in 1644. Indeed, the following year a Jesuit was given the important post of Director of the Astronomical Board. Several Jesuits took part in surveys of the Great Wall, reporting back to Peking and the world on the state of the barrier. The Emperor's enthusiasm for such reports would suggest that the Court's knowledge of the Great Wall was far from complete. At the beginning of the eighteenth century, the great Emperor K'ang Hsi (who reigned for sixty-one years from 1661) was persuaded to commission a complete survey of his realm. The project was begun in July 1708 and lasted ten years. Father Jean-Baptiste Regis and a team of cartographers set out from the sea terminus of the Wall at Shan Hai Kuan, then followed the outer line of the Wall all the way to Suchow, where Goes had died. They found the western sections of the barrier to be in far less admirable a state than the Ming fortifications north of Peking. The Wall in Shansi was only about 5 feet high, made of earth and with no protective battlements, whereas west of Shansi it was even lower, sometimes no more than a sandy ridge. Between Suchow and Kiayükwan the rampart was well maintained, presumably because it played an important role as the frontier post with the West. From Suchow the Jesuits went south and mapped some of the spurs of the Wall but appear to have been totally unaware of the existence of Han Wu-ti's western Wall that had stretched from Kiayükwan to Tun-huang. The map of the Great Wall the Jesuits produced was fifteen feet long, and their atlas of China, printed in 1718, was, despite omissions, recognised as the most accurate map of any part of the world at that time.

The early years of the Ch'ing dynasty (Manchu) saw several embassies and travellers from Russia, who naturally passed through the Wall on their way to Peking. A Russian named Spathary left a detailed account of the barrier.

There are frequent towers, 100 sazhens [700 feet] one from the other. The Wall is built in this way: at the foundation, cut stone of huge dimensions, undressed granite, and above that, brick. The height is four sazhens [twenty-eight feet], the breadth is two sazhens [fourteen feet]. In some places, among the mountains it has fallen down. The Chinese, speaking of it, boast that when it was built there remained no stone in the mountains, no sand in the desert, in the rivers no water, in the forest no trees.[13]

The gate that Spathary used to pass through the Wall was a complicated affair in three stages. A Chinese escort met him at the outer wall, then escorted him to the first gate, beside which was a large tower. Officials checked everyone passing through, writing down in great detail who they were and what weapons they carried. The first gate was about thirty feet wide, while thirty yards on was a second wall and similar gates, and beyond these a third series.

And all those gates and towers are very strong, the third [inner] wall thicker than the others, and all three are built across the stony ravine about fifty-six feet wide, with a high and rocky cliff on either side. The doors themselves in the gate towers are sheathed in iron.[14]

The Russians, like the Westerners who made overtures to the Celestial Empire, sent their embassies in the hope of establishing trading relations with the Chinese. The Chinese were not especially keen to have much contact with their northern neighbours, and greatly resented Russian interference in northern Mongolia, a traditionally Chinese zone of influence. A vaguely and superficially similar situation has existed ever since, and it is interesting to note that the Chinese and Russians fought battles along the Amur River way back in 1684.

One of the alleged reasons for the lack of success in Russian approaches to China was the question of protocol before the Sun of Heaven. The Manchu emperors would receive foreign ambassadors only if they performed an elaborate and debasing series of kowtows. Most non-Asians felt this was beneath their dignity, and refused. Many embassies failed because of this impasse, including the first British delegation under Lord Macartney in 1793. The issue was blown up out of all proportion in the eyes of Western governments, who felt that the dignity of Europe was at stake, though it is doubtful whether flexibility on this point would have made much difference. A Dutch ambassador who threw pride to the wind and agreed to go through the kowtowing process only brought howls of laughter when his wig fell off during the execution of a particularly extravagant bow. He did not win any special concessions for his efforts.

The English were comparative latecomers to the Chinese scene, but once they had arrived, became the most persistent and troublesome Foreign Devils of all, against whom the Great Wall, the antique weaponry of the Chinese army and all the other elements of the Chinese defence system were useless.

13   From Baddeley, John F., *Russia, Mongolia and China* (Macmillan; London, 1919).
14   Ibid.

Lord Macartney's embassy arrived at Tientsin, the nearest major port to Peking, in the summer of 1793. Macartney had received the title of viscount after a distinguished career as a diplomat in Russia, where he had negotiated a treaty with the Empire of Catherine the Great, then later served in the West Indies. In the early 1780s he had been Governor of Madras in India, and was therefore considered the most experienced man capable of a delicate mission to China. George III and the British government wanted a treaty with China which would put both powers on equal terms, and would allow the British to run trading missions within the Middle Kingdom. This was a stance without precedent, as the other barbarians, despite their dislike of Chinese court procedure, never directly asked the Son of Heaven to recognise their equality. The mission was greeted in China by nervous officials who repeatedly questioned Macartney about his knowledge of Manchu protocol. In fact, when Macartney was ushered into the Emperor Ch'ien Lung's presence, he merely knelt on one knee, as he would before his own monarch, and the dignified Emperor pretended not to notice the hairy barbarian's fearful lack of manners. Needless to say, the embassy was not a success, and the English were subjected to many humiliations during the visit, not least of which was the appalling accommodation which they were given. Many members of the mission wrote books on their return, ranging from lucid travel accounts to lurid descriptions of the evil Chinese.

Ch'ien Lung received Lord Macartney not at Peking but at Jehol, a royal retreat north of the Great Wall which the Manchu rulers used in summer to escape the heat and dust of Peking. Macartney was pleased about this as it gave him the opportunity of examining the Wall, about which he shared his good friend Dr Johnson's great curiosity. In his Journal, Macartney describes how he and his party dismounted at the Wall to take a close look at the famous structure, much to the amazement and consternation of their Chinese escort who could not understand such curiosity about a line of stone, then later became worried that there may be some sinister motive behind the halt. The party passed through the Wall at Kupeikou Pass, where they found it in disrepair, even though this section had been built only a couple of hundred years before. Macartney wrote that the Wall was 'built of blueish coloured brick, not burnt but dried in the sun'.[15] This was untrue. The bricks were baked and gained their blueish colour from iron in the original clay and ashes and coal used in the kiln. He went on:

> [They were] raised upon a stone foundation, and as measured from the ground on the side next to Tartary, it is about twenty-six feet high in the perpendicular. The stone foundation is formed of two courses of granite equal to twenty-four inches or two feet. From thence to the parapet including the cordon which is six inches are nineteen feet four inches, the parapet is four feet eight inches...At the bottom the walls are five feet thick, and diminish gradually as they rise... The space or terrepleine between the walls, which is filled with earth and rubbish up to the level of the bottom of the cordon and paved with square bricks, is eleven feet in the clear, so that there is room for two coaches or five horsemen abreast.[16]

15   From Cranmer-Byng, J. L., *An Embassy to China: Lord Macartney's Journal* (Longmans; London, 1962).
16   Ibid.

172

John Barrow, who accompanied Macartney, had, as already noted, estimated that the amount of building material used in the Wall was more than that used in all the houses of England and Scotland. This fanciful notion was based on the fallacious assumption that the Wall was as massive along its whole length as it was north of Peking. Macartney wrote,

If the other parts of it be similar to those which I have seen, it is certainly the most stupendous work of human hands, for I imagine that if the outline of all the masonry of all the forts and fortified places in the whole world besides were to be calculated, it would fall considerably short of that of the Great Wall of China. At the remote period of its building[17] China must have been not only a very powerful empire, but a very wise and virtuous nation, or at least to have had such foresight and such regard for posterity as to establish at once what was then thought a perpetual security for them against future invasion.[18]

Macartney had no reason to be rhapsodic on his return journey through the Wall. The Chinese kept him waiting nervously for several days, then informed him that the Emperor thanked George III for his 'tribute' but that 'strange and costly objects do not interest us. As your ambassador can see for himself, we possess all things. We set no value on objects strange and ingenious and have no use for your country's Manufactures.' Now Macartney too knew what the Great Wall signified. He returned to England greatly discouraged, but was eagerly greeted at home by people thirsty for knowledge of China and his experiences.

The Chinese insult to his Britannic Majesty only served to strengthen the position of the hawks in the British government who believed that armed intervention was the only way of dealing with the Chinese. The history of the nineteenth century in the Middle Kingdom is a sad tale of misunderstanding, bigotry, corruption and wars and it must rank as one of the most ignoble periods of modern man. The British and their fellow Europeans, rivals yet allies against the Chinese, pressed their claims by force of arms, thrusting opium onto the Chinese, and sending gunboats every time Christian missionaries seemed threatened. It is a long and well-recorded story, of which few could be proud. Small wonder the Great Wall fell into serious decay, the victim of erosion and wilful destruction by peasants seeking building materials. China had neither the interest nor the possibility to preserve its great monument at a time when the whole imperial system was under threat. Several times the imperial family was forced to make hasty retreats from Peking north of the wall.

The late nineteenth and early twentieth centuries brought many kinds of foreigners to China, representing almost every conceivable nationality. Antique hunters, scientists and adventurers rubbed shoulders with diplomats, soldiers, traders and missionaries. Travellers began to arrive in droves as China became a fashionable target for the more imaginative tourists. Everyone had heard of the Great Wall and wanted to see it, and as the great

17 Macartney seems to have been under the impression that he was looking at part of Ch'in Shih Luang-ti's original Wall, instead of one built 1700 years later.
18 Ibid.

monument was so close to Peking, it made a delightful trip to visit the ramparts for a day, returning to the elegant houses in Peking in time for tea. Only the more dedicated saw anything more than the Ming towers and crenellated walls behind the capital. One man who did make the effort to acquire more than a summary knowledge of the Wall was the highly individualistic American traveller and author, William Edgar Geil, author of such period gems as *A Yankee in Pigmy Land*. Despite his butterfly mind and an inability to remain serious for more than three consecutive sentences, his tome on his 1908 journey from Shan Hai Kuan to Kiayükwan remains the classic description of the Wall as it was and presumably still is, though nobody has been allowed to retrace Geil's steps since the People's Revolution. The mood of the book is set by a compatriot's witticism: 'The most important building in China is the Great Wall, built to keep the Tartars out. It was built at such enormous expense that the Chinese never got over it. But the Tartars did. And the way they accomplished the feat was as follows – one went first and t'others went after.'[19] Interspersed with the Doylestown Pennsylvania humour and numerous classical allusions, are many of the legends of the Wall and Geil's own folksy version of the history of the principal emperors behind the project.

Geil began his journey at Shan Hai Kuan on the coast. The Great Wall joins the city wall of Shan Hai Kuan two miles from the sea, while the town itself served in Geil's day as a seaside resort for European troops on leave. The town had only a thousand families, yet boasted both Catholic and Methodist missions. Walking along the top of the Wall to the junction with the city wall, Geil recorded,

> Where one would expect to find cannon, rapid-fire guns, mortars and terrible dynamite throwers, as in the West, here on this most wonderful fortification of human history we find instead a white lighthouse, a searchlight and a temple to literature. Is it possible that after all the Chinese are right and that these are a better protection for a state than death-dealing machinery of the modern diabolical kind?[20]

Not far outside the town were the blackened ruins of a foreign compound where 200 people had met their deaths in the turmoil of the Boxer Rebellion only eight years before, when all foreigners lived in fear of their lives, and the foreign legations in Peking were besieged by the Boxers while the Empress Dowager sat in her palace allegedly powerless to stop them. Strangely enough, the Great Wall itself is sometimes cited as one of the causes of the Boxer Rebellion. In 1899 four bored American journalists were sitting on a railway platform one night in Denver waiting for a celebrity who failed to turn up. To while away the time, the four newsmen cooked up a story that American engineers were on their way to China to demolish the Great Wall. The Chinese had given in to Western pressure to demolish the Wall, so the story said, as a symbolic gesture of a more open policy to foreigners and international trade. The spoof report duly appeared in the *Denver Times*, and was picked up by a New York Sunday paper which amplified the report with pictures. Not surprisingly, the articles soon

19   Geil, W. E., *The Great Wall of China*.
20   Ibid.

reached China, where sensationalist newspapers, anxious for any item that discredited the Foreign Devils, announced in terms of outrage that the Americans were coming to forcibly knock down the Wall. The situation between the Boxers and the Westerners was already beyond hope, so that the fictitious reports cannot be seriously considered a cause of the rebellion, but they certainly cannot have helped the tense situation.

To return to Geil's account, he had considerable difficulty locating the 'Eastern Y' of the Wall, where one part of the Wall branches off north-west to Kalgan and the other south-west to Nankow. None of the locals he asked seemed to have any idea where the fork was, and indeed he discovered that Chinese knowledge of the geography of the Wall was almost zero. One coolie, when asked where the Wall was, replied correctly that it was three miles away, but added pathetically, 'But I have not seen it; to gather fuel takes me from early morning till toward sunset in the woods; then the heavy burden prevents me from looking up, and I have never set eyes upon it.'[21] Geil added,

> Turning to human nature, much is to be desired. The people dwelling near the Great Wall are mostly poor. Our one thousand li of travel was through a thousand li of poverty; a thousand li of ignorance, for the natives knew as little of the history and condition of the only wonder of the Far East as an American University graduate! One thousand li of goiter! This disease we have seen in many mountain lands among different peoples, but never with the same proportion as among the people of the Great Wall.[22]

Geil had the choice of two routes after the Eastern Y, and chose the inner Wall, travelling past the Ming Tombs that are now shown to tourists in China on the same day as the famous Nankou Pass, which appears on the jacket of this book. Near the Ming Tombs was the site of a massacre of Christians, where the Chinese converts were forced to drink the blood of their European missionaries in cruel mockery of the Holy Sacrament. 'Are the Chinese bloody?' Geil asked himself, for although the story of the Great Wall is a story of blood and suffering, China had shed less blood over the previous fifty years than any nation half its size, he claimed. As his journey progressed, Geil had occasion to note the reactions of his Chinese companions.

> Many towers of the Great Barrier remain intact, and even much of the Wall. Thus far on our trip of six hundred miles we appreciate the work of the engineers who brought masses of stone, brick and mortar and built them solidly. But our native companions appreciate yet more highly the work of the geomancers who fixed the sites of the towers, and so brought down good influences on the fields around. One guide would never enter a tower without kotowing thrice and repeating a formula for luck, a prayer to the god of war.[23]

21 Ibid.
22 Ibid.
23 Ibid.

In the regions of the strong Ming Wall, Geil found many tablets and inscriptions, some of which were quoted in Chapter Eight. At one point he discovered a stone slab bearing a poem by Wen Ju-chang, a censor in charge of Border Garrison Inspections, written around 1570. The following is a prose translation:

The Arrowhead Mountain rears its vast mass against the crystal sky; the rocky fortress to the west appears, and farther away a well-known battleground. Two mountain ranges unite to inclose a camp of the ancient Chin Tartars [the Nuchen]. A stream of water flows athwart, with iron bridge and lock. The north is veiled in clouds, the ripe grain is all gathered in, the autumn rains from the north-west begin to increase. The times are tranquil; from the Great Desert is neither smoke nor dust [from the camps or marching of soldiers]. After sunset the drifting leaves alone disturb our dreams [of home].[24]

Geil shared the poet's enthusiasm for the magnificent mountain scenery, and for the dramatic rises and falls of the Wall which at times reaches 10,000 feet above sea-level.

The further west Geil went, the less impressive the Wall became, for erosion had taken a much heavier toll in the loess lands. He noticed that the engineers who had built the Wall, finding that dust drifted up against it forming a slope on the desert side, laid out a second wall behind and in very wind-swept parts, a third. They also made a moat along the Wall, equal in width and depth to the width and height of the Wall, and made it water-tight. For long stretches, the Wall had simply been hewn out of the natural formation of the loess. 'It has been sneeringly said that the Wall in Shensi and Kansu is only a heap of hard mud; but if mud will do to keep people out, why not use it?'[25] Even though much of the structure had decayed, he did find towers still in existence 30 feet high and 35 feet square at the base.

It was in the loess regions that Geil came across the colourful legend of the wild, hairy pigmies. According to the story, a race of dwarfs was conscripted along with the other workers to build the Great Wall. Being so small, their output was well below the norm and accordingly they were harshly treated and abused. Many of them were thrown into the Wall and trampled down as an example to their colleagues. They were so resentful at this treatment that they all ran away and hid from sight. The local people of Geil's day still believed these pigmies existed, that they ran away from any humans whom they saw, and that they were naked, covered in hair like wolves. The *Manchester Evening News* seized on this particular story as an occasion to lecture its readers, surely one of the strangest of the many examples of association of ideas triggered off by the Great Wall.

A Lesson for 'Work Shys'—An instructive moral may be drawn from the discovery of a pigmy race in central China by Dr. William Edgar Geil. The ancestors of the pigmies, Dr. Geil declares, fled to the mountains to escape the curse of labour in the shape of assisting in the task of building the Great Wall of China. Whether or not they were

24 Ibid.
25 Ibid.

justified in acting thus does not concern us now, but the fact remains that the present representatives of the race have degenerated into hairy pigmies, living in a state of savagery. This awful example should be a warning to those people in civilised communities who, blindly refusing to recognise the blessings of labour, pine for a life of ease and idleness![26]

Geil stopped at the city of Ninghia, which nestles in a corner of the Wall. Ninghia is 4000 feet above sea-level and apart from its remarkable position in the right-angle bend of the Wall, it was famous for its fish, which made Geil violently ill. While recuperating in Ninghia, Geil wrote a series of extraordinary letters to a Miss X in America which included the interesting rough calculation that China had an estimated 1700 walled towns, with approximately four miles of city walls on average, thus totalling 6800 miles or twice the length of the Great Wall. Added together, the walls were more than the diameter of the earth. Apart from a few interesting details of Ch'in Shih Huang-ti's Magic Horse, an example of what the Chinese called 'Long Wall Wild Talk', the contents of Geil's letter do not bear repetition.

From Ninghia, Geil followed the line of the desert loop of the Wall through Kansu. He noted that the local residents referred to this part of the Wall as the Eight Hundred Li Wall instead of the more normal Ten Thousand Li Wall, suggesting that they considered their stretch independent from the rest. The land is flat in the area and a telegraph wire followed the line of the Wall. The American discovered that Chinese travellers had scratched remarks on the Wall, the most succinct of which read 'The men on this earth are no good'. Sandstorms made Geil lose his way several times, and he dolefully struggled on past forsaken villages and deserted towns. Eventually with relief he sighted the town of Liangchow. Pausing once more for reflection, he decided that the Chinese had built at least a dozen Great Walls in the past two thousand years, as witnessed by at least a dozen methods of construction. Liangchow was known locally as the '9 by 3' city on account of the dimensions of its own walls. The Great Wall near Liangchow is full of eccentric bends for which no adequate explanation has been forthcoming. At some stage, a man working on repairs to the Great Wall near Liangchow was reputed to have come across a secret cache of gold, which gave rise to the legend that the Great Wall was full of gold.

The highest altitude reached by the Great Wall is at a pass between Liangchow and Lanchow, where it is approximately 10,000 feet above sea level. That stretch is in fact a southern loop, which Geil found in bad repair and overgrown. At the pass was a little temple to guard the highest part of the Great Barrier. From Lanchow, Geil's party explored the Tibetan loop of the Wall, including the nearby 'Seat of Ten Thousand Images' at Gumbum, the second most important lamasery after Lhasa. He was justifiably excited by this stretch of the Wall as it did not appear on contemporary maps. Three miles south-east of Gumbum the ruins of the Wall measured 10 feet at the base and were 20 feet high. He makes a characteristically odd statement that 'as the Tibetans cannot walk, the combination of moat

26   Ibid.

177

and wall was effectual in preventing a charge by the fierce horsemen'.[27] At Gumbum he came across a cripple who was waiting patiently, bent double under a sacred tree, in the hope that a holy leaf would fall and cure him.

Regaining the main line of the Great Wall at Liangchow, Geil set off on the last stage of his journey to Kanchow, Suchow and the western end of the Great Wall. The course of the Wall is through a wide and lofty valley, frequently following the line of least natural resistance. Geil noticed that the outer casing of the Wall had broken down, revealing the inner core, but when he asked local inhabitants why they did not restore the Wall they replied that they could not repair their own town wall, let alone the Great Wall. One man also seriously informed the visitor that the mammoth Barrier was built to prevent a barbarian tribe to the north bringing their mules and donkeys in to eat Chinese peas! From Kanchow (called the City of Liars) Geil advanced to Suchow, where Goes had died, and which had become famous for jade and rhubarb. Finally he arrived at Kiayükwan, which Geil took to be the end of the Wall, and stared out at the wilderness beyond. In his inn at Kiayükwan, Geil found the walls covered in poems written by Chinese who had departed west. One read,

> The road leads westward to the seventy cities in the far country. The mountains and rivers of ten thousand kingdoms return to everlasting antiquity. The majesty of this pass is spoken about inside and outside of the kingdom and it protects heaven and earth.[28]

Geil had come to the end of his magnificent journey, seemingly unaware that only a few months before a Hungarian born archaeologist Aurel Stein had rediscovered the real western section of the Wall, Han Wu Ti's western extension that extended for another three hundred miles as far as Tun-huang. Stein's expedition was sponsored by the British Museum, and he left scholarly records of his findings, very different in tone from those of Geil. Fighting his way across the inhospitable desert, Stein discovered tower after tower, and then observed that reed bundles in the desert were in a noticeably straight line. Stein,

> saw the line stretching away perfectly straight towards another tower visible some three miles to the east, and assuming in the distance the form of an unmistakable wall. It was manifested by part of that early 'Chinese Wall' for which M. Bonin's observation had made me look out, and a little prospecting on the knoll soon revelaed with clearness that I actually stood on remains of it![29]

Han Wu Ti's wall had completely disappeared in some parts, but in others it was as much as eight feet thick and twelve feet high. Han dynasty bamboo writing spills, and materials found in the sand, gave Stein conclusive proof that the area had been occupied in Han times. Often his research work was interrupted by sandstorms, but in the course of his 1907

27   Ibid.
28   Ibid.
29   Stein, Sir Mark Aurel, *Ruins of Desert Cathay*, Vol. 1 (Macmillan; London, 1912).

expedition Stein amassed a large collection of documents and artefacts recovered from the sands, giving valuable historical information about the silk trade along the western route and the establishment of military posts by the Han in 102 and 101 BC, westwards from Tun-huang to the 'Salt Marsh'.

Only a handful of other men ever attempted to make significant journeys along the Great Wall, but none ever equalled that of Geil. Two reports on the Great Wall appeared in American geographical publications in the 1920s, but they added little to existing knowledge of the Wall, apart from the discovery that an unknown part of the Great Wall existed buried in the sands of the Ordos desert, far north of the accepted line. Nobody has ever seen the whole length of the Wall, and no two authoritative maps agree as to its exact course. Until the present Chinese government decides that a full-scale survey of the Wall would be worthwhile, no one can give a conclusive account; the Wall will, therefore, always retain at least some of its mystery.

10

Of Walls and Bamboo Curtains

CHAPTER TEN

Of Walls and Bamboo Curtains

DURING the worst months of the Cultural Revolution (mid-1966 to early 1968) when Red Guards were involved in street fighting and foreign residents in Peking were submitted to humiliation reminiscent of the Boxer Rebellion, Western journalists had a field day describing China's 'orgy of self-destruction', 'mass violence', 'hysterical robots' and 'screaming fanatics'. Western readers followed events as well as they could (information being scarce and patchy), horrified and fascinated by an intellectual and social upheaval which they could not understand. The Chinese had always been traditional villains in European eyes – sly, clever and cold-blooded. Popular novelists and film-makers pandered to the idea. Communists were also villains; respectable newspapers and politicians said so. Chinese Communists were about the most dangerous people the average man in the street could imagine, particularly as there were 750,000,000 of them and they all looked alike. They were shut behind their bamboo curtain (the favourite term for China's abstract Great Wall) but might explode through at any moment. They had 'The Bomb'. They would not allow visitors in to see what was going on behind the Great Wall, and their leaders never travelled outside China. Many governments and organisations in the West were secretly pleased with the situation in the Middle Kingdom because it helped justify their own policies. Journalists were happy to vent their outrage against the Red Guards and Chairman Mao because it made good copy. The media were full of pictures and descriptions of Chinese intellectuals forced to undergo self-criticism sessions, demonstrators in their hundreds of thousands chanting slogans of hate outside embassies in Peking, students defacing historic monuments and buildings with their 'Large Character Posters'.

Only now is the Cultural Revolution falling into perspective. The full story is way outside the scope of this book, but it is of concern to the Great Wall because it brought to light two important and deeply misunderstood factors: the Chinese attitudes to their past and to the outside world.

Early reports of Red Guards on the rampage caused great concern around the world for the future of China's rich heritage. In reality, there was very little wanton destruction, and historic relics suffered far less than they have done at the hands of municipal planners. Slogans were daubed on buildings, street walls and even the Great Wall, but that is fairly common student practice around the world in times of unrest, and most of the disfiguring paint has been successfully removed. Indeed, the Chinese authorities were at pains to protect cultural treasures from over-enthusiastic elements. Precious and breakable museum pieces were removed from show and carefully stored away. The Forbidden City was closed to visitors. Ideologists said that the closing of museums and old libraries was to stop corrupting old influences interfering with the revolutionary process, but the real reason was far more practical. When the situation quieted down, exhibits reappeared, institutions reopened and the government produced many new and beautiful archaeological discoveries that had been unearthed during the late 1960s and kept secret until the mood was right.

It took the Chinese Communist Party some time to formulate an exact policy for dealing with cultural relics. Sung celadon-ware or delicate T'ang dancing figures were universally acclaimed to be of exquisite loveliness, yet a strong faction argued that such pieces were symbols of the evil old society and should therefore be despised. They were made for the wealthy 'slave-owning, feudal or semi-feudal' classes who survived by subjugating the working people. Another faction argued that the works of art were produced by working men, so that whatever their intention or ownership may have been, they should be treasured as witness to the genius of the Chinese worker. This latter view fortunately prevailed.

The Great Wall is the largest and most spectacular of the preserved monuments. The favourite visiting spot at Nankou Pass has been smartened up, strengthened, weeded and equipped with a little tea-shop. It has all the appearance of a tourist attraction, complete with carved initials in the stone work from Western visitors and the legend 'Viva Castro!'. No details are forthcoming about the Wall's state further west, where it is seen only by local shepherds and the occasional Chinese archaeologist.

The Great Wall seems to have been more fortunate than its many similar counterparts, the city walls. While the Dragon Screen survived a period of neglect, other walls have been vigorously demolished. The planners declared the old walls hazardous in a modern city and restrictive to growth, and the health authorities complained about their dirtiness and their blocking out of the sun. The narrow old walled alleys, or 'hu-t'ung' of Peking and other cities have been giving way to broad streets, open spaces and workers' flats.

Historical figures as well as cultural relics have come under the ideological scrutiny of the Party. Thus for the whole of 1974, Chinese newspapers and magazines were full of articles criticising Confucius, who had died more than 2000 years before. To the Westerner, the preoccupation with ancient figures seems inappropriate to a political debate, but it is consistent with the pattern of Chinese education and polemic. Men learn from models. Chairman Mao himself has often stressed the need to learn from history, to 'use the past to serve the present'.

Contemporary China has grown out of the China of the past; we are Marxist in our historical approach and must not lop off our history. We should sum up our history from Confucius to Sun Yat-sen (the first great Chinese republican leader) and take over this valuable legacy. This is important for guiding the great movement of today![1]

In keeping with many other Socialist countries, the People's Republic of China set about rewriting its history, from a Marxist-Leninist standpoint. In doing so, they were also following the example of every previous Chinese dynasty or government, who all employed scholars and writers to give the latest official version of history. Unlike some of their predecessors, the Communists did not wilfully distort the facts but instead reinterpreted history in keeping with Marxist theories of class struggle. Heroes of the past became villains of the present, and vice versa. Latterly, Confucius has been the main target for attack, suddenly demoted after hundreds of years of veneration as China's greatest sage. Confucius' main crime is that he supported the 'slave system'. He preached virtue, but his virtue extended only to the members of the aristocracy. He talked of benevolence, but benevolence was merely a tool used to consolidate the unity between the exploiting classes, or so say the modern theorists. He despised productive labour, and believed that there should always be two classes of men – those who ruled and those who were ruled. As always, there is a lesson for the present to be learnt from Confucius and his élitist attitude to life, not least because of one of his alleged admirers, Lin Piao, the former army chief and Mao Tse-tung's former 'heir apparent', who crashed to his death in a plane over Mongolia following an abortive coup.

> The bourgeois careerist, conspirator, double-dealer, renegade and traitor Lin Piao was an out-and-out devotee of Confucius. Like all reactionaries in Chinese history when on the verge of extinction, he revered Confucius and opposed the Legalist School, and attacked Ch'in Shih Huang [Ti], the first emperor of the Ch'in Dynasty (221–207 BC). He used the doctrines of Confucius and Mencius as a reactionary ideological weapon in his plotting to usurp Party leadership, seize state power and restore capitalism.[2]

The builder of China's original Great Wall, Ch'in Shih Huang-ti, appears in many contemporary magazines and books. His reputation has been white-washed and his detractors abused. Significantly, the fact that he was responsible for the Great Wall is almost never mentioned. The Great Wall does not fit neatly into any ideological compartment. It is neither overtly good nor overtly bad. It represents a certain achievement on the part of Chinese building workers of the past, and an enormity of vision by Shih Huang-ti, yet its history is bloody, its building hardly complimentary to its creator's attitude to the toiling masses, and its symbolism contrary to the spirit of unity between the peoples of the world. From Chinese officials sometimes comes the feeling that the Wall is something of an embarrassment. There is nothing in the Wall that directly points to progress, and progress is the lifeblood of the continuing Revolution.

1   Mao Tse-tung, 'The Role of the Chinese Communist Party in the National War', *Selected Works of Mao Tse-tung*, Vol. II (Foreign Languages Press; Peking, 1967).
2   Publisher's note to 'Selected Articles Criticising Lin Piao and Confucius'.

The controversy over Ch'in Shih Huang [Ti] is not only a question of how to evaluate a historical character, but a manifestation of the political struggle between progress and retrogression. In the present epoch, it is, in the final analysis, a struggle between the proletariat and the bourgeoisie and their world outlook.[3]

Ch'in Shih Huang-ti's rise to favour after 2000 years of calumny no doubt has something to do with Mao Tse-tung's own liking for the First Emperor. Chairman Mao and most of the other members of the old guard in the Peking hierarchy are very well read in Chinese history, and inevitably have their favourites amongst the men of the Empire's past. It is interesting to note that the two 'heroes' mentioned in Mao Tse-t'ung's most famous poem 'Snow' were the two early builders of the Great Wall, Ch'in Shih Huang-ti and Han Wu-ti, who built the great Han extension to Ch'in Shih Huang-ti's 'Long Rampart'.

SNOW

This is the scene in that northern land;
A hundred leagues are sealed in ice,
A thousand leagues of whirling snow.
On either side of the Great Wall
One vastness is all you see.
From end to end of the great river
The rushing torrent is frozen and lost.
The mountains dance like silver snakes,
The highlands roll like waxen elephants,
As if they sought to vie with heaven in their height.
And on a sunny day
You will see a red dress thrown over the white,
Enchantingly lovely!
Such great beauty like this in all our landscape
Has caused unnumbered heroes to bow in homage.
But alas, these heroes—Ch'in Shih Huang-ti and
    Han Wu-ti
Were rather lacking in culture;
Rather lacking in literary talent
Were the Emperors T'ang T'ai Tsung and
    Sung T'ai Tsu;
And Genghis Khan,
Beloved Son of Heaven for a day,
Only knew how to bend his bow at the golden eagle.

3 *Peking Review*, 13 December 1974.

Now they are all past and gone:
To find men truly great and noble-hearted
We must look here in the present.[4]

The advent of Communist power in China in 1949 saw a mass exodus of foreigners. Within two or three years the number of Europeans resident in the Middle Kingdom was a mere fraction of that before the Second World War. Of those who remained, almost all lived in Peking or Shanghai. The door into China which had been brutally prised open during the nineteenth century was suddenly slammed shut. Every request for an entry visa was subject to delays and more often than not refused, unless the applicant was an invited visitor or a member of a group likely to be sympathetic to the People's Revolution. In the early years of the People's Republic, Western students and lecturers were still accepted at some of China's universities, and old China hands who revisited the country from which they had fled were often eloquent in their praise for the speed with which the Communists were stamping out corruption, poverty, disease and inefficiency, just some of the characteristics that many cynical Westerners had considered inherent in Chinese society. In the late fifties and early sixties, however, the number of entry visas granted fell sharply. China became far more selective about the nationality of its visitors, with Communist and Third World 'friends' taking priority. Western aspirants who were interested in things Chinese became disheartened after receiving refusals or no replies to their visa applications, and turned to Taiwan, where Generalissimo Chiang Kai-shek had installed his Nationalist government, taking with him many of China's intellectuals and a large part of the great museum collections. On the mainland, the Bamboo Curtain had been drawn.

The leaders in Peking justified their decision to turn their back on the world in several ways. They said China was about to realise a unique experience in social revolution in which freedom from foreign interference was essential. They had every reason to assume that foreign governments would interfere in China's internal affairs, just as they had for the past hundred years. The Americans had interfered even during the Civil and anti-Japanese Wars which stretched from 1937 to 1949. The Nationalists and Communists often fought against each other when they should have been concentrating their forces against the Japanese. The Americans continued to support financially and militarily the official Nationalist government in Chungking, long after a top American adviser on the spot, General Stilwell, had informed Washington of the corruption and manoeuvring that existed around Peanuts, as he nicknamed the Generalissimo. The Americans in turn felt bitter when China was 'lost' to the Communists because Mao Tse-tung looked to Moscow, not Washington, for a special relationship. When the friendship treaties between Russia and China broke down and the Russians suddenly withdrew their technical advisers in 1960, the Chinese withdrew even further into their shell. They never forgave Kruschev for degrading Stalin, and considered the Russian back down over Cuba an appeasement equal to Munich.

The Cold War and China's clumsy war with India only heightened the Middle

4   From Mao Tse-tung, *Nineteen Poems* (Foreign Language Press; Peking, 1958).

187

THE GREAT WALL OF CHINA

Kingdom's isolation. Reports coming out of China spoke of millions of people being killed in the compulsory take-over of land in the 1950s, of thousands of intellectuals being purged after the 'Hundred Flowers Movement' when the government suddenly liberalised freedom of speech and censorship laws, and then equally suddenly clamped down on the flood of criticism that poured out. Refugees making the daring swim by night across the bay into Hong Kong spoke of hunger, political coercion and quickly snuffed-out revolts. Information was scarce and often contradictory, so several Western governments installed permanent China-watching teams in Hong Kong to attempt to keep track of events in China. Every Western newspaper report about China for a while seemed to be based on the hypotheses of learned sinologists who sat bound to their desks and earphones in Britain's tiny colony. Every text was full of 'maybe', 'might', 'could be', 'X was not present at the last banquet for Y which is generally thought to be indicative of...'. China had constructed a Great Wall around herself far more effective than the stone construction had ever been. The unique barrier which Mao Tse-tung and his government had built around their country was reflected in the titles of many of the books published in the West about China during the fifties and sixties, such as *Through the Bamboo Curtain, The Wall has Two Sides* and *The Red Book and the Great Wall.* Occasionally a bombshell would be dropped on the unsuspecting world, such as the denunciation and disappearance of the President of the People's Republic, Liu Shao-ch'i, during the Cultural Revolution, as if to tell the West that behind the Wall the dragon was still very much alive.

The speed with which political situations and attitudes can change is a source of amazement to any serious student of history. Usually such changes come about by revolution or the election of a government radically different from its predecessor. In China there was no such change of government, yet the end of the 1960s saw a complete volte-face in relations between China and the West. In 1968, China must have been the most abused country in the world, yet by the summer of 1971 scarcely a newspaper in Europe or the United States had a bad word to say about the 'Land of the Eight Hundred Million'. The turning point was marked symbolically by a remarkably banal but historic speech made by the then President Richard Nixon, standing on the Wall one snowy morning, which began, 'I think you would have to conclude that this is a great wall, and it had to be built by a great people...'. The impossible had been achieved. The figurehead of Western Society and Capitalism had come to pay homage to the rulers of the Middle Kingdom, to usher in a new era of peace and co-operation. Suddenly it seemed that barriers of stone were of no significance, that walls no longer existed, even in politicians' minds.

Over the last few years, China has stepped out tentatively into the world. People's China has occupied its rightful seat in the United Nations and has been accepted into many international organisations. The number of foreign visitors to China increases slowly but steadily; even passengers on luxury liners are permitted a quick glimpse of the People's Revolution. China's new openness is indicative of a fresh confidence in herself, an awareness that the task of revolution, although not finished, is at least ensured. When the People's Republic celebrated its twenty-fifth anniversary on 1 October 1974, it was as if everything had been beautifully timed so that New China would be at peace with almost all the world. A special book was published in Peking to mark the anniversary; at the end was a large picture of the Great Wall, along which hundreds of people of different nationalities were walking hand in hand with Chinese. The caption read, 'The friendship between the Chinese people and the peoples of the world is as long and everlasting as the Great Wall of China.' In just over 2000 years of turbulent history, the meaning of the Great Wall had turned completely around. Born as a symbol of fear between nations, it had become the symbol of international trust and friendship.

Appendices

The Chinese Dynasties

Hsia (possibly legendary)	2205 (?)–1766 (?) BC
Shang	1766 (?)–1122 (?) BC
Chou	1112 (?)–221 BC
Ch'in	221 –207 BC
Han	206 BC –AD 220
Three Kingdoms (Wei, Shu and Wu)	AD 220 280 (?)
Tsin	265 –420
Southern and Northern Dynasties	420 –589
Sui	589 –618
T'ang	618 –906
Five Dynasties	907 –960
Sung	960 –1279
Yüan	1260 –1368
Ming	1368 –1644
Ch'ing	1644 –1912
Republic (continues in Taiwan)	1912 –
People's Republic	1949 –

NOTE: Many of the dates above should be taken as rough estimates only. The earliest dates, although accepted by traditional Chinese historians, are extremely suspect, and several others are made approximate by the long-drawn-out transfer of power or regional variations within China.

The Length of the Great Wall

There have been hundreds of estimates for the total length of the Great Wall, ranging from as little as 850 miles to over 4000 miles. The most plausible figures were drawn up by an American geographer, Frederick Clapp, who put the total at 2150 miles of main wall and 1780 miles of spurs and offshoots, making a total of 3930.

Main Line:	Shanhaikuan to the Eastern Bifurcation	300
	Eastern Bifurcation to the Yellow River (outer)	500
	North Shensi Frontier Wall	350
	Ninghsia to Liangchow	250
	Kansu to Kiayükwan via Silk Road	450
	Kiayükwan to Yumen-kuan and Yang-kuan	300
		2150
	Manchurian Extension (Willow Pale)	400
	Eastern Bifurcation to the Yellow River (inner)	400
	South Branch Wall (Shansi border)	230
	Lanchow Loop	250
	Ch'inghai Loop	400
	Miscellaneous offshoots	100
		1780
	Total	3930

Figures quoted here are from Joseph Needham's *Science and Civilisation in China* Vol. IV, part 3 (Cambridge University Press, 1971).

Bibliography

Select Bibliography of Western Language Book Sources

Andō, Hikotaro. *Peking* (Ward Lock; London, 1968)

Backhouse, E. and Bland, J. O. P. *Annals and Memoirs of the Court of Peking* (William Heinemann; London, 1914)

Baddeley, John F. *Russia, Mongolia and China* (Macmillan; London, 1919)

Balazs, Etienne. *Chinese Civilisation and Bureaucracy* (Yale University Press; 1964)

Bodde, Derk. *China's First Unifier* (Brill; Leiden, 1937)

—— *Statesman, Patriot and General in Ancient China* (American Oriental Series Vol 17; New Haven, Conn., 1940)

Cable, Mildred and French, Francesca. *The Gobi Desert* (Hodder and Stoughton; London, 1942)

Cail, Odile. *Fodor's Guide to Peking* (Hodder and Stoughton; London, 1972)

Cheng Te-K'un. *Archaeology in China* (Heffer; Cambridge, 1959)

Colombo, Furio. *The Chinese* (Grossman; New York, 1972)

Cottrell, Leonard. *The Tiger of Ch'in* (Evans Brothers; London, 1962)

Cranmer-Byng, J. L. *An Embassy to China: Lord Macartney's Journal* (Longmans; London, 1962)

Creel, Herrlee G. *The Birth of China* (Frederick Unger; New York, 1954)

Cressey, George B. *China's Geographical Foundation* (McGraw Hill; New York, 1934)

—— *Land of the 500 Million* (McGraw Hill; New York, 1955)

Cronin, Vincent. *The Wise Man from the West* (Fontana Books; London, 1961)

Dawson, Raymond. *El Cameleon Chino* (Alianza Editorial; Madrid, 1970)

De Crespigney, R. R. C. *China, the Land and Its People* (Thomas Nelson; Melbourne, 1971)

Fitzgerald, C. P. *China: A Short Cultural History* (The Cresset Press; London, 1935)

Fung Yu-lan. *A History of Chinese Philosophy* (Henri Vetch; Peking, 1937)

Geil, William Edgar. *The Great Wall of China* (Sturgis and Walton; New York, 1909)

Greene, Felix. *The Wall Has Two Sides* (The Reprint Society; London, 1963)

Grousset, Rene. *The Rise and Splendour of the Chinese Empire* (Geoffrey Bles; London, 1952)

Gunther, John. *Inside Asia* (Hamish Hamilton; London, 1939)

Hsia Nai, et al. *New Archaeological Finds in China* (Foreign Languages Press; Peking, 1973)

Hucker, Charles O. *The Censorial System in Ming China* (Stanford University Press; 1966)

Hummel, A. W. *Eminent Chinese of the Ch'ing Period* (United States Government Printing Office; Washington, 1943)

Karlbeck, Orvar. *Treasure Seeker in China* (The Cresset Press; London, 1957)

Lach, Donald. *China in the Eyes of Europe* (University of Chicago Press; 1965)

Lamb, Harold. *Genghis Khan: Emperor of All Men* (Bantam Books; New York, 1953)

Lattimore, Owen. *Inner Asian Frontiers of China* (Capitol Publishing Co; New York, 1951)

Ley, C. D. (ed). *Portuguese Voyages 1498–1663* (J. M. Dent; London, 1960)

Li, Dun J. *The Ageless Chinese* (J. M. Dent; London, 1965)

Liddell, T. Hodgson. *China, Its Marvel and Mystery* (George Allen and Sons; London, 1909)

Loewe, Michael. *Everyday Life in Early Imperial China 202 BC–AD 220* (Batsford; London, 1968)
—— *Records of Han Administration* (Cambridge University Press; 1967)

Lum, Peter. *The Purple Barrier* (Robert Hale; London, 1960)

MacFarquhar, Roderick. *The Forbidden City* (Newsweek Books; New York, 1972)

Mao Tsu-tung. *Selected Works of Mao Tse-tung* (Foreign Languages Press; Peking, 1967)
—— *Nineteen Poems* (Foreign Languages Press; Peking, 1958)

Maspero, Henri and Balazs, Etienne. *Histoire et Institutions de la Chine Ancienne* (Presse Universitaire de France; Paris, 1967)

Mendoza, Juan G. de. *History of the Great and Mighty Kingdom of China* (The Haklyut Society; London, 1854)

Needham, Joseph. *Science and Civilisation in China* (Cambridge University Press; 1954 et seq)

Pickthall, Mohammed Marmaduke. *The Meaning of the Glorious Koran* (New American Library; New York, 1953)

Reichwein, Adolf. *China and Europe* (Routledge & Kegan Paul; London, 1968)

Reischauer, Edwin O. and Fairbank, John K. *East Asia: The Great Tradition* (Houghton Mifflin; Boston, 1958)

Roberts, Francis Morley. *Western Travellers to China* (Kelly and Walsh; Shanghai, 1932)

Roy, Jules. *Journey Through China* (Faber and Faber; London, 1967)

Russell, Bertrand. *The Problem of China* (George Allen and Unwin; London, 1922)

Segalen, Victor. *Chine: Le Grande Statuaire* (Flammarion; Paris, 1972)

Siao, Eva. *Peking* (Sachserverlag; Dresden, 1956)

Silverberg, Robert. *The Great Wall of China* (Chilton Books; New York, 1965)

Stein, Sir Mark Aurel. *Ruins of Desert Cathay* (Macmillan; London, 1912)

Terrill, Ross. *800,000,000: The Real China* (Dell; New York, 1974)

Tregear, Tom. *The Chinese, How They Live and Work* (David & Charles; Newton Abbot, 1973)

Tsui Chi. *Het Eeuwige China* (W. de Haan; Utrecht, 1949)

Tuchman, Barbara, *Stilwell and the American Experience in China* (Macmillan; London, 1971)

Waley, Arthur (trans). *Ballads and Stories from Tun-huang* (George Allen and Unwin; London, 1960)
—— *The Book of Songs* (George Allen and Unwin; London, 1937)

Watson, Burton (trans). *Records of the Grand Historian of China* (Columbia University Press; New York, 1961)

Watson, William. *Early Civilisation in China* (Thames and Hudson; London, 1966)

Wei, Winifred. *The Great Wall of China* (China Publishing; Taipei, 1963)

Yang, Jung-kuo, et al. *Selected Articles Criticising Lin Piao and Confucius* (Foreign Languages Press; Peking, 1974)

Yule, Sir Henry and Cordier, Henri. *Cathay and the Way Thither* (The Haklyut Society; London, 1914–16)

Index

Index

Wherever possible in Chinese proper names which do not include a description, an indication has been added in brackets to show to whom or to what the name refers, such as 'city of', 'author', 'historian' etc.